The Art of Command

THE ART OF COMMAND

Military Leadership
from
George Washington
to
Colin Powell

Edited by
HARRY S. LAVER AND JEFFREY J. MATTHEWS

THE UNIVERSITY PRESS OF KENTUCKY

Copyright © 2008 by The University Press of Kentucky

Scholarly publisher for the Commonwealth,
serving Bellarmine University, Berea College, Centre College of Kentucky,
Eastern Kentucky University, The Filson Historical Society, Georgetown
College, Kentucky Historical Society, Kentucky State University, Morehead
State University, Murray State University, Northern Kentucky University,
Transylvania University, University of Kentucky, University of Louisville,
and Western Kentucky University.
All rights reserved.

Editorial and Sales Offices: The University Press of Kentucky
663 South Limestone Street, Lexington, Kentucky 40508-4008
www.kentuckypress.com

12 11 10 09 08   5 4 3 2 1

Library of Congress Cataloging-in-Publication Data

The art of command : military leadership from George Washington to Colin
Powell / edited by Harry S. Laver and Jeffrey J. Matthews.
    p. cm.
  Includes bibliographical references and index.
  ISBN 978-0-8131-2513-8 (hardcover : alk. paper)
  1. United States—Armed Forces—Officers—Biography. 2. Generals—United
States—Biography. 3. Admirals—United States—Biography. 4. Command of
troops—Case studies. 5. United States—History, Military. 6. United States—
History, Naval. I. Laver, Harry S. II. Matthews, Jeffrey J., 1965-
  U52.A77 2008
  355.3'3041092273—dc22   2008028017

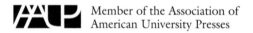 Member of the Association of
American University Presses

To our mentors:
    Lance G. Banning
    Joseph A. Fry
    George C. Herring
    James Johnson
    Willard H. Rollings

Contents

Foreword

In March 1969, I, along with two dozen other young men, stumbled off a chartered bus in front of the white World War II–era barracks at Fort Lewis, Washington. Waiting for us and already barking orders was Drill Sergeant Mata. I had joined the United States Army. I was a volunteer, a private who planned to serve his three-year enlistment and return home to Oregon. (Two weeks after entering boot camp, I received an official induction notice in the mail.) Unbeknownst to me, boot camp was actually the start of a thirty-eight-year military career—a four-decade journey of public service and leadership development.

The year 1969 was the midpoint of the cold war and the peak of the Vietnam War. Four years earlier, in Vietnam's Ia Drang Valley, Lieutenant Colonel Harold "Hal" Moore had exercised masterful leadership that resulted in America's first major battlefield victory in that long and bloody conflict. As a new recruit, I knew little of Vietnam or military leadership, but I quickly embraced the culture of duty and honor that is the core of America's armed forces. Remarkably, twenty-five years after my enlistment, I would lead two of Hal Moore's sons, Lieutenant Colonel Steve Moore and Colonel Dave Moore. For me, the Moore family embodies the selfless values taught, learned, and practiced by the best leaders in our country's military.

During the course of my career, I had the tremendous benefit of being stationed in various billets around the world. I served under and with numerous superb commanders, each of whom influenced my own leadership development. During my tour as a staff officer for the Joint Chiefs of Staff, for example, I came to appreciate fully the complex and innumerable challenges faced by high-level military leaders. During this time, the Joint Chiefs, chaired by General Colin Powell, oversaw Operation Just Cause in Panama, Operation Desert

Storm in the Middle East, and the fall of communism in Eastern Europe. Furthermore, my cruise aboard the nuclear submarine USS *Pennsylvania* served as a clear and direct reminder of Admiral Hyman Rickover's accomplishments and the importance of technology leadership in the military. Then-colonel Norman Schwarzkopf at Fort Lewis and Major General Henry "Gunfighter" Emerson in Korea taught me invaluable lessons about charismatic, visionary, adaptive, and willful leadership.

The Art of Command: Military Leadership from George Washington to Colin Powell provides insightful and informed analyses of nine leadership qualities that have been central to effective American military leadership. Do these historic leadership qualities have relevance for military officers leading servicemen in the twenty-first century? In other words, can the traits and practices of leaders such as George Washington, Ulysses Grant, Henry "Hap" Arnold, and Lewis "Chesty" Puller be effectively applied by military officers in places like Iraq, Afghanistan, Korea, and the Balkans? The answer is yes. The lessons offered in the following chapters are timeless and should be adopted by current and aspiring military leaders. In fact, a renewed focus on integrity, persistence, vision, adaptability, institutional development, and technological advancement is needed now more than ever. In a unipolar world of intense globalization driven by revolutionary technological change and the free flow of goods, services, and capital, U.S. military leaders will be challenged like never before.

The prelude to 11 September 2001 and its immediate aftermath brought to the foreground the exceptional leadership skills of two very different people: Osama bin Laden and Rudy Giuliani. Bin Laden orchestrated the audacious attacks on the Pentagon and World Trade Center; in response, Giuliani rallied the citizens of New York City and inspired the country as a whole. Neither of these leaders, however, was born great. They, and the commanders discussed in this book, spent decades learning and developing as leaders. As legendary football coach Vince Lombardi once remarked, "Leaders are made; they are not born. They are made by hard effort, which is the price all of us must pay to achieve any goal that is worthwhile."

One of my many mentors, General Montgomery "Monty" Meigs, personified the leader who is a lifelong learner. In the late 1990s, I was responsible for exploring the application of Internet and other computer technologies to the army mission. Then–lieutenant general Meigs, commanding general of the U.S. Army Combined Arms Center at Fort Leavenworth, Kansas, inquired where he could learn more about the application of emerging technologies, including the Internet, space-based systems, and commercial software, to military operations. My colleagues and I prepared for General Meigs a customized course of instruction. He was thoroughly engaged in theoretical and practical discussions about the future role of technology in the military art. The success of this informal course led many other general officers to request similar instruction. As a result of General Meigs's interest, we began monthly technology seminars for flag officers from the U.S. Army, Navy, Air Force, and Marine Corps and for select members of Congress. General Meigs went on to successfully command NATO forces in the Balkans and continually pressed his forces to learn and apply technical solutions as an enabler for stability operations. His commitment to adding technological expertise as a personal competency and accepting the risk of and accountability for the early employment of commercial technical practices was emblematic of a professional leader and successful commander. General Meigs set the example, demonstrating through his actions the importance of continual learning to leadership development.

When we developed the technology course for General Meigs, I also pressed junior officers to assume personal responsibility for staying abreast of the fast-paced technological changes occurring in the private sector rather than waiting for such information to be introduced at the various military educational institutions. I recall, in particular, a keynote address before some five hundred young lieutenants and captains at Fort Gordon, Georgia. Afterward, one young officer asked, "How do we learn these new technologies that are so quickly appearing in the commercial sector, and how do we apply them to the army?" I answered that in the fast-moving area of computers and software, the institutional schools could not keep up, and as upcoming leaders and professionals, they must seek out information from publications, the Internet, and industry partners. Self-study, I emphasized, is the realm of the professional; it is sometimes inconvenient and harsh but is always rewarding. This answer received a mixed reaction. The junior officers who were not receptive to my advice were on a path to become managers, whereas the others were destined to become leaders.

Successful leaders, like Meigs, Marshall, and Moore, understand that failing to make a lifetime study of the profession abrogates the responsibility of command and provides the high ground to one's adversary. The pages that follow detail nine traits that have helped define nine preeminent American leaders. Each of those traits is as relevant today as it was in Washington's Revolutionary army. Several stand out, in this age of information and globalization, as requiring additional leader focus and emphasis. The cross-cultural skills of Eisenhower should be emphasized and honed by our leaders. We must be prepared to face a world in which "we will not and should not fight alone," as evolving cultures, non-nation-states, enemies with no boundaries, the erosion of Westphalian agreements, and traditional members of the world community combine to create an unstable strategic environment, as witnessed in the Balkans. The visionary and technology-based leadership of Arnold and Rickover must be repeated and our young leaders given fertile ground to bloom. Technology and the Internet empower the individual but also, ominously, for the first time in history, enable individuals, through a free flow of information, to inflict death and destruction on tens of thousands without the sponsor of a nation-state. Today's leaders must continue to develop their integrity, determination, adaptability, and the other leadership qualities discussed in this book.

We are at a tipping point for the leadership of our armed forces that will define the future of the nation. Driven by the pervasiveness of information, the exponential growth of technology, and the availability of commercial technology to friends and adversaries alike, leaders must preserve the leadership qualities of the past while learning new skills at an ever increasing pace. Military leaders must be willing to accept the possibility of failure and not, like unimaginative managers, avoid all risk. As social philosopher Eric Hoffer points out, "In times of change, learners inherit the earth, while the learned find themselves beautifully equipped to deal with a world that no longer exists."

The quality of our young men and women today in the armed forces is without equal. After almost six years of war—longer than either world war lasted—we have the most experienced and best-seasoned force in our nation's history. At the end of the current conflicts in Iraq, Afghanistan, and other untold places involved in fighting the War on Terror, our military will reconstitute and rebuild. The traits and skills of the leaders you will read about here must remain at the core of our armed forces' leadership. The nation and the world, however, are changing at an increasingly fast pace. Our leaders must adapt, as Moore did in Vietnam and as Arnold did in World War II. I believe the former chief of staff of the U.S. Army, General Eric "Rick" Shinseki, said it best when in 2002 he observed, "If they [army leaders] don't like change, they will like irrelevance even less."

Lieutenant General Steven W. Boutelle
U.S. Army (Ret.)

Acknowledgments

The core concepts and framework for this book took meaningful shape in late spring 2005 when we participated in the National Security Forum at the Air War College in Montgomery, Alabama. As a result, we would like to thank our sponsors at the Air War College, Lieutenant Colonel J. J. Lamers and Captain Bill Hendrickson. We would also like to express our deep appreciation for Colonel Catherine E. Lee, our forum seminar leader. We also acknowledge the invaluable continuing support of Colonel George E. Reed, the former director of command and leadership studies at the U.S. Army War College in Carlisle, Pennsylvania. Like Colonel Reed, Stephen Wrinn, the director of the University Press of Kentucky, was an early and enthusiastic supporter of this project. Wrinn and his staff, especially Anne Dean Watkins, are consummate professionals, and together they have worked diligently to improve the quality of this book. Our eight chapter authors also deserve special recognition for producing thoughtful contributions on the history and art of military leadership. We want to give particular praise to the late Larry Bland, the author of our chapter on General George C. Marshall. Larry was a superb scholar and collaborator who for years had served masterfully as the editor of *The Papers of George Catlett Marshall* and the managing editor of the *Journal of Military History*. Together, we also want to thank people who helped to secure photographs or reviewed the original book proposal, early chapter drafts, or the entire manuscript; these include Lieutenant General Steven W. Boutelle, Brigadier General Earl D. Matthews (select), Colonel Larry Wilkerson, Lieutenant Colonel Steve Moore, Joe Galloway, Lisa Johnson, Thomas Appleton, Andy Fry, George Herring, and two anonymous outside readers.

In editing various chapters and in writing the book's chapter on General Colin Powell, Jeff received significant support from many sources. The University of Puget Sound provided financial resources for travel research and granted him a most timely sabbatical. His university and department colleagues, especially Lisa Johnson, Keith Maxwell, Jim McCullough, and Tami Hulbert, have been demonstratively supportive of the project throughout. His many stellar students, including those in the Business Leadership Program, provided regular and invaluable inspiration. Many other friends lent support in personal ways; they include Tony and Rhonda, Ed and Cheryl, Mark and Allison, Tom H., Dave, Scott, Russ, Dan, Nick and Mirelle, Mark and Nancy, Doug and Lisa, Rob and Gail, Tom S., Steve, Randy and Barb, Brandon, Doug, Bruce, Ross, Kate, Matt, Scott, and Steve. Finally, Jeff benefited enormously from the encouragement of his brothers, Andy and Earl; his mother, Margareta; his supportive wife, Renee; and his beautiful daughters, Kathryn and Emily. They, along with the spirit and memory of his father, Lieutenant Colonel Cleve Matthews, are at the center of his motivation for teaching and learning.

Like Jeff, Harry benefited from the assistance of a number of individuals. During his tenure as an instructor in the Military History Division of the Department of History at West Point, the faculty, led by Colonel James Johnson, provided both financial and moral support for his research. William Robison, head of the Department of History and Political Science at Southeastern Louisiana University, has been kind enough to create a teaching schedule conducive to research and writing. Terrance Winschel, historian at Vicksburg National Military Park, gave invaluable feedback on the Ulysses S. Grant essay. During numerous discussions while walking a number of Civil War battlefields, Dean Burchfield, Greg Hospodor, Paul Starkey, and John Thornell pushed Harry's thinking on military leadership. And most important, his wife, Tara, has shown inexhaustible patience.

Introduction

Leadership for War and Peace

Harry S. Laver and Jeffrey J. Matthews

Few people would challenge the assertion by presidential biographer James MacGregor Burns that "leadership is one of the most observed and least understood phenomena on earth."[1] Yet, in the three decades since the publication of Burns's seminal work *Leadership*, our understanding of the leadership process has improved tremendously. Among the most important developments is the widespread recognition that successful leaders, operating at any level of responsibility, are not simply endowed at birth with great leadership ability. As General William Tecumseh Sherman once observed, "I have read of men born as generals peculiarly endowed by nature but have never seen one."[2] Instead, leadership skills are learned and developed over the course of an individual's life and career through education, mentoring, and experience. Today, there is no longer a debate on this question. Leadership can be learned and applied.

What has not been fully recognized, however, is that leadership development is an active process that requires the conscious and consistent attention of aspiring and proven leaders. To fulfill their leadership potential, individuals must make deliberate choices to improve their leadership skills throughout their careers. This may seem readily apparent, but consider that one may have had the benefits of graduating from a prestigious educational institution, working with the best possible mentors, and gaining experience in a range of circumstances and yet still fail to lead effectively. One must want to become a better leader and strive consistently to achieve that goal. Leaders such as George Washington, Dwight Eisenhower, and George Marshall worked to cultivate their abilities and fulfill their potential through effort and commitment. From their first days as junior officers to their appointments as commanding generals, time and again they chose the difficult path of working to improve their leadership.

The most effective leaders have recognized that they can best enhance their abilities through diverse means. Hands-on, practical experience is perhaps the best way to learn the art of leadership. Learning by doing, however, must always be reinforced with learning by thinking. Those who aspire to improve their leadership—and their followership, for that matter—must reflect on their personal experiences and the experiences of others and learn from both. Consequently, a central component of informed leadership development is studying the past. The political philosopher Niccolò Machiavelli provided wise counsel to the prince when he advised him to use history as a guide for political and military action: "A prudent man should always enter those paths taken by great men [of history] and imitate those who have been most excellent, so that if one's own skill does not match theirs, at least it will have the smell of it." While such counsel might seem obvious, there is growing concern that many of our contemporary leaders see little to be learned from the past. In their thought-provoking book *The Past as Prologue*, historians Williamson Murray and Richard Hart Sinnreich lament that "few current civilian and military leaders seem willing to indulge in a systematic reflection about the past. . . . How else to explain political and military assumptions preceding the 2003 invasion of Iraq that largely ignored the history of the region, [and the] planning that discounted post-conflict challenges . . . and the slowness only thirty years after Vietnam to recognize and deal with the insurgency that followed the collapse of Saddam Hussein's regime."[3]

The primary purpose of our book is to provide both aspiring and experienced leaders, especially those in the military but also civilians in every field and profession, with a historically grounded exploration of leadership development, giving special attention to nine essential qualities of effective leadership. While their working environments may be dramatically different, military and civilian leaders must exercise essentially the same skills. The themes and attributes emphasized here were derived from our experiences as military historians and professors of leadership and from countless discussions with active duty and retired military personnel. We identified nine leadership themes and then selected nine commanders whose leadership styles exemplified those themes. Not surprisingly, each leader personified many, if not all nine, of our key themes. For example, Ulysses S. Grant showed remarkable adaptability and fierce determination during the 1863 Vicksburg campaign. A century later, during the Battle of the Ia Drang Valley, Hal Moore demonstrated flexibility and tenacity equal to Grant's. The purpose of each essay, however, is to put a spotlight on one particular quality as illustrated by one leader. By this simplification of leadership's complexity, the individual elements become more apparent, more easily studied, and therefore more readily learned. The most effective leaders will strive to develop as many of these traits as possible. Some readers may wish to challenge our choices of qualities and leaders or our decision to focus on American military officers. We are confident, nevertheless, that these traits and their associated leaders are appropriate and that the essays present essential qualities of leadership.

Several subthemes emerge from the experiences of these nine leaders. Their careers demonstrate that the quality of one's leadership ability develops over years, even decades. None of them began their careers in the military as exceptional leaders. They did, however, have the good fortune to serve under effective mentors, and, more significantly, each had the good sense to learn from the examples set by these role models. Finally, these nine officers all made deliberate commitments throughout their careers to work consciously and consistently at improving their leadership ability. They understood that, since no one is born an exemplary leader, they too could enhance their efficacy through conscious study and practice.

Today, there are a variety of resources designed to improve leadership effectiveness, including literature that explores military command from a historical perspective. Many such works take a biographical approach to distill lessons to be learned. Others explore how leadership has evolved from the ancient world to contemporary society, highlighting the philosophical and practical changes in command. Some indulge in hagiography; others offer only brief vignettes.[4] Our book is a study of nine essential leadership qualities that span time, place, rank, and branch of service.

In the book's opening chapter, historian Caroline Cox illustrates the preeminent role that integrity plays in the leadership process by examining the military career of George Washington. Early on, Washington recognized the value and power of establishing a reputation for integrity. As a prosperous planter-businessman and militia veteran of the French and Indian War, he came to epitomize the eighteenth-century ideal of gentlemanly honor. Washington's proven abilities and impeccable stature, especially his renown as a person of high moral character, led to his appointment as commander in chief of the Continental Army in 1775. As Cox shows, Washington's integrity, which he demonstrated consistently and guarded carefully throughout the war, was instrumental to his overall leadership effectiveness. In short, moral character and altruism were at the center of Washington's greatness as a leader. According to Thomas Jefferson, the general's "integrity was most pure. . . . His character was, in its mass, perfect," and if not for his well-known "moderation and virtue," the Revolution might have been "closed, as most others have been, by a subversion of that liberty it was intended to establish."[5]

In the second chapter, historian Harry S. Laver studies the evolution of Ulysses S. Grant's military career to reveal the importance of a leader's unremitting resolve in achieving critical objectives. Committed leaders, like Grant, are undeterred by obstacles, constraints, or distractions. As a young officer serving under Zachary Taylor and Winfield Scott in the Mexican-American War, Grant saw firsthand the difference a determined leader could make. He himself showed signs of a developing inner strength during those campaigns, but not until the Civil War did his own force of will become fully apparent. Through the Shiloh, Vicksburg, and Overland campaigns, General Grant, time and again, made the conscious decision to drive on, to push himself and his men forward, and in each instance, his determination was rewarded with battlefield success. General John C. Fremont observed fittingly that Grant "was a man of . . . dogged persistence, and of iron will."[6]

Next, historian Larry I. Bland analyzes the unique domain of institutional leadership by examining the career of George C. Marshall, the U.S. Army's chief of staff from 1939 through 1945. Leaders of large institutions face daunting challenges. Even when their organizations are remarkably efficient, the sheer size gives rise to managerial complexities that can produce bureaucratic inertia, infighting, and a loss of vision and vitality. As Bland demonstrates, Marshall possessed the experience, commitment, assertiveness, and intelligence necessary to meet the challenges of reforming and reenergizing the U.S. military. By emphasizing simplicity, flexibility, and decentralization, Marshall's institutional leadership delivered undeniable effectiveness and efficiency. Near the close of the war in Europe, Winston Churchill cabled Washington and noted, "What a job it must be [for Marshall] to see how the armies he called into being by his own genius have won immortal renown. He is the true 'organizer of victory.'"[7]

The Allied campaigns of World War II proved the absolute necessity of international cooperation, and in the fourth chapter, historian Kerry E. Irish examines the idea of cross-cultural leadership through the military career of Dwight D. Eisenhower. Irish makes evident that Eisenhower's successful leadership as the supreme Allied commander stemmed from nearly two decades of preparation. Serving overseas during the interwar period under generals such as Fox Conner and Douglas MacArthur, Eisenhower came to appreciate both the need for truly unified allied commands and the leadership behaviors essential for their effectiveness. He recognized the importance of flexibility, accountability, humility, consultation, patience, and trust in his relationships with fellow officers and foreign leaders. During the war, Ike proved especially deft at working with political leaders like Franklin Roosevelt and Winston Churchill, with Allied military commanders like Bernard Montgomery and Charles de Gaulle, and with his senior military subordinates like George Patton. As one scholar notes, in his cross-cultural leadership Ike "was patient, tactful, and willing to compromise when the situation allowed, but he was just as able to dig in his heels, cut off debate, and hold his ground."[8]

In the fifth chapter, Colonel Jon T. Hoffman, U.S. Marine Corps Reserves, explores the nature of charismatic leadership in his study of Lewis B. "Chesty" Puller. Charismatic leaders possess exceptional qualities that excite, inspire, and influence followers on an individual, emotional level. As Hoffman demonstrates, Puller's leadership style, most evident during World War II and the Korean War, developed over several decades of military service and education. In the years prior to Pearl Harbor, Puller served in multiple assignments abroad, including marine combat tours in Haiti and Nicaragua; in the United States, he completed military studies at the Virginia Military Institute, in the officer candidate program, and at the U.S. Army Infantry School. The essence of Puller's dynamic leadership was leading by example from the front, developing a personal connection with his subordinates, and ensuring the welfare of his men. Such behavior established strong bonds and unwavering loyalty. One dedicated marine remarked, "He was one of you. He would go to hell and back with you. He wouldn't ask you to do anything that he wasn't doing with you."[9]

Historians François Le Roy and Drew Perkins next analyze Henry H. "Hap" Arnold and the concept of visionary leadership. Visionary leaders craft clear and compelling visions that motivate followers through a shared sense of direction. Unlike institutional leaders, who draw on managerial and administrative skills, visionary leaders must identify long-term objectives and maintain their organizations' focus and momentum. By steadfastly pursuing deliberate objectives, leaders such as Arnold change the status quo and provide their organizations with control over their operating environments. Along with other pioneering aviators of the early twentieth century such as General Billy Mitchell, Arnold developed an appreciation for the potential role of air power in modern warfare. His vision was to create a massive, technically advanced air force that was organizationally independent of the army and thus operationally capable of strategic bombing campaigns.

Research and development were central to Arnold's conception of building and sustaining America's air dominance, and he envisioned close and continuous collaboration between air force personnel and civilian scientists in academia and industry. Unlike other air power visionaries, Mitchell included, Arnold demonstrated considerable political skill to oversee the transformation of America's air power. His leadership success was defined by the clear articulation of a comprehensive vision, an extensive knowledge of aeronautics and logistics, and a fierce resolve to achieve his objectives. Theodore von Kármán, a leading aeronautical engineer and Arnold's colleague, appropriately described the general as "the greatest example of the U.S. military man—a combination of complete logic, mingled with farsightedness and superb dedication."[10]

In the book's seventh chapter, Tim Foster, a former business executive with the U.S. Naval Nuclear Propulsion Program, assesses the career of his former boss, Hyman G. Rickover, to uncover important attributes of effective leadership in the field of high technology. Technological shifts can significantly alter institutional capabilities, leader-follower dynamics, and the broader operating environment. Consequently, leaders like Rickover are tasked with developing, implementing, and adapting to technological change. As the father of the nuclear navy, Rickover epitomized effective technological leadership. The essential elements of his success included his innovative approaches to problem solving, his unshakable determination to succeed, and his high standards for performance and accountability. According to the U.S. Atomic Energy Commission's official historian, Rickover's "greatest legacy was training people how to achieve technical excellence, not only in the navy but in industry and other walks of life."[11]

In chapter eight, Colonel H. R. McMaster, U.S. Army, analyzes the importance of a leader's adaptability when operating in uncertain and complex environments. Adaptive leaders understand that leadership is a contingent and situational practice and that effective action in one situation will not necessarily bring success in a different context. McMaster focuses on Harold G. "Hal" Moore, the battalion commander who demonstrated an extraordinary ability to adapt during the Battle of the Ia Drang Valley in Vietnam. According to McMaster, central to Moore's successful leadership was his thorough preparation for command, along with his creative intellect, physical courage, and sheer resolve. "Again, the principle which must be driven into your own head and the heads of your men," Moore instructed, "is: *Three strikes and you're NOT out!* . . . There is always one more thing you can do to influence any situation in your favor."[12]

In the book's final chapter, historian Jeffrey J. Matthews examines the unsung yet critical role of effective followership in the leadership process and notes that most people in positions of organizational authority must assume the complicated dual roles of follower and leader. Rare is the leadership position that is not simultaneously a position of followership. Too often, followership evokes a negative connotation, implying that those who follow are inherently submissive, dependent, passive, and unimaginative. To the contrary, the best and most effective followers share many characteristics with successful leaders, including enthusiasm, competence, commitment, courage, assertiveness, moral conduct, and independent critical judgment. To illustrate exemplary followership and its connection to leadership development, Matthews traces the military career of Colin L. Powell, who spent much of his remarkable career in advisory, not command, positions. In the aftermath of the Persian Gulf War, President George H. W. Bush praised Powell for his concurrent performance as an exemplary follower and leader: "If there's anybody that has the integrity and the honor to tell a president what he feels, it's Colin Powell, and if there's anybody that is disciplined enough and enough of a leader to instill confidence in his troops, it's Colin Powell."[13] By demonstrating the qualities of an exemplary follower, a leader presents an appropriate and realistic role model for everyone within his organization.

From George Washington to Colin Powell, individuals have sought ways to improve their leadership abilities. In the training manual *Infantry in Battle*, first published in 1934, then-colonel George C. Marshall instructed soldiers on the importance of leadership development: "To master his difficult art [a leader] must learn to cut to the heart of a situation, recognize its decisive elements and base his course of action on these. The ability to do this is not God-given, nor can it be acquired overnight; it is a process of years. He must realize that training in solving problems of all types, long practice making clear, unequivocal decisions, the habit of concentrating on the question at hand, and an elasticity of mind, are indispensable requisites for the successful practice of the art of war." No single book on leadership development can be comprehensive, but we believe that students and practitioners who master and apply the leadership concepts herein will be well served.[14]

Notes

1. James MacGregor Burns, *Leadership* (New York: HarperCollins, 1978), 2.

2. Sherman quoted in Maxwell D. Taylor, "Military Leadership: What Is It? Can It Be Taught?" in *Concepts for Air Force Leadership* (Montgomery, AL: Air University Press, 2001), 423–26.

3. Niccolò Machiavelli, *The Prince*, trans. and ed. Peter Bondanella (New York, 1979), 20; Williamson Murray and Richard Hart Sinnreich, *The Past as Prologue: The Importance of History to the Military Profession* (Cambridge: Cambridge University Press, 2006), 1.

4. Robert Taylor and William E. Rosenbach, eds., *Military Leadership: In Pursuit of Excellence*, 5th ed. (Boulder, CO: Westview/Perseus, 2005); Edgar F. Puryear Jr., *Nineteen Stars: A Study in Military Character and Leadership* (New York: Presidio, 2003); Edgar Puryear Jr., *American Generalship: Character Is Everything; The Art of Command* (Novata, CA: Presidio, 2000); Christopher Kolenda, ed., *Leadership: The Warrior's Art* (Carlisle, PA: Army War College Foundation, 2001); Harry J. Maihafer, *Brave Decisions: Fifteen Profiles in Courage and Character from American Military History* (Dulles, VA: Brassey's, 1999); Roger H. Nye, *The Challenge of Command: Reading for Military Excellence* (New York: Perigee, 2002).

5. Thomas Jefferson to Madame de Tesse, 8 December 1813, in Thomas Jefferson, *Writings*, ed. Merrill Peterson (New York: Library of America, 1984), 1318–21; Thomas Jefferson to George Washington, 6 April 1784, in Thomas Jefferson, *Papers*, ed. Julian P. Boyd (Princeton, NJ: Princeton University Press, 1950–2006), 7:106.

6. Fremont quoted in Jean Edward Smith, *Grant* (New York: Simon and Schuster, 2001), 117.

7. Winston Churchill to Field Marshal Wilson, 30 March 1945, in Forrest C. Pogue, *George C. Marshall* (New York: Viking, 1963–1987), 3:585.

8. David A. Smith, "Dwight David Eisenhower," in *Encyclopedia of Leadership*, ed. George R. Goethals, Georgia J. Sorenson, and James MacGregor Burns (Thousand Oaks, CA: Sage, 2004), 414–17.

9. Jim Butterfield, interview by Jon T. Hoffman, 1995.

10. Kármán quoted in James L. Stokesbury, *The Rise of American Air Power* (New York: William and Morrow, 1986), 186.

11. Francis Duncan, "Hyman George Rickover," in *American National Biography*, ed. John A. Garraty and Mark C. Carnes (Oxford: Oxford University Press, 2001), 483.

12. Harold G. Moore, "Battlefield Leadership," 16 December 2003, http://www.au.af.mil/au/awc/awcgate/documents/moore.htm.

13. Bush quoted in Karen DeYoung, *Soldier: The Life of Colin Powell* (New York: Knopf, 2006), 216.

14. George C. Marshall, *Infantry in Battle*, 2nd ed. (Washington: Infantry Journal, 1939), 1.

1

Integrity and Leadership

George Washington

Caroline Cox

In March 1783, when peace negotiations with Great Britain were under way and the end of the Revolutionary War was in sight, the American army faced one of its greatest crises. The restless officers of the Continental Army believed they had endured enough hardship. Their pay was in arrears, as usual, and their accounts had not been settled for the food and clothing that they had provided for their men. From their winter quarters at Newburgh, New York, the officers petitioned Congress in Philadelphia to address their grievances. They even hinted of a possible mutiny. Some congressional delegates were sympathetic to their plight, and perhaps a few hoped that discontent in the army would lead to a change in the constitutional arrangements that would give Congress the authority to tax the states. But whatever political intrigue swirled, the Continental Congress had no funds to pay the officers what they were owed. General George Washington wrote to his former aide de camp, Alexander Hamilton, "The sufferings of a complaining Army on the one hand and the inability of Congress and tardiness of the States on the other, are the forebodings of evil." He feared the situation would "end in blood."[1]

The evil that Washington feared manifested itself on 10 March, and in facing it, he staked his own integrity. The crisis began when he was handed an anonymously written flyer that called the officers of the army to a meeting. The note warned ominously, "The army has

GEORGE WASHINGTON
(Metropolitan Museum of Art, New York)

its alternative." One alternative was for the army to refuse to disarm if a peace treaty were struck with Britain. If no peace were negotiated, the army could also disband, leaving the nation to deal with the British without armed forces.[2]

Shocked by the threat of disobedience, Washington acted quickly. He issued general orders the next day that strongly condemned such "disorderly proceedings." Recognizing that the groundswell of unhappiness had to be quelled, Washington called for his own meeting of the officer corps. Before it could take place, however, the anonymous author issued another flyer. It claimed that Washington's agreement to meet with the officers indicated his sympathy for their cause, and he had thus "sanctified" their complaints.[3] The meeting would be tense.

On 15 March, promptly at noon, Washington addressed his assembled officers and, in one of the most moving speeches of his long public life, defused the crisis and transformed his disgruntled, mutinous officer corps into dutiful servants of the new nation. He accomplished this feat by interlocking his own reputation for integrity with their actions, by speaking with eloquence, and by having a small measure of luck. Washington embodied the ideal of the officer and gentleman. An unflinching commitment to safeguard his reputation for personal honor had always guided his actions. Thus his call for his officers to remember their own "sacred honor" had profound meaning. He encouraged them to rebuff those who sought to "overturn the liberties of our Country." He implored them to do nothing "which, viewed in the calm light of reason, will lessen the dignity and sully the glory you have hitherto maintained." In addition to reminding them of their own honor and integrity and of the great cause for which they all labored, Washington spoke of his own commitment and integrity and linked his star to their conduct: "I have never left your side one moment. . . . I have been the constant companion and witness of your Distress, and not among the last to feel and acknowledge your Merits. . . . I have ever considered my own Military reputation as inseparably connected with that of the Army."[4]

Washington's speech was eloquent and moving, infused with candor and genuine emotion. A happy accident also served him well. In explaining the country's dire financial difficulties, he read aloud a letter written by Joseph Jones, a congressional delegate from Virginia. Washington struggled to read this densely written text, which did not make for scintillating speechifying. He pulled his spectacles out from his pocket to read more easily. As he did so, he casually commented to the crowd, "Gentlemen, you must pardon me. I have grown gray in your service and now find myself growing blind." The aside profoundly moved his audience and dissipated the tension. After Washington left the room, the officers reasserted their loyalty to Congress and entrusted the general to negotiate with that body on their behalf. The so-called Newburgh conspiracy was over.[5]

In a military career that endured a variety of crises—fiscal, logistical, and military—the crisis at Newburgh during the last winter of the war exemplified the importance of Washington's integrity to his effective leadership. Later generations of historians were not alone in citing the centrality of his integrity. Washington himself had consciously brought this quality to his duties as commander in chief. It was one of the primary characteristics that contemporaries recognized in him and that earned him the generalship of the American army. In the eighteenth century, the word "integrity" was not used lightly. Its meaning was profound. To have integrity meant to be independent, incorruptible, selfless, dedicated, honest, and of sound moral principle. One had to be perceived as responsible and trustworthy in every setting and circumstance, whether social, financial, or political. A person of integrity was true to all personal commitments and, as a result, was capable of building and sustaining trusting relationships.[6]

When Washington forestalled a possible mutiny, it was an accomplishment borne of his stellar reputation for integrity. He had consistently demonstrated his commitment to the patriotic cause. He had built trusting relationships with his officers. When he reminded them of their common larger purpose against the British, he was in fact reminding them of their own obligation to act with integrity. Through his war service, Washington had come to epitomize the cultural ideals of military and gentlemanly honor, of which integrity was the central quality, and his officers admired him accordingly.

Washington's influence over his officers would have been limited had his integrity been an abstract virtue. However, he had demonstrated it continuously throughout the war and thus earned the respect of the army and Congress. Both had given him enormous power over all their lives. Congress had channeled huge sums of money through his hands and granted him considerable latitude in war planning and in matters of civilian and military relations. He never once abused that trust. Indeed, he had been reluctant at times to use the full range of authority granted him. The officers and men of the army had accepted his leadership and his authority to make life-or-death decisions. Washington had used his integrity and the trust that it generated to keep the army together as it struggled against the British, then the most powerful army in the world. As commander in chief, he wielded considerable influence yet led by example, demonstrating personal courage, financial honesty, and steadfast political commitment. Drawing on modern theories of management, we can see that Washington offered his men both transactional leadership, an exchange of interests and responsibilities to meet individual needs, and transformational leadership, a chance to participate in something larger than themselves. Washington, of course, knew nothing of these academic theories; instead he acted on the bases of character and experience.

Even as a youth, Washington sought to act in ways that would bring him respect as a gentleman of integrity. Although he never actually chopped down a cherry tree and then refused to lie about it, young Washington consciously thought about how to acquire a good reputation. To be a gentleman was a social necessity for a prosperous man in eighteenth-century Western society generally and in Virginia society particularly. Financial independence was part of the equation, but one also had to be a man of knowledge, manners, and honor. Many men who aspired to be gentlemen failed to live up to this cultural ideal, but Washington was determined to be respected. When he was about fifteen years old, he famously transcribed 110 rules of civility, which he copied from a widely available courtesy book on good manners. Two central themes of these rules were that respect should be given to others when due and that respect from others was earned by one's personal conduct. Guided by these cultural values, Washington always tried to act in ways that would earn him respect.[7]

Washington's integrity was shaped by his father and his older half brother, Lawrence, by his own sociability, by his ambition, and by his inquiring mind. His quick temper might have derailed him, but he controlled it reasonably well. Born in 1732 to a prosperous planter, Washington received a mostly informal education, provided at different times by his father, Lawrence, tutors, and teachers. This improvised schooling served him well. He possessed a curious mind and loved grappling with detail. His father died when he was eleven years old, and Lawrence, fourteen years George's senior, became the family patriarch. Although Lawrence left George in order to manage Mount Vernon, a family property, he stayed in close contact with his younger brother, offering him guidance, adventure, direction, and an education. Lawrence's marriage to Ann Fairfax connected the Washingtons to one of Virginia's wealthiest families and swept George into a higher social world, where a reputation for integrity was paramount.[8] After Lawrence's death, young George seized the opportunity to demonstrate his managerial and leadership abilities. Not only did he skillfully organize and administer his brother's confused business affairs, but he also assumed Lawrence's position in the Virginia militia—becoming a regional adjutant at twenty-one.[9]

Washington's experiences leading the militia and subsequently provincial troops in the Ohio Valley in 1754 and through the French and Indian War were formative, and they laid the foundation for his public reputation as a leader of ability, energy, and integrity. He developed his skills in the field, observing experienced British officers and gaining practical knowledge by building fortifications, managing scarce men and materiel, and administering the complex details necessary to operating an army. He augmented this learning with extensive reading of classical literature, such as Julius Caesar's *Commentaries*, and contemporary training manuals, such as Humphrey Bland's *Trea-*

tise of Military Discipline. While youthful inexperience caused him to make critical mistakes in tactics, he demonstrated his ability to think clearly in the midst of chaos. During the infamous defeat of the British forces under General Edward Braddock at the hands of the French and Indians in 1755, he remained coolheaded and competent. As the British troops embarked on an ignoble retreat and many officers lay dead or dying, including Braddock himself, Washington brought order to the confusion and ensured the safe return of the survivors. He secured Braddock's body, gave him a dignified funeral, and took news of the disaster back to military and civilian leaders. Washington's integrity was exemplified by his honest financial management while in command of the Virginia provincial troops. The exigencies of war required him to manage significant sums of money, and unlike some other leaders, Washington consistently resisted the temptation to pad his own expenses. In fact, he brazenly assured the governor of Virginia, Robert Dinwiddie, that "no man, that ever was employed in a public capacity, has endeavored to discharge the trust reposed in him with greater honesty, and more zeal for the country's interest, than I have done." Having thus conducted himself with honor and excelled as an administrator and leader, Washington emerged from the war with a well-deserved reputation for ability and integrity.[10]

Washington's reputation as a man of honor and competence was solidified in the postwar era when he fully entered public life. He served as a vestryman in his church, as a representative in the House of Burgesses, and eventually as a member of the Continental Congress. He continued to read widely, mastered new farming methods, and studied his community. His personal fortune, which was enhanced greatly by his marriage to the wealthy widow Martha Custis, helped to secure him further prominence. One could be a man of integrity without amassing substantial wealth, of course, but it was widely considered that only a gentleman of financial independence could serve the public interest without obligation to any individual or political faction. Not many of Washington's contemporaries attained the ideal of financial independence. As the colonial political crisis with Great Britain intensified in the years before the Revolutionary War, even the most prosperous Virginia gentlemen experienced cash flow problems as tobacco prices fell and western land speculation failed to yield immediate profits. Washington also encountered such problems. He was in debt to his London agent, but unlike many others, he had diversified his crops and had not recklessly gambled on frontier real estate. In short, Washington's prudent management kept his wealth secure, and he came to epitomize the ideal public servant: independent and incorruptible.[11]

Washington's reputation as a man of character and integrity preceded him as he moved from Virginia to the national stage. His moral character was especially admired by members of the Continental Congress and other leaders. American patriots often suspected that many of their travails with the British government came from the intrigues of placemen, men who held patronage appointments and who were forever maneuvering for personal advancement rather than the public good. Thus, when congressional delegates were considering who should command armed forces, they were dismayed by men who actively lobbied for the position, such as John Hancock and Charles Lee. Washington, in contrast, did not aggressively court the office—though he did wear his Virginia militia uniform to meetings to signal his military experience. His renowned prudence, his military record, his general reputation, and his residence in the most populous colony all made him a prime candidate to lead the army.

Washington's prominent reputation led to his appointment as commander in chief of the Revolutionary Army in June 1775. When he rejected any salary, settling only for the reimbursement of his expenses, he embodied the eighteenth-century notion of an honorable public servant. Yet there are two issues that, for some modern scholars, stain his reputation for integrity and disinterested public service: he was a slave owner and a speculator in western lands. On both matters, British policies weakened his financial interests. In 1775, the royal governor of Virginia, Lord Dunmore, offered freedom to all slaves who came to British lines, and some of Washington's slaves were among those who answered this call. Like other Virginia planters, Washington was outraged by this challenge to Virginia's authority and to colonial property rights. Additionally, the British closed western lands to new settlement in the hope of staving off conflict between settlers and native peoples, and that delayed any financial return Washington might have made on his land investments there. Neither of these matters lessened his reputation for integrity in the eyes of his contemporaries. That the British had violated his property rights simply fortified his patriotic credentials and did nothing to injure his reputation as a man who stood above faction and passion. His willingness to risk his fortune for those rights attested to his high principles. Thus John Adams could recommend Washington as "an Officer, whose independent fortune, great Talents and excellent universal Character" made him an ideal candidate to be commander in chief.[12]

At the time of his appointment, Washington expressed serious personal doubts about his ability to mold an army that would be capable of defeating the British. He hoped his moral compass would serve as his guide. In his acceptance speech to Congress, he expressed his concern that he "may not be equal to the extensive & important Trust" given to him. Many in Congress interpreted this as modesty, but he had also confided his insecurity to his wife and friends. He confessed his fear to Martha that Congress had bestowed a "trust too great for my Capacity." He told Burwell Bassett that he worried over his "want of experience in the conduct of so momentous a concern." In the end, he believed his role as the American military commander was "a kind of destiny." He wrote to Bassett that he would be sustained by three factors: "a firm belief in the justice of the cause—close attention to the prosecution of it—and the strictest Integrety [*sic*]." The first two sustained Washington in the field when he was most disheartened. It was his personal integrity, however, that guided his daily actions and stands as the hallmark of his leadership.[13]

One important aspect of Washington's integrity was that he always assumed responsibility for his decisions, even when they had arisen from lengthy consultations with others. As the newly appointed commander of the army, he willingly accepted Congress's injunction to consult frequently with a "council of war" that consisted of senior military officers. Congress favored the advisory council because it was suspicious of standing armies and the unrestrained power of its commander. This stipulation did not offend Washington. Uncertain of his command abilities, he relied heavily on the council. In fact, during the first year of the war, he allowed it to overrule him. For example, the council challenged him when he presented plans for a full-scale attack on Boston in February 1776. One biographer suggests that his plans were so optimistic that council members "questioned his grasp on reality." Washington later admitted that his planned attack was "more than could be warranted by prudence." As General Washington gained experience and confidence, he continued to seek the council's advice, but increasingly he followed his own instincts, and he always accepted the burden of responsibility.[14]

The importance of integrity to effective military leadership in the eighteenth century cannot be overstated. Harsh and brutal punishments were often seen as the keys to maintaining discipline, and coercion certainly occurred. However, another cornerstone of military authority was trust. Soldiers in the Continental Army needed to trust their officers' integrity—their fairness, honesty, morality, and courage. Because soldiers lived in harsh conditions with poor food and intermittent pay, they had to trust that their officers and the commander in chief would be just and active agents on their behalf. Whereas soldiers in European armies often served for life, American soldiers in the Revolutionary War were mostly volunteers who served under a variety of short-term contracts, ranging from several months to three years. It was crucial, then, that Washington's soldiers acquire sufficient confidence in the officer corps so that when they left the military, they were willing to reenlist or support it in other ways.[15]

Because officers possessed the authority to make life-or-death decisions, they needed to inspire an extraordinary degree of trust and confidence. These crucial decisions took place most commonly on the battlefield, but officers had additional settings in which to exercise critical leadership power. Since death from diseases such as dysentery and typhus far outstripped battlefield deaths in this period, policing camp life had implications beyond daily comfort. Moreover, military courts had the authority to dole out fines, imprisonment, corporal punishment, or execution by hanging or a firing squad. In short, the power of military leaders over their men encompassed almost every aspect of daily life. Nevertheless, the fact that most men were volunteers meant that officers had to demonstrate their integrity by treating soldiers fairly and with a modicum of respect. The army was desperate for men, and despite harsh conditions, low pay, and, in the words of one veteran, "marching and countermarching, starving and freezing," it needed soldiers to sign up for multiple years of service.[16]

In this challenging leadership environment, Washington relied on inspirational tactics and his personal reputation for integrity to keep the Continental Army together. He offered his men an opportunity to transform themselves, to pursue something larger than their individual interests. He reminded the officers that they were "contending for liberty," a political objective that most appealed to the propertied men, who possessed voting rights and served on juries. Washington understood that enlisted men had limited political rights and believed they had little stake in the legal issues of the Revolution. He had no illusions about "such People as compose the bulk of an Army." He believed they were probably not motivated to serve "by any other principles than those of [material] interest." Unfortunately, Washington also knew that he could not always supply enlisted soldiers with the promised pay, food, and supplies. Instead, he had to draw on his personal integrity to instill in soldiers a pride in being part of the army itself and part of the larger Revolutionary cause.[17]

This inspirational tactic became increasingly effective as American soldiers gained experience, professional skills, and the confidence to compete with the legendary British armed forces. During the terrible winter of 1777–1778 at Valley Forge, Washington was continually visible to his men. Regardless of weather conditions, he inspected the encampment daily and directed its maintenance. Beyond such a regimen, he also attended to the larger war strategy and trained the troops. The army suffered harsh conditions at Valley Forge but emerged a more confident and professional fighting force. Moreover, the experience there deepened the soldiers' personal connection to Washington, as he had earned their trust and loyalty.[18]

An exemplary officer and gentleman, Washington instilled confidence, skill, and pride through leadership by example. He fully understood that he had to model appropriate behavior and promote high standards of conduct, including personal integrity in financial matters. He demanded that his officers be equally virtuous, and that was no easy task. After all, he later noted, "the most enviable of all titles" was to have "the character of *an honest man*." It was an enviable reputation not only because it added to personal honor but also because it was so difficult to accomplish. Even so, it was basic to Washington, and he was surprised at having to chastise junior officers for financial irregularities. Because officers bought food and clothing for their men, a good deal of money passed through their hands. In 1775, Washington was outraged that some engaged in "low & dirty arts . . . to filch the public." He campaigned successfully for improved pay, which he hoped would solve the problem. It did, along with rigorous courts-martial of those suspected of embezzling.[19]

Washington also used much subtler means to promote integrity in his officers. For example, he arranged regular dinners with senior subordinates to become better acquainted with them, to assess their talents, and to model effective leadership. Such events were key to his ability to earn trust and respect, and the dinners, inspired by the British army's regimental mess system, integrated new officers into their regiments. There was no comparable institution in the Continental Army, but through this extension of his Virginia hospitality, Washington accomplished many of the same goals, and he expected in turn that his senior staff socialize with junior officers.[20]

Within his relatively small army, Washington also used his reputation for integrity to build trust with junior officers in direct ways. He met frequently with them to discuss petitions for the redress of grievances and to forge influential personal connections. Lieutenant John Bell Tilden of Pennsylvania, a twenty-year-old college graduate, met Washington for the first time in 1781 at Williamsburg, Virginia. In his journal, he described the fanfare of the commander in chief's arrival and noted that Washington invited all officers of the Pennsylvania line to his quarters, where "he received them very politely and shook each officer by the hand." Tilden was thrilled at this mark of warmth and affability, as bowing was the formal way of acknowledging someone. The young lieutenant was in awe of Washington's informality and accessibility, which only increased his trust in him.[21]

In his attempts to build trust with subordinates, Washington was careful not to become overly friendly. He was frequently reserved, even aloof. He did not suffer fools gladly and only rarely engaged in idle chitchat. Yet he understood both the power of his reputation as a man of great integrity and the value of visibility and personal interaction. He realized that young officers such as Tilden, who admired him as a man of honor, would be motivated by the contact. On select occasions, Washington even bantered with enlisted men and with the women of the camp. As in other eighteenth-century armies, a large number of women—wives, laundresses, sutlers, and others— traveled with the Continental Army. One of these women was the young Sarah Osborn, who had followed her husband to the army camp. She cooked, sewed, and washed for him and his messmates. One day, when his unit was in an entrenchment besieging York- town, she braved flying missiles to carry "beef, bread, and coffee" to the soldiers. She later remembered that Washington had called out to her and asked if she were not afraid of the cannonballs. She replied, "No, the bullets would not cheat the gallows," joking that she had a rougher destiny. It was a small exchange but indicative of a commander whose followers believed they had an intimate connec- tion to him. Such ties were critical to the soldiers and camp followers who often marched on empty stomachs and served in physically try- ing conditions. For Tilden and Osborn, Washington's conduct rein- forced their image of him as a leader with integrity who had earned their trust and loyalty.[22]

Washington's personal reputation among soldiers and officers was crucial for an army that had little to celebrate. From the dis- tance of more than two centuries, we measure Washington's effectiveness by his ultimate military victory over the British. However, for much of the war, the army's engagements with the British were largely unsuccessful. Even as peace was being negotiated, the enemy still controlled important North American cities. Thus the measure of leadership success in the Revolution was not the kind that we usually expect in military conflicts. Success for Washington was not in battlefield victory alone but also in simply keeping the army together. No matter what disappointments the army faced in the field, as long as it continued to exist, the Revolution was alive. The longer the Continental forces fought, the more secure Congress and the new nation became, the more other nations accepted the legitimacy of the new government, and the more disgruntled and war weary the British became.

Despite a steady string of military setbacks through 1776, Washington's evident integrity and selflessness quickly gained the trust of Congress and the army. As a result, Congress invested Washington with broad decision-making powers to enhance his effectiveness in the field and to improve organizational efficiency. The powers it granted went far beyond the needs of the moment, allowing him to raise and "equip three thousand light horse, three regiments of artillery, and a corps of engineers, and to establish their pay," appoint officers, requisition supplies from local populations, and "to arrest and Confine Persons who refuse to take the Continental Currency." This authority was given to him by politicians who were highly suspicious of the concentration of power and who were struggling against British parliamentary usurpation of authority. In an era without a president, Washington became the closest thing to a chief executive. It is a testament to his integrity that, in this crisis, Congress entrusted him with such unprecedented authority. This trust was not misplaced, as the general was uncomfortable with these immense powers and rarely used them.[23]

The military situation deteriorated through 1777, and while no one questioned Washington's integrity, some questioned his competence. There were murmurs of discontent from various American political and military leaders who thought that others—perhaps even they themselves—would make better commanders in chief. These criticisms coalesced into the so-called Conway cabal, named after Brigadier General Thomas Conway, who authored several damning letters. Although most historians discount the existence of an organized cabal against his authority, Washington clearly suspected one. This tempest gathered after American general Horatio Gates's victory at Saratoga, New York, in October 1777, while Washington was struggling in vain against the British near Philadelphia. Always sensitive to criticism, Washington was disturbed by a letter from Conway to Gates that questioned his leadership abilities. Washington believed that these two men, along with their supporters in Congress, might attempt to remove him. He went on the offensive, going public with their criticisms and objecting to these slights to his reputation. Some people wondered whether Washington's quick response was politically calculated. Regardless, the crisis passed when the men who had privately doubted the general leapt to his defense. The affair forced Congress to consider more openly its military leadership alternatives. This challenge to Washington's authority, however, only served to cement his positive reputation. As Washington biographer James Flexner notes, there were few leaders capable of performing better. The much respected Washington, it seems, was indeed "the indispensable man."[24]

In this affair, as in all other matters, Washington ultimately submitted himself to the will of Congress. The Conway cabal only added to his stature as a disinterested public servant, and no matter how he chafed against the slow pace of congressional or state assembly action, he kept his frustrations private. His correspondence with those bodies was always respectful, if firm, and he always deferred to civilian authority. Thus, as the war progressed, his own stature rose because of what he did not do—abuse his power. This was striking to foreign observers such as the Marquis de Chastellux, a French major general, who noted that Washington always had "obeyed the Congress; more need not be said, especially in America, where they know how to appreciate all the merit contained in this simple fact."[25]

Praise for Washington's integrity during the Conway cabal added greatly to his stature among his contemporaries from all walks of life. By his honorable conduct in relations with Congress, he ful-filled a contemporary political ideal. In the eighteenth century, Whig sentiment was deeply entrenched in the colonies. Whigs saw power as expansive, always needing to be checked, and liberty as delicate, needing protection and nurturing. Patriot Samuel Adams observed that "ambition and lust of power above the law are . . . the predomi-nant passions in the breasts of most men." Thus General Washing-ton's continual deference to civilian authority was much more than a "simple fact." He embodied the Whig ideal, and this fortified the country's trust in him.[26]

It was not only the political elite who trusted Washington; so too did the soldiers of the army. This was reflected in the reenlist-ment rates. On one occasion, knowing that the size of his army might dwindle, Washington risked an attack on Hessian troops at Tren-ton, New Jersey, and achieved an overwhelming victory. To follow through on that success and press the enemy, however, he needed his army to reenlist. The men, filthy, tired, and homesick, resisted all en-treaties, flatteries, and inducements until Washington's personal plea on New Year's Eve turned the tide. One sergeant remembered that Washington's prepared speech elicited little response. Then the com-mander in chief exclaimed, "My brave fellows, you have done all I asked you to do and more than could be reasonably expected . . . but we know not how to spare you. . . . The present is emphatically the crisis, which is to decide our destiny." The sergeant recalled that the "soldiers felt the force of the appeal." Although hundreds did leave, many more stayed on. Washington was both inspiring and lucky. On New Year's Day, a sack of hard cash arrived at camp, and he was able to pay the reenlistment bounties he had offered his men.[27]

Washington's commitment to the patriot cause and his willing-ness to risk his own life for it were at the core of his integrity. On the battlefield, he led by example. At the Battle of Monmouth in June 1778, for example, he saved the day with what Alexander Hamilton called "the skill of a master workman." There was considerable con-fusion on the battlefield when General Charles Lee ordered American forces to withdraw. Washington claimed this directive was against his express instructions. Some historians have been kinder to Lee, arguing that Washington's orders were unclear. Whatever the case, Washington rallied and exhorted the exhausted troops to reengage the enemy. In doing so, he exposed himself to considerable personal danger from enemy fire. Alexander Hamilton remembered that Washington "brought order out of confusion, animated his troops and led them to success." At best the battle was a draw, but that was much better than a defeat. Hamilton was correct in noting that Washington had "turned the fate of the day." It was one of his finest moments as a battlefield leader. It was also an occasion in which he forged a bond with his soldiers who had fought hard in intense heat that day. He had inspired them, and they identified their own bravery with his.[28]

There is another, less-known leadership accomplishment that depended on, and also deepened, the trust of his soldiers: the containment of the terrible smallpox epidemic that swept through the army. The disease made its appearance in 1775. Although nothing could be done to treat it, Americans already knew about a practice of inoculation known as variolation. Infectious material was taken from the smallpox pustules of a sick person and inserted under the skin of a healthy person, who, if well rested, usually contracted only a slight case of the disease. This brief experience conferred a lifetime of immunity. Because there was some risk of contracting a full-blown case of the often fatal illness, however, many people were afraid of the inoculation procedure.[29]

Washington faced the difficult decision of whether to inoculate his soldiers. Characteristically, he sought input from his subordinates. Washington, who had experienced smallpox as a young man, thought that inoculation was too dangerous for the army. He not only questioned the viability of the practice but also feared a British attack if the enemy learned that many soldiers were on enforced rest. Still, many doctors and surgeons were in favor of variolation, and some soldiers, contrary to Washington's orders, had inoculated themselves. Washington decided to attempt to prevent the disease from spreading by quarantining sick soldiers and burning contaminated clothes.[30]

Washington's preventive measures were only temporarily successful. In January 1777, while he was celebrating important victories
at Trenton and Princeton, the disease struck again. Washington was
initially still indecisive as to whether to proceed with inoculation. The
task was immense. The soldiers had to be polled to find out who
had already had the disease. Those at risk had to be separated from
their units, nursed through the process, and then returned to duty.
The medical procedure had to be conducted with "the necessity of as
much secresy [sic] as the nature of the Subject will admit" to prevent
the British from learning of it. Finally, Washington decided to take
the risk, and over the next year or so, doctors inoculated hundreds of
men. Thereafter, the army experienced only occasional outbreaks of
the disease. Washington never fully grasped the magnitude of his accomplishment, but in the words of historian Elizabeth Fenn, he had
carried out the "first large scale, state-sponsored immunization campaign in American history." The program had required an immense
commitment of resources, administrative energy, and the cooperation
of the soldiers themselves. Washington had made a bold and risky
decision. In a time when many more soldiers died from disease than
on the battlefield, it was an extraordinary achievement made possible
because of Washington's deep commitment to his troops and their
absolute trust in him.[31]

In a military career filled with demonstrations of his integrity, perhaps the most symbolic one, and arguably the most significant, came
when Washington resigned his commission at the end of December
1783. Valuing reputation above all else, he made certain that his final
acts as commander in chief exemplified and enhanced his credibility.
At the beginning of the war, Congress had trusted him with immense
power because of his reputation for integrity. Throughout the long
years of the war, he had given Congress every reason to be secure in
that trust. His actions continually testified to his belief that civilian
control of the army was sacrosanct. It was his adherence to this moral
principle, his absolute integrity on this matter, that was his greatest
legacy to the new nation. Rarely in human history had anyone in such
a strong position to usurp power shied away from doing it. Washing-

ton insisted that his resignation as commander in chief be a public event. It was important that everyone know that he had fulfilled this immense public trust and walked away. Historian Robert Middlekauff notes that when Washington arrived in Annapolis, where Congress was sitting, "some hoped—and others feared—that he was Caesar," that he would fail this final test of his willingness to subordinate himself to civilian authority. However, as Middlekauff observed, Washington might "have admired Caesar [but] he admired the republic more."[32] In what he thought would be his last significant public act, Washington demonstrated his deference to civilian authority.

The carefully planned resignation on 23 December 1783 was well attended. The president of Congress, Thomas Mifflin, met Washington as he entered the capitol. The general read his prepared speech to Congress. His hands trembled with emotion, but his voice gained in confidence as he spoke: "Having now finished the work assigned me, I retire from the great theater of Action; and Bidding an Affectionate farewell to this August body under whose orders I have so long acted, I here offer my Commission, and take my leave of all the employments of public life." Mifflin's reply, written by Thomas Jefferson, acknowledged Washington's gift to the nation: "You have conducted the great military contest with wisdom and fortitude, through invariably regarding the rights of the civil government power through all disasters and changes."[33]

Many years later, after Washington's death, Jefferson recalled the commander in chief he had known. Not all of his memories were complimentary. Washington's "mind," he wrote, "was great and powerful without being of the very first order . . . slow in operation, being little aided by invention or imagination." He also remembered Washington's sharp temper but noted that "reflection and resolution had obtained a firm and habitual ascendancy over it." Perhaps most important, Jefferson recalled that Washington's integrity was "most pure, his justice the most inflexible I have ever known, no motives of interest or consanguinity, of friendship or hatred, being able to bias his decision. . . . His character was, in its mass, perfect."[34] Washington's wartime service in "the great theater of Action" exemplified the many meanings of leadership integrity. We, in the present day, know how the story ended, but for much of the war, Washington could not foresee the outcome. Indeed, for many years, he saw only a bleak future. His commitment to the Revolutionary cause and his sense of duty, honor, and integrity sustained him through the darkest days. That same integrity bound the army, Congress, and the public to him and led to an improbable victory over the world's strongest military power.

Notes

1. Edward G. Lengel, *General George Washington: A Military Life* (New York: Random House, 2005), 345–46; Robert Middlekauff, *The Glorious Cause: The American Revolution, 1763–1789*, 2nd ed. (New York: Oxford University Press, 2005), 603–4; George Washington to Alexander Hamilton, 4 March 1783, in *The Writings of George Washington from the Original Manuscript Sources, 1745–1799*, ed. John C. Fitzpatrick (Washington, DC: GPO, 1931–1944), 26:186.

2. "First Newburgh Address," in *Journals of the Continental Congress, 1774–1789*, ed. Worthington C. Ford (Washington, DC: GPO, 1904–1937), 24:297.

3. George Washington, general orders, 11 March 1783, in *Writings*, 26:208–9; "Second Newburgh Address," in *Journals*, 24:298–99.

4. George Washington, address to the officers of the army, 15 March 1783, in *Writings*, 26:224, 226–27.

5. Douglas S. Freeman, *George Washington: A Biography* (New York: Scribner, 1948–1957), 5:435.

6. *Oxford English Dictionary*, 2nd ed., s.v. "integrity." For a synthesis of the scholarship on the range of meanings of "integrity," see *Stanford Encyclopedia of Philosophy*, http://plato.stanford.edu/entries/integrity/.

7. Caroline Cox, *A Proper Sense of Honor: Service and Sacrifice in George Washington's Army* (Chapel Hill: University of North Carolina Press, 2004), 27.

8. James T. Flexner, *Washington: The Indispensable Man* (Boston: Little, Brown, 1969), 6–7; Lengel, *General George Washington*, 10–15.

9. Lengel, *General George Washington*, 16–18.

10. Cox, *Proper Sense of Honor*, 181; Julius Caesar, *The Commentaries of Caesar* (London: Tonson and Draper, 1755); Humphrey Bland, *A Treatise of Military Discipline* (London: Buckley, 1740); Fred Anderson, *Crucible of*

War: The Seven Years' War and the Fate of Empire in British North America, 1754–1766 (New York: Vintage, 2000), 289–93; George Washington to Robert Dinwiddie, 17 September 1757, in *The Papers of George Washington, Colonial Series*, ed. W. W. Abbot (Charlottesville: University of Virginia Press, 1983–1995), 4:412.

11. Woody Holton, *Forced Founders: Indians, Debtors, Slaves, and the Making of the American Revolution in Virginia* (Chapel Hill: University of North Carolina Press, 1999), 4, 45.

12. Lengel, *General George Washington*, 86–89; Middlekauff, *Glorious Cause*, 298–302; John Adams, *Diary and Autobiography*, ed. L. H. Butterfield (Cambridge, MA: Belknap Press of Harvard University Press, 1961), 3:322–23.

13. George Washington, address to the Continental Congress, 16 June 1775, in *The Papers of George Washington, Revolutionary War Series*, ed. Philander D. Chase (Charlottesville: University Press of Virginia, 1985–2006), 1:1; George Washington to Martha Washington, 18 June 1775, in ibid., 8–9; George Washington to Burwell Bassett, 19 June 1775, in ibid., 12–13.

14. "Instructions from the Continental Congress," 22 June 1775, in ibid., 21–22; Lengel, *General George Washington*, 120; George Washington to Joseph Reed, 6 February–9 March 1776, in *Papers of George Washington, Revolutionary War Series*, 3:370.

15. Cox, *Proper Sense of Honor*, xiii.

16. *Ordinary Courage: The Revolutionary War Adventures of Joseph Plumb Martin*, ed. James Kirby Martin (New York: Brandywine Press, 1993), 50.

17. George Washington, general orders, 1 January 1777, in *Papers of George Washington, Revolutionary War Series*, 7:499; George Washington to John Hancock, 25 September 1776, in ibid., 6:394.

18. Middlekauff, *Glorious Cause*, 417–23. For an in-depth analysis of the army's experience at Valley Forge, see Wayne Bodle, *The Valley Forge Winter: Civilians and Soldiers in War* (University Park: Pennsylvania State University Press, 2002).

19. George Washington to Alexander Hamilton, 28 August 1788, in *The Papers of George Washington, Confederation Series*, ed. W. W. Abbot and Dorothy Twohig (Charlottesville: University Press of Virginia, 1992–1997), 6:481; George Washington, general orders, 2 August 1775, in *Papers of George Washington, Revolutionary War Series*, 1:212; George Washington to Richard Henry Lee, 29 August 1775, in *Papers of George Washington, Revolutionary War Series*, 1:373.

20. Bodle, *Valley Forge Winter*, 166; John W. Jackson, *Valley Forge: Pinnacle of Courage* (Gettysburg, PA: Thomas, 1992), 41.

21. "Extracts from the Journal of Lieutenant John Bell Tilden, Second Pennsylvania Line, 1781–82," *Pennsylvania Magazine of History and Biography* 19 (1895): 51–63.

22. Holly Mayer, *Belonging to the Army: Camp Followers and Community during the American Revolution* (Columbia: University of South Carolina Press, 1996), 1–2; Sarah Osborn quoted in John Dann, ed., *The Revolution Remembered: Eyewitness Accounts of the War for Independence* (Chicago: University of Chicago Press, 1980), 245.

23. *Journals*, 6:1045–46; Flexner, *Washington*, 170; Bodle, *Valley Forge Winter*, 164.

24. Flexner, *Washington*, 116.

25. Barry Schwartz, "George Washington and the Whig Conception of Heroic Leadership," *American Sociological Review* 48 (1983): 27; François-Jean, Marquis de Chastellux, in Gilbert Chinard, *George Washington as the French Knew Him: A Collection of Texts* (Princeton, NJ: Princeton University Press, 1940), 56.

26. Schwartz, "George Washington," 18–33; Samuel Adams quoted in Bernard Bailyn, *Ideological Origins of the American Revolution* (Cambridge, MA: Belknap Press of Harvard University Press, 1967), 60.

27. Lengel, *General George Washington*, 196, 198; Sergeant R., "The Battle of Princeton," *Pennsylvania Magazine of History and Biography* 20 (1896): 515–16.

28. Lengel, *General George Washington*, 305; Middlekauff, *Glorious Cause*, 430–34; Alexander Hamilton to Elias Boudinot, 5 July 1778, in *The Papers of Alexander Hamilton*, ed. Harold C. Syrett (New York: Columbia University Press, 1961–1987), 1:512.

29. Elizabeth Fenn, *Pox Americana: The Great Smallpox Epidemic of 1775–82* (New York: Hill and Wang, 2001), 28–36.

30. Ibid., 46–51.

31. George Washington to Nicholas Cooke, 10 February 1777, in *Papers of George Washington, Revolutionary War Series*, 8:297; Fenn, *Pox Americana*, 102.

32. Middlekauff, *Glorious Cause*, 603.

33. Ibid., 605; *Journals*, 25:837–38.

34. Thomas Jefferson to Walter Jones, 2 January 1814, Thomas Jefferson Papers, American Memory, Library of Congress, http://memory.loc.gov/ammem/collections/jefferson_papers/index.html.

2

Determination and Leadership

Ulysses S. Grant

Harry S. Laver

In a downpour on 6 April 1862, Brigadier General William Tecumseh Sherman spent the early evening searching for his superior, Major General Ulysses S. Grant, commander of the Union Army of the Tennessee. He found him crouched under a tree with rain dripping from his down-turned hat and a dim lantern providing meager light. "Well, Grant, we've had the devil's own day, haven't we?" "Yes," Grant replied. "Lick 'em tomorrow, though."[1]

Undoubtedly Sherman was taken aback by Grant's unremitting resolve. The day's fighting around Shiloh Church had ended with the coming of twilight, but the federals found little comfort in the darkness. The Confederate Army of the Mississippi had surprised the bluecoats with a morning attack, driving back Grant's farm boy soldiers nearly three miles, to the banks of the Tennessee River. General P. G. T. Beauregard, who took command of the Southern army after General Albert Sidney Johnston died in the thick of the fighting, telegraphed Richmond that Grant and his men were finished, or they would be the following day. Few could have argued with Beauregard. The Union army had lost its cohesion, energy, and spirit, and it teetered on the edge of annihilation. Its fate rested with its commander, who might well have ordered a retreat, as his subordinates,

ULYSSES S. GRANT
(National Archives, College Park, MD)

even Sherman, recommended. But Grant decided to fight. His reply
to Sherman revealed a tenacity and commitment to press forward. In
spite of the day's setbacks, Grant's experience confirmed his determination that the next day would bring victory. In that crisis, confronted with overwhelming obstacles, Grant demonstrated perhaps
his greatest quality as a leader, what Carl von Clausewitz described as
"a great force of will."[2]

Grant did not begin his military career armed with an unshakable resolve. His perseverance in war developed from studying the
examples of mentors and from learning the hard lessons of experience. During his years in the army, Grant had the good fortune
to serve with men like Zachary Taylor and Charles F. Smith, who
possessed the drive to succeed and who served as worthy leadership role models. Yet practical, firsthand experience proved Grant's
most effective teacher. With every decision, he gained experience
and confidence and developed further into a commander who embodied Clausewitz's "great force of will." But make no mistake,
Grant's persistence was not mere stubbornness. A stubborn leader
unthinkingly stays the course, failing to recognize the subtleties in
strategic, operational, or tactical situations. Major General Ambrose
E. Burnside's repeated, bloody, and failed assaults at Fredericksburg
revealed a leader unable to distinguish perseverance from an unrea-
sonable inflexibility. Grant, however, exercised resolve tempered by
an eye for the complex and evolving nature of military operations.
As his Vicksburg campaign revealed, he was always prepared to
adapt, unwilling to allow tactical problems to distract from or over-
whelm strategic objectives.

Little in Grant's youth hinted at the presence of great inner
strength. An unremarkable childhood in Ohio ended in 1839 with
his admission to West Point through an appointment arranged by
his father. Grant lacked self-confidence and doubted that he could
succeed at the academy, but his father was adamant that he would
go, and that settled the matter. As a cadet, Grant was no more than
average. He easily conquered math but barely survived two years of
French. He excelled at horsemanship, and his high jump record was

not surpassed for more than a quarter century. During his third year, Grant suffered demotion from cadet sergeant to private because he failed to accept the responsibilities of the rank. "The promotion was too much for me," Grant later recalled. Nevertheless, he graduated twenty-first out of thirty-nine cadets in 1843, impressing most with his mediocrity despite his superior command of horses. Assigned to the U.S. Army's Fourth Infantry Regiment—itself an indicator of his undistinguished record, as the best graduates became engineering or artillery officers—the newly commissioned brevet second lieutenant began what all expected to be an unremarkable military career.[3]

During Grant's first years in the army, there emerged hints of untapped energy and resolve. One afternoon in 1846, while serving in Mexico under Zachary Taylor, Grant dismounted to help his men clear underwater obstructions that lay in the path of the advancing army. His enthusiasm for the wet and muddy work drew smirks from a few junior "dandy officers," who poked fun at the young lieutenant. Grant, however, was determined to accomplish the mission at hand. General Taylor, who witnessed the event, was impressed: "I wish I had more officers like Grant, who would stand ready to set a personal example when needed." Promotion to full second lieutenant soon followed. During the Mexican campaign, Grant did some observing of his own and learned from Taylor's example. In March 1846, Taylor's force came to the Colorado River and faced the challenge of a contested crossing. Under fire, Old Rough and Ready took command of the situation and pushed his army across the river. Young Lieutenant Grant saw that determination was the parent of success, whereas equivocation invited defeat.[4]

Following the Mexican-American War, Grant continued to show a developing strength of will. In 1852, the Fourth Infantry was ordered to the West Coast by way of Panama, and Lieutenant Grant was responsible for the regiment's logistics. The complexity of the task became apparent when he arrived on the Panamanian coast, where prior arrangements for the regiment's transport fell apart. Undeterred, Grant negotiated with local suppliers, bent a few military regulations, and eventually secured sufficient mules to organize a caravan, which

he led across the isthmus. Arrival at Panama City brought its own
challenges as cholera struck the regiment. Grant carried out his normal duties while tending to the sick, earning admiration as a "man
of iron" and "the coolest man I ever saw."[5] Grant's steady leadership
in Panama, like his service with Taylor in Mexico, demonstrated his
maturing confidence and grit. Unfortunately, Grant's military career
was about to enter purgatory. The next seven years, in fact, decep-
tively suggested a distinct lack of determination as he struggled to
overcome boredom, isolation, and adversity.

From Panama, Grant was transferred to the Pacific Northwest,
where he lived a life of dullness and despair. Postings at Fort Vancouver on the Columbia River and Fort Humboldt in northern California, along with the hollow solace of drink and longing for his family,
left him in deep melancholy. Unwilling or perhaps unable to continue such a disheartening existence, the young captain resigned his
commission in 1854 to seek a better life with his family. Rather than
finding comfort and prosperity, however, Grant experienced continuing failure. His financial investments soured, his business ventures
lost money, and his farming produced mostly heartbreak. By the late
1850s, Grant found himself on the streets of St. Louis, hawking fire-
wood to feed his family. Deliverance came in 1861. With the outbreak of civil war, the retired captain saw an opportunity to escape the
poverty, aimlessness, and despondency that had plagued him since
leaving the army seven years earlier.[6]

In June 1861, Grant secured an appointment as colonel of the
Twenty-first Illinois Volunteers. As he took command, the determination that would see him through the next four years of war re-
emerged.[7] While leading the Twenty-first toward its initial encounter
with the enemy, Grant learned that the will to succeed stemmed from
a deliberate decision to press forward, a conscious choice to confront,
not avoid, adversity. Recalling lessons learned from Taylor in Mexico,
Grant realized that the successful commander could not surrender to
doubts and misgivings.

The Twenty-first Illinois Volunteers' first mission was to break up
a group of Confederate irregulars who were operating on the western

side of the Mississippi River near Florida, Missouri. As Grant's men went into camp on the evening of 17 July 1861, contact with the enemy seemed imminent. The following morning the federals broke camp and were soon in column, moving toward the rebels. Grant, beginning to feel the weight of command, grew anxious:

> As we approached the brow of the hill from which it was expected we could see [Colonel Thomas] Harris' camp, and possibly find his men ready formed to meet us, my heart kept getting higher and higher until it felt to me as though it was in my throat. I would have given anything then to have been back in Illinois, but I had not the moral courage to halt and consider what to do; I kept right on. When we reached a point from which the valley below was in full view I halted. The place where Harris had been encamped a few days before was still there and the marks of a recent encampment were plainly visible, but the troops were gone. My heart resumed its place. It occurred to me at once that Harris had been as much afraid of me as I had been of him. This was a view of the question I had never taken before; but it was one I never forgot afterwards. From that event to the close of the war, I never experienced trepidation upon confronting an enemy, though I always felt more or less anxiety. I never forgot that he had as much reason to fear my forces as I had his. The lesson was valuable.[8]

Here Grant fully realized that a commander's resolve was crucial, perhaps more important than logistics, firepower, or numerical superiority. As he contemplated the enemy's empty encampment, he recognized that what separated one commander from another was something simple yet elusive: tenacity. Anticipating conflict, all soldiers suffer from fear, anxiety, and doubt, but an effective leader overcomes those mental obstacles and drives forward. Had Grant decided to turn back, to retreat from the brow of that hill, he would have failed, if not militarily then psychologically, and such defeats may be the most difficult to overcome. The lesson that determination can overcome fear would serve Grant well throughout the Civil War.

In November 1861, Grant again led his men on an expedition, this time against a slightly better-organized Confederate force at Belmont, Missouri. After crossing the Mississippi a few miles below Cairo, Illinois, the federals landed on the river's west bank and, meeting minimal resistance, drove the Southerners back to their camps and beyond. For the Union soldiers, victory had come too easily; they turned to looting and celebrating while officers made patriotic speeches. Grant had lost control of his command. Discipline and order dissolved in the Union ranks, while the Confederates formed for a counterattack. Recognizing that his force might be cut off from the safety of his riverboats, Grant scrambled to reorganize and march the federals back to their boats. In the chaos, despair began to spread through the ranks, with the most fainthearted calling for surrender to the Southerners. Grant, concerned but steady, insisted that "we had cut our way in and could cut our way out just as well." Fighting through brisk Confederate musket fire, the federals retraced their path to the river transports and escaped to Cairo.[9]

The Belmont excursion provided Grant with his first meaningful test as a combat commander, and he had nearly failed. His lack of situational awareness and his poor command and control might have resulted in higher casualties, if not capture and defeat, but at the battle's critical moment, Grant's fortitude pushed his men through the rejuvenated Confederates. The brigadier general from Illinois survived his first engagement as commander, but only by the thinnest of margins.

In the following year, Grant commanded his first major operation, a campaign that nearly ended in disaster on the Tennessee River at Shiloh. January found Grant and his command in Cairo, restless and anxious to strike south. Looking to break the stalemate, Grant decided to force the issue. He traveled to St. Louis to convince General Henry W. Halleck, his immediate superior, to approve a campaign against the rebel stronghold at Fort Henry. Located on the Tennessee River just south of the Kentucky-Tennessee state line, Fort Henry was a key point in Confederate general Albert Sidney Johnston's defensive line that ran from Paducah, Kentucky, in the west to the Cumberland Gap in eastern Tennessee. The fort's artillery blocked Union naval forces from advancing along the river into northern Alabama. Just ten miles to the east on the Cumberland River was Fort Donelson, which was designed to stop the federals from moving south to Nashville. Grant secured Halleck's approval for an attack, and on 2 February 1862, his men departed Cairo on Union riverboats bound for Fort Henry. Once on location, the infantry disembarked from transports while flag officer Andrew H. Foote's gunboats turned their sights on Fort Henry. The Union's naval guns proved more effective than anticipated, forcing the fort's garrison to surrender on 6 February, before Grant's soldiers could work their way through the muck and mud along the riverbank.[10]

Grant might have paused to enjoy the successful operation, which was one of the first significant victories won by any Union commander. Instead, he pushed on, barely stopping long enough to notify Halleck of the outcome: "Fort Henry is ours. . . . I shall take and destroy Fort Donelson on the 8th and return to Fort Henry." Grant's approach to war was beginning to take shape: "I intend to keep the ball moving as lively as possible."[11] And keep it moving he did.

By 14 February, Grant's command, now named the Army of the Tennessee, had encircled Fort Donelson. Compared to Fort Henry, Donelson's defenses were better engineered, and Confederate artillery crews drove away the gunboats, severely wounding Foote. The task of capturing the fort fell to Grant's soldiers. On 15 February, while Grant conferred with Foote onboard his flagship, the Southerners suddenly struck the Union right flank in an attempt to escape south to Nashville. When Grant returned to the field, he found chaos and confusion. Listening to the panicked reports of generals John McClernand and Lew Wallace, Grant, quickly and with understated determination, made clear his intent: "Gentlemen, the position on the right must be retaken." Having experienced a similar crisis three months earlier during the Belmont engagement, Grant recognized that this moment would decide the battle's outcome. General Wallace, writing after the war, identified what the situation revealed about his commander's developing leadership: "In every great man's career there is a crisis exactly similar to that which now overtook General Grant, and it cannot be better described than as a crucial test of his nature. . . . His admirers and detractors are alike invited to study him at this precise juncture. It cannot be doubted that he saw with painful distinctness the effect of the disaster to his right wing. . . . But in an instant these signs of disappointment or hesitation . . . cleared away."[12]

Sensing that the Southerners were as disorganized and demoralized as his own army, Grant recognized that victory awaited the commander who seized the initiative. He ordered his men forward, despite the army's confusion: "The one who attacks first now will be victorious and the enemy will have to be in a hurry if he gets ahead of me." The Confederates did not get ahead, and the following day Grant dictated the terms of surrender that established his reputation: "No terms except unconditional and immediate surrender can be accepted." On 19 February, "Unconditional Surrender" Grant was promoted to major general of volunteers.[13]

During the Forts Henry and Donelson campaign, Grant benefited from the experience and mentoring of Brigadier General Charles Smith, a subordinate but most able officer. Smith had been the commandant at West Point while Grant was a cadet, and as the 1862 campaign progressed, Grant frequently turned to the aging Smith for advice and support. The two enjoyed something of an awkward relationship, with Grant being overly deferential, but they were of a like mind. Smith believed that a leader must always be prepared for the fight: "Battle is the ultimate to which the whole life's labor of an officer should be directed. He . . . must always be getting ready for it exactly as if he knew the hour of the day it is to break upon him. And then, whether it come late or early, he must be willing to fight—he *must* fight."[14] This tenacity was also apparent in Grant's philosophy of war: "The art of war is simple enough. Find out where your enemy is. Get at him as soon as you can. Strike him as hard as you can, and keep moving." Smith later died from an infected leg wound, and while Grant missed his steadying influence, he never forgot Smith's lessons.[15]

The successes at Forts Henry and Donelson ironically brought Grant's first setback of the war, which came not from the Confederates but rather from his commander, Henry Halleck. Rumors continued to circulate about Grant's having returned to the bottle, but more worrisome to Halleck was Grant's apparent refusal to maintain communications while in the field. Halleck, never fond of overachieving subordinates, relieved Grant and gave command of the army to the ailing General Smith. Grant, in fact, had not fallen to drink and had responded to all of Halleck's telegrams, but a Confederate sympathizer in the telegraph office had waylaid his replies. Halleck's accusations bewildered Grant, who struggled to defend himself. Within a few weeks, in part because President Lincoln had taken an interest in the matter, Halleck reinstated Grant as the Army of the Tennessee's commander. Grant had survived his first significant engagement in army politics, but future battles in that arena would test his determination as much as combat.[16]

Grant returned to command just as the army was preparing to move against Johnston's Confederate force, concentrated at the railroad junction of Corinth, Mississippi. Halleck had ordered Don Carlos Buell's Army of the Ohio to advance southwest from Nashville, link up with Grant, and with their combined armies strike a death-blow at Corinth. Johnston, however, did not follow the Union script and caught Grant and his men by surprise, attacking the federals' encampment near Shiloh Church at dawn on 6 April 1862. Riding amid the chaos, Grant showed no "evidence of excitement or trepidation" as he encouraged his men to hold firm.[17] As dusk fell and the thunder of battle faded, a beleaguered federal soldier overheard Grant mutter, "Not beaten yet by a damn sight." Few others seemed to share his opinion.[18] When pressed by a newspaper reporter to comment on the desperate situation, Grant replied, "They can't break our lines tonight—it is too late. Tomorrow we shall attack them with fresh troops and drive them, of course."[19] Later that evening, Colonel James B. McPherson, a respected officer destined to command a corps at Vicksburg, raised the issue of withdrawal: "General Grant, under this condition of affairs, what do you propose to do, sir? Shall I make preparations for retreat?" Again Grant brushed aside any thought of withdrawal: "No. I propose to attack at daylight and whip them."[20] Despite the day's brutal fighting that seemingly gave the Southerners the upper hand, Grant recognized that the enemy was likely spent, and Union reinforcements were at hand. He was certain he could "lick 'em tomorrow," and indeed, that is what he did. The next day, encouraged by the timely arrival of Buell's reinforcing army, the federals drove the rebels from the field, a victory that secured the Union's hold on western Tennessee and assured the initiative in the region for the remainder of the war.

The 1862 spring campaign revealed the incremental development of Grant's resolution and strength of will. At the critical moment outside Fort Donelson when the battle hung in the balance, Grant chose to attack, putting into practice the lesson that he had learned the previous summer in Missouri. A few months later, at Shiloh, the stakes were higher when the army itself faced destruction on the banks of the Tennessee. With the steadying hand of General Smith gone, with his subordinate officers counseling withdrawal, and with the battle spiraling out of control, Grant faced his most critical combat crisis of the war. Sensing that the Confederates had exhausted themselves in the day's fighting and that the arrival of Buell's divisions gave him the edge, he did not consider withdrawing from the field. His decision to stand firm, a deliberate choice made under stress and against the recommendations of his staff, resurrected the fighting spirit of the army and its commanders. Grant had learned the lessons of earlier engagements: "So confident was I before firing ceased on the 6th that the next day would bring victory . . . if we could only take the initiative that I visited each division commander . . . [and] directed them . . . to engage the enemy as soon as found. To Sherman I told the story of the assault at Fort Donelson, and said that the same tactics would win at Shiloh."[21] Grant's leadership at the end of the first day's fighting at Shiloh exemplified the nature of Clausewitz's "great force of will": "By the spark in his breast, by the light of his spirit, the spark of purpose, the light of hope, must be kindled afresh in others: in so far only as he is equal to this, he stands above the masses and continues to be their master."[22] Grant was no longer the same man who had approached Colonel Harris's Missouri encampment with trepidation and fear. He had learned from that experience, from General Smith's mentoring, and from the Forts Henry and Donelson campaign. He had developed a firmness of mind that matured on the bloody battle-field at Shiloh.

The Union army had won an important, if narrow, victory at Shiloh, but Grant had made mistakes. He neglected to ensure the preparation of adequate defenses, and as at Fort Donelson, he had been caught away from his army when the battle commenced. Grant had completely failed to anticipate the stratagems of his Confederate counterpart. A few officers were quick to blame him directly. Halleck, giving more credence than he should have to these recriminations and the relentless but unfounded rumors of Grant's drinking, took direct command of the armies at Shiloh and elevated Grant to the preeminently impotent position of second in command, with no troops under his control. Promoted to irrelevance, Grant nearly succumbed to self-doubt and depression. Two events saved him from resigning his commission. First, as Grant packed in preparation for his resignation, General Sherman convinced him to stay. He assured Grant that the setback was temporary, and he was right. Then, on 10 June, Halleck returned Grant to command of the Army of the Tennessee. A month later, President Lincoln summoned Halleck to Washington to serve as general in chief, allowing Grant to operate without oppressive scrutiny. Grant had survived another political crisis, but his resolve had faltered, demonstrating that a great strength of will is neither innate nor permanent but requires vigilance and self-awareness. For Grant, it took the intervention of a trusted subordinate and a fortunate turn of events to keep him in the war. In July 1862, once more in command of himself and his army, Grant went to work, establishing his headquarters in Memphis, where he set about planning the capture of Vicksburg, the Confederate "Gibraltar of the West" and the key to control of the mighty Mississippi.[23]

Situated on soaring bluffs that towered over a hairpin turn in the Mississippi River, Vicksburg and its defenders presented a seemingly insurmountable obstacle to Union control of the river. Unassailable from the Mississippi, the town was vulnerable only, if at all, in its eastern approaches, roads that cut through deep ravines and under looming Southern defenses. From November 1862 to the following March, Grant orchestrated a series of operations to place his army on those roads east of Vicksburg. When each of those attempts failed, Grant remained undeterred. He asserted that "to make a backward movement as long as that from Vicksburg to Memphis would be interpreted . . . as a defeat. . . . There was nothing left to be done but to *go forward to a decisive victory*."[24] As he had done during the Forts Henry and Donelson campaign, Grant turned to his naval counterpart for assistance. With Rear Admiral David Dixon Porter, he drew up a daring plan to float Porter's squadron south, under the cover of darkness, past the guns of Vicksburg. The gunboats and transports survived the hair-raising passage and met Grant's soldiers a few miles south on the west bank. On 30 April, Porter's boats began ferrying men across the river at Bruinsburg, Mississippi. No Southerners opposed the landing, in part because a Union cavalry raid led by Benjamin Grierson rode from the Mississippi-Tennessee state line to Baton Rouge, Louisiana, drawing Southern attention to the east. Grant, with his troops safely across the river, quickly pushed inland. General McClernand's corps led the advance, driven by Grant's admonition to "push the enemy from the field or capture him."[25] Push they did, capturing Port Gibson the next day.

Grant reflected upon his army's success, born of determination and perseverance, "I was now in the enemy's country, with a vast river and the stronghold of Vicksburg between me and my base of supplies. But I was on dry ground on the same side of the river with the enemy. All the campaigns, labors, hardships and exposures . . . that had been made and endured, were for the accomplishment of this one object." Grant's army would have to operate on a tenuous supply line, but he was on the eastern side of the Mississippi, with only Confederate soldiers between him and the city of Vicksburg. His confidence and tenacity were becoming infectious, affecting those who served both above and below him. As the army pushed farther inland, he assured Halleck in Washington, "This is a long and precarious route but I have every confidence in succeeding in doing it. . . . [We will] not stop until Vicksburg is in our possession." The men who would do the fighting had also developed a trust in their commander, not the fleeting parade-ground cheers sought by a McClellan but a quiet resolve that mirrored their general's own subdued determination. He continued to push his soldiers, and they responded, "march[ing] as much by night as by day, through mud and rain, without tents or much other baggage, and on irregular rations, without complaint and with less straggling than I have ever before witnessed."[26]

Grant knew that hesitation or delay could lead to disaster. Lieutenant General John C. Pemberton's Vicksburg army was strengthening its defenses and beginning to maneuver in his direction. Confederate forces near Jackson under Joseph E. Johnston were adding recruits and hoped to unite with Pemberton. In contrast, the federals expected no reinforcements. The success of the operation depended ultimately on Grant's will to see it through. Sherman had expressed his doubts, Grant later remembered, "saying that I was putting myself in a position voluntarily which an enemy would be glad to maneuvre [sic] a year—or a long time—to get me in." But Grant suffered no such qualms; he simply pushed forward.[27]

The federals departed Port Gibson on 2 May 1863, and for the next two weeks Grant befuddled his enemy with diversion, deception, and superior generalship. Grant bypassed the most direct road to Vicksburg and instead moved his army northeast, toward the state capital, Jackson. There Confederate forces were gathering to trap the federals against Pemberton's Confederates to the west. Learning of the Confederate concentration in Jackson, Grant immediately issued orders: attack Johnston to destroy or drive him away, then turn and catch Pemberton before he could withdraw into the fortifications at Vicksburg. Despite his being deep in enemy territory with a tenuous supply line and confronted by two Confederate armies that combined held numerical superiority, Grant never contemplated retreat. He would "not stop until Vicksburg is in our possession."[28] For the next few days, his will to succeed dominated the theater of operations. From 12 to 17 May, the Army of the Tennessee fought and won four engagements, prevented the joining of the two Confederate armies, and trapped Pemberton's defenders in Vicksburg. Grant had pushed his men and commanders to pursue the retreating Confederates, hoping to bring about their destruction or surrender. Unable to strike that fatal blow before the Southerners withdrew into their Vicksburg defenses, he had nevertheless bottled up the enemy in their earthworks with little hope of relief. Hoping to avoid siege operations, Grant ordered two frontal assaults to batter his way into the town. Daunting fortifications manned by resolute Confederates turned back each attack. Trenches and the slow but inexorable movement of siege warfare followed, finally bearing fruit on 4 July 1863, when Pemberton and his exhausted command surrendered.

The Vicksburg campaign, still a model of operational-level warfare, revealed the extent of Grant's will to succeed and his maturation as an army commander. For more than eight months, he had battled inclement weather, public criticism, obdurate subordinates, uncooperative superiors, logistical nightmares, the doubts of his most trusted corps commander, and a numerically superior enemy. The Army of the Tennessee, in overcoming these challenges, had come to reflect the determination of its commander. As Grant's men slogged through months of mud, cold, and imminent despair, it became clear that he had won their confidence. "General Grant still retains his hold upon the affections of his men," a reporter wrote in February. "No Napoleonic displays, no ostentation, no speed, no superfluous flummery" kept these men in camp; they stayed because of their commander's "energy and disposition to do something." Sherman, despite his earlier skepticism, acknowledged that Grant had directed "one of the greatest campaigns in history."[29] Grant's perseverance had also won over his commander in chief. In early 1863, Lincoln had brushed aside Grant's critics, who called for the general's dismissal when the army encountered one roadblock after another. "I think Grant has hardly a friend left, except myself," Lincoln observed. But "what I want, and what the people want, is generals who will fight battles and win victories. Grant has done this and I propose to stand by him." In July, with the siege in its final days, the president again made clear he would stick by his winning general: "If Grant only does this thing down there—I don't care much how, so long as he does it *right*— why, Grant is my man and I am his the rest of the war!"[30]

Even with Vicksburg broken, Grant kept his grip on the enemy, ordering Sherman to pursue Johnston's army, which was hovering near Jackson. On the day of Vicksburg's surrender, Grant directed Sherman to "drive [Johnston] out in your own way . . . and inflict on the enemy all the punishment you can."[31] Having won a significant victory, Grant denied his opponent even a moment's rest and demonstrated the relentlessness first revealed during the Forts Henry and Donelson campaign. His determination was no longer the reckless sort that had nearly brought disaster at Shiloh but rather a force of will, tempered by confidence and adaptability that derived from experience and reflection. Vicksburg confirmed Grant's status as one of the war's preeminent generals, but the greatest challenge to his leadership and will to win was yet to come.

After Vicksburg, Grant hoped to move against the Confederate stronghold at Mobile, Alabama, but leaders in Washington had other plans. In September, the Union Army of the Cumberland, under General William S. Rosecrans, narrowly avoided destruction along Chickamauga Creek in Georgia. The defeated and dispirited federals retreated to Chattanooga, where mountainous terrain and General Braxton Bragg's Confederates threatened to destroy Rosecrans's force by siege. A few weeks later, on a railcar in Indianapolis, Secretary of War Edwin Stanton gave Grant command of the Military Division of the Mississippi, encompassing a huge swath of land from the Alleghenies to the Mississippi, from the Ohio River to the Gulf of Mexico. That was the good news; the bad news was that the territory included the crisis in Chattanooga. Grant acted swiftly. He immediately replaced Rosecrans with Major General George H. Thomas and, on 19 October, cabled the new commander, "Hold Chattanooga at all hazards. I will be there as soon as possible." Thomas, fully understanding the tenor of Grant's message, responded with equal determination: "I will hold the town till we starve."[32]

Grant arrived four days later to find a Union army that was indeed on the verge of starvation. Establishing a secure supply line became the first priority; Rosecrans had developed a plan to do just that, but neither he nor Thomas had put it into motion. Grant reviewed the plan and thought it sound. He issued the necessary orders, and soon the "cracker line" was delivering desperately needed goods. Thomas had planned well, but it took a leader like Grant to act, a difference in leadership that did not escape one of Grant's staff officers: "It is decisiveness and energy in action that always accomplishes grand results, and strikes terror to the heart of the foe, it is this and not the conception of great schemes that make military genius."[33] As Grant began planning offensive operations in Chattanooga, he could not ignore his responsibilities to subordinate generals in other theaters, especially Ambrose Burnside, who was struggling to hold Knoxville, Tennessee. Looking to steel Burnside's resolve, Grant wrote on 17 November, "You are doing exactly what appears to me to be right. I want the enemy's progress retarded at every point, all it can be, only giving up each place when it becomes evident that it cannot longer be held without endangering your force to capture."[34]

Grant's primary concern remained the federals' situation at Chattanooga, and he was again determined to seize the initiative. To his superiors in Washington he telegraphed reassurances of his intention to advance, which undoubtedly brought a nod of relief and approval from the president. "I will," Grant wrote, "endeavor to get the troops in a state of readiness for a forward movement at the earliest possible day."[35] On 23 November, Union forces advanced against the center of the Confederate line at Missionary Ridge with the limited objective of capturing outposts. The following day, federals struck both flanks of the enemy position but failed to make significant gains. Grant was determined to make 25 November the decisive day and ordered his generals on the flanks to renew their attacks, but by midday both assaults had bogged down. Seeing that a crisis was at hand, Grant ordered Thomas to advance the troops in the center, looking to draw Confederates away from the flanks. Minutes passed, however, with no movement from Thomas's men. Grant, impatient at the delay, bypassed Thomas, who opposed the assault, and went directly to the division commander responsible for the attack, "asking him why he did not charge as ordered an hour before. He replied very promptly that this was the first he had heard of it. . . . I told him to make the charge at once. He was off in a moment, and in an incredibly short time loud cheering was heard." The advancing federals swept up the slope of Missionary Ridge and drove back Bragg's Confederates, achieving one of the most spectacular feats of the war. Chattanooga and the Union army were now secure as the Southern army made a rapid retreat into Georgia. True to form, Grant did not pause to collect well-deserved accolades but rather ordered reinforcements north to support Burnside at Knoxville and other elements of the army to keep the pressure on the enemy elsewhere. Grant again hoped to move against Mobile, but the president had another course in mind.[36]

Like the Vicksburg campaign a few months earlier, the Chattanooga campaign demonstrated that Grant applied his determination to succeed at the operational as well as the tactical level of war. Before the battle could be joined, Grant had to solve the army's supply crisis, and whereas others had developed an appropriate plan, Grant pushed it to completion. At the critical moment, Grant again revealed not only his ability to adapt to changing circumstances but also the will to drive his men forward when others faltered. And as before, the men in Grant's army recognized their commander's force of will. In a December 1863 letter, the Eleventh Corps' commander, O. O. Howard, assessed the Chattanooga campaign: "This department was completely 'out of joint' when we first arrived. A *most complete and perfect want* of system prevailed, from Louisville to Chattanooga. I can now feel the difference. . . . I cannot be too thankful for the policy that placed these three Depts. under Grant." A colonel echoed Howard's observations, writing, "You have no conception of the change in the army when Grant came. He opened up the cracker line and got a steamer through. We began to see things move. We felt that everything came from a plan. He came into the army quietly, no splendor, no airs, no staff. He used to go about alone. He began the campaign the moment he reached the field."[37] After Chattanooga, Grant was clearly Lincoln's man for the rest of the war.

In March 1864, Lincoln demonstrated his faith in Grant by approving his promotion to lieutenant general and general in chief of all Union forces. From this new position, Grant formulated plans for simultaneous campaigns in different theaters, a strategy Lincoln had been promoting since the early months of the war. Lincoln's new commander did not allow the multiple operations to distract him from his primary concern, the eastern theater and Lee's Army of Northern Virginia. If matching wits with Lee was not enough to keep Grant up nights, he also faced the challenges of overseeing Major General George G. Meade and the Army of the Potomac, an army of veterans with a less than aggressive record. Grant did not know these generals, and they did not know him. Moreover, to them Grant was a diminutive westerner who had battled the likes of Pemberton and Bragg, not Robert E. Lee. Such skepticism was not limited to the federal side of the war line; a number of Southerners doubted Grant was up to the job. Lieutenant General James Longstreet, who had known Grant for decades, knew better. "I tell you," Longstreet warned his Confederate colleagues, "we cannot afford to underrate him and the army he now commands. We must make up our minds to get into line of battle and stay there; for that man will fight us every day and every hour till the end of the war."[38] Sherman, who had remained in the West and knew Grant better than any other officer, reminded his friend and commander why he was chosen to lead the war and what effect he had on his men: "The chief characteristic [of your nature] is the simple faith in success you have always manifested. . . . This faith gave you victory at Shiloh and Vicksburg. . . . When you have completed your preparations, you go into battle without hesitation, as at Chattanooga—no doubts—no reserves; and I tell you, it was this that made us act with confidence."[39]

Despite his having the respect of Sherman, Lincoln, and even Longstreet, Grant still had to convince his new army of his leadership abilities and instill in the men the same self-confidence. He began with the army commander, General Meade, the victor of Gettysburg. Grant kept Meade on but made clear to him the objective of the Army of the Potomac: "Lee's army will be your objective point. Wherever Lee goes, there you will go also."[40] Meade would require additional reminders in the months to come. Among the rank and file, word spread quickly of their new commander and his reputation. A New Englander recalled, "We all felt at last that *the boss* had arrived"; likewise, another soldier noted, "He looks as if he would stay with 'em till somebody cried enough."[41]

On 4 May 1864, the Army of the Potomac crossed the Rapidan River into Virginia and moved south in pursuit of Lee's army. The next day, even as Lee turned to engage the federals in what would become known as the Battle of the Wilderness, Grant reminded Meade, "If any opportunity presents itself for pitching into a part of Lee's army, do so without giving time for disposition."[42] For two days, the armies fought in the smoke and tangled underbrush of the Wilderness, inflicting substantial casualties on each other. As the second day's fighting dragged on amid rumors of impending Union disaster, a flustered brigade commander rode into Grant's camp with news that Lee was about to envelop the entire army and trap them south of the Rapidan. Grant had heard enough. "I am heartily tired," he fumed at the brigadier, "of hearing about what Lee is going to do. Some of you always seem to think he is suddenly going to turn a double somersault, and land in our rear and on both flanks at the same time. Go back to your command, and try to think what we are going to do ourselves, instead of what Lee is going to do."[43] With that, Grant left no doubt that the Army of the Potomac had a new boss, one who was not intimidated by Lee and was determined to succeed.

After two days of battle, Lee had not been moved and the federals had suffered considerable casualties, but Grant's army was not going to follow the well-worn path of retreat. Grant was committed to moving his men forward. This became apparent as the soldiers began marching out of camp after the battle, expecting to head back north as they had always done, but instead found the army winding its way south, after Lee and toward Richmond. Veteran soldier Elisha Hunt Rhodes reflected, "If we were under any other General except Grant I should expect a retreat, but Grant is not that kind of soldier, and we feel that we can trust him." In a scene reminiscent of Napoleon's firelight procession prior to the Battle of Austerlitz, soldiers held torches to light the way and cheered Grant as he passed. Grant's determination was infectious, winning over not only his men but civilian observers as well. Sylvanus Cadwallader, a newspaper reporter traveling with the army, likened his realization of the depth of Grant's will to win as "the grandest sunburst of my life. I had suddenly emerged from the slough of despond, to the solid bed-rock of unwavering faith." Grant reassured Lincoln that "there will be no turning back." Sherman, writing after the war, observed that the heavy casualties of the Wilderness did little to diminish Grant's determination: "Undismayed, with a full comprehension of the importance of the work in which he was engaged, feeling as keen a sympathy for his dead and wounded as anyone, and without stopping to count his numbers, he gave his orders calmly, specifically, and absolutely—'Forward to Spotsylvania.'"[44]

On 8 May, after retreating a few miles south, Lee turned to give battle at Spotsylvania Court House, Virginia. Lee's beleaguered veterans hurriedly threw up a series of breastworks that presented a formidable obstacle to a Union assault. Grant notified Halleck that the Southerners "hold our front in very strong force and evince strong determination to interpose between us and Richmond to the last." Still, there was no thought of withdrawal: "I shall take no backward step." The next day brought more heavy fighting, with a considerable addition to the butcher's bill. Again reassuring his superiors in Washington of his commitment to see the campaign through, the general in chief averred, "I propose to fight it out on this line if it takes all summer." For the next three weeks, Grant pushed and maneuvered the Army of the Potomac through a series of large and small battles, inflicting and suffering casualties daily. On 2 June, his battle-weary force arrived at Cold Harbor, Virginia, where Lee once more pulled up to offer battle. Grant, facing heavy rains and believing his men exhausted from a month of unrelenting campaigning, postponed the attack until the following day, a delay that would prove disastrous. The respite gave the Confederates sufficient time to fortify what was already good defensive ground. On 3 June, sixty thousand federals surged forward against Lee's earthworks, only to be driven back after suffering seven thousand casualties. In this instance, Grant displayed either too much or too little force of will. Had he pushed his men to attack on 2 June, they would have charged less formidable Southern fortifications. Had he shown less determination and postponed the attack, further reconnaissance and reflection might have convinced him of the folly of a frontal assault. Grant himself recognized his mistake, a decision better characterized as stubborn than steadfast: "I regret this assault more than any one I have ever ordered."[45]

Despite the attack's disastrous consequences, Grant never contemplated an operational pause or retreat. A colonel on Grant's staff recalled that "nothing deterred him [or] depressed or discouraged, so far as those nearest him could discover, this imperturbable man. . . . His confidence never wavered. . . . He was yet advancing, not only . . . towards Richmond, but towards the goal he had proposed to himself, the destruction of Lee and the rebellion." Equally important, the army's fighting men continued to follow the lead of their commander, showing the same resolve to see the matter through. Five days after Cold Harbor, a New York soldier wrote, "We have the gray backs in a pretty close corner at present and intend to keep them so. There is no fall back with U. S. Grant." And because of Grant, there was little fall back in the ranks either. Even the dour Meade had started to reflect some of Grant's attitude, writing a few days earlier, "There is a determination on all sides to fight it out, and have an end put to the war."[46]

While Meade's respect for Grant grew, the Army of the Potomac's corps commanders remained less pliable. After Cold Harbor, the army once again maneuvered south, hoping to take the rail center of Petersburg, Virginia. In mid-June 1864, the federals launched a series of assaults against Confederate fortifications but failed to press the attack, especially on 15 June, when General William F. "Baldy" Smith hesitated before thinly held earthworks. Grant later lamented, "I believed then, and still believe, that Petersburg could have been easily captured at that time." But Smith was not the only Union officer to falter. Historian Bruce Catton writes that the corps commanders' "reflexes were sluggish. Between the will and the act there was always a gap. Orders received were executed late, sometimes at half-stroke; now and then they were reinterpreted on the spot so that what was ordered was not done at all." Almost alone Grant could maintain the army's strategic momentum, but operational momentum and tactical success often depended on the skill and tenacity of the generals, especially the corps commanders. During this phase of the campaign, Grant failed to instill in his subordinates sufficient determination.[47]

At Petersburg, as at Vicksburg, once Grant recognized the futility of repeated frontal assaults, he turned to siege operations. The lack of an immediate victory did not discourage the Union commander, who sent a note of reassurance and confidence to the president: "You will never hear of me farther from Richmond than now, till I have taken it. I am just as sure of going into Richmond as I am of any future event. It may take a long summer day, as they say in the rebel papers, but I will do it." Lincoln visited Grant in late June, and upon the president's return to Washington, Secretary of the Navy Gideon Welles recalled that the president seemed rested physically and "strengthened . . . mentally." Grant's unyielding determination, though it was less than fully successful in driving his corps commanders, continued to buck up the man who was ultimately responsible for maintaining the nation's commitment to victory.[48]

As the Petersburg siege devolved into a war of trenches, Grant, as general in chief, continued to carry out his responsibilities to ongoing operations elsewhere, encouraging and driving his theater commanders. Grant informed Halleck in early July that Philip Sheridan's troops in the Shenandoah Valley were "to eat out Virginia clear and clean as far as they go, so that Crows flying over it for the balance of this season will have to carry their provender with them." General George H. Thomas, commanding the Army of the Cumberland near Nashville, also received encouragement from Grant, albeit with a sharp edge. John Bell Hood had taken a force of Confederates north in the hopes of reviving Southern morale and capturing Nashville. Thomas, who was expected to turn back the invasion and destroy Hood's army, was moving with less energy than the War Department or Grant had hoped. Grant instructed Halleck to relieve Thomas if he failed to move, commenting, "I fear he is too cautious ever to take the initiative." To Thomas, Grant wrote, "I have as much confidence in your conducting a battle rightly as I have in any other officer. But it has seemed to me that you have been slow and I have had no explanation of affairs to convince me otherwise." Improved weather, along with Grant's less than subtle prodding, put Thomas in motion.[49]

Back at Petersburg, both armies had settled into the tedious attrition of static warfare. Grant resisted demands to shift troops to other theaters or to Northern cities to put down unsettling draft riots. He argued that the army's priority must remain Lee and his besieged Confederates. In this instance, Grant found his own determination strengthened by the president. "I have seen your despatch [sic] expressing your unwillingness to break your hold where you are," Lincoln telegraphed the general on 17 August. "Neither am I willing. Hold on with a bull-dog grip, and chew & choke as much as possible."[50] These two men shared, and reinforced in each other, an unswerving commitment to military victory.

Grant did not break his hold, and he continued to poke and prod Lee's defenses through the fall and into the spring of 1865. The standoff came to a head in late March, when Lee realized that his paucity of supplies and men dictated that the Confederates must abandon the Richmond-Petersburg line and move south in the hope of continuing the fight in the Carolinas. Grant, moving with a tenacity refined over a long military career, relentlessly pursued Lee. To Sheridan and his cavalry, Grant telegraphed, "I now feel like ending the matter. . . . In the morning push around the enemy if you can and get on to his right rear."[51] Push Sheridan did, racing ahead of Lee's army to block the only line of escape. Grant accepted Lee's surrender on 9 April, confirming the faith Lincoln had placed in "his man" to finish the war.

Those who had expected little of West Point cadet Ulysses S. Grant grossly underestimated him. He endured failures and despondency and worked his way to the top of his profession, earning a reputation as one of the best military commanders in U.S. history. A great force of will explains much of his success, and that determination was cultivated by the examples of his mentors and by hard experience. Zachary Taylor's and Charles Smith's leadership styles modeled the doggedness that Grant emulated during the Civil War. In the later months of the war, Grant discovered in Lincoln a determined partner, if not mentor. Indeed, they had a common cause and a shared dedication to seeing the matter through.

Grant applied lessons from the Mexican campaigns during the early engagements of the Civil War and demonstrated a confident determination by the Vicksburg campaign. At Chattanooga, he refined this determination in seeming preparation for his confrontation with Robert E. Lee in the 1864 Overland Campaign. At each step, Grant applied the lessons learned from previous experience to reach a deliberate decision to push forward. Each campaign revealed the maturation of his plain-spoken philosophy of war to strike the enemy hard and keep moving.

Such firmness of purpose was not stubbornness born of an obtuse mind. Grant demonstrated operational-level flexibility in maneuvering his army to the gates of Vicksburg and pursuing a siege and in improvising a breakout at Chattanooga. During the Overland Campaign, contrary to the label "butcher," Grant attempted to avoid—with the exception of Cold Harbor—blunt frontal attacks. He continually sought to envelop rather than frontally assault Lee's right flank. Despite his facing the tactical obstacles of terrain and a brilliant opponent, Grant kept his army moving forward and focused on the strategic objective, Lee's army. At Petersburg, the general in chief continued to reinforce the determination of his subordinates in other theaters as well as of his men in the trenches. Sherman, who knew Grant so well, recognized the essential quality of his commander's leadership: "Grant is the greatest soldier of our time, if not of all times. . . . He fixes in his mind what is the true objective point, and abandons all minor ones. . . . If his plan works wrong, he is never disconcerted, but promptly devises a new one, and is sure he will win in the end."[52]

Notes

1. Quoted in Jean Edward Smith, *Grant* (New York: Simon and Schuster, 2001), 201.

2. Carl von Clausewitz, *On War*, trans. Anatol Rapoport (New York: Penguin, 1968), 145.

3. Ulysses S. Grant, *Memoirs and Selected Letters* (New York: Library of America, 1990), 1:33; Brooks D. Simpson, *Ulysses S. Grant: Triumph over Adversity, 1822–1865* (Boston: Houghton Mifflin, 2000), 9–17; Smith, *Grant*, 23–28.

4. Lafayette McLaws, interview, *New York Times*, 24 July 1885; Smith, *Grant*, 40, 44.

5. Simpson, *Ulysses S. Grant*, 54–56; Smith, *Grant*, 78.

6. Simpson, *Ulysses S. Grant*, 63–77; Smith, *Grant*, 80–91.

7. Smith, *Grant*, 107–8.

8. Grant, *Memoirs and Selected Letters*, 1:164–65.

9. Ibid., 180; Simpson, *Ulysses S. Grant*, 98–103; Smith, *Grant*, 125–34.

10. Simpson, *Ulysses S. Grant*, 108–12; Smith, *Grant*, 139–47.

11. U. S. Grant to H. W. Halleck, 6 February 1862, in War Department, *The War of the Rebellion: A Compilation of the Official Records of the Union and Confederate Armies* (Washington, DC: GPO, 1880–1901), series 1, vol. 7, pt. 1, p. 124; Ulysses S. Grant to Mary Grant, 9 February 1862, in *The Papers of Ulysses S. Grant*, ed. John Y. Simon (Carbondale: Southern Illinois University Press, 1967–2005), 4:179.

12. Simpson, *Ulysses S. Grant*, 113–18; Smith, *Grant*, 147–66; Lew Wallace, "The Capture of Fort Donelson," in *Battles and Leaders of the Civil War*, ed. Robert U. Johnson and Clarence C. Buel (New York: Century, 1887–1888), 1:422.

13. Grant, *Memoirs and Selected Letters*, 1:205, 208; Simpson, *Ulysses S. Grant*, 113–18; Smith, *Grant*, 147–66.

14. Smith quoted in Lew Wallace, *An Autobiography* (New York: Harper, 1906), 1:345.

15. *Personal Memoirs of John H. Brinton: Civil War Surgeon, 1861–1865* (Carbondale: Southern Illinois University Press, 1996), 239; Smith, *Grant*, 208; Simpson, *Ulysses S. Grant*, 138.

16. Simpson, *Ulysses S. Grant*, 121–25; Smith, *Grant*, 172–77.

17. Quoted in Smith, *Grant*, 193.

18. Quoted in Wiley Sword, *Shiloh: Bloody April* (Dayton, OH: Morningside House, 1974), 368.

19. Grant quoted in Bruce Catton, *Grant Moves South, 1861–1863* (Edison, NJ: Castle Books, 2000), 237–38.

20. Quoted in ibid., 241.

21. Grant, *Memoirs and Selected Letters*, 1:234.

22. Clausewitz, *On War*, 145.

23. Smith, *Grant*, 206–16; Simpson, *Ulysses S. Grant*, 136–46.

24. Grant, *Memoirs and Selected Letters*, 1:296.

25. U. S. Grant to Major General McClernand, 1 May 1863, in *Papers of Ulysses S. Grant*, 8:140.

26. Grant, *Memoirs and Selected Letters*, 1:321; U. S. Grant to Major General H. W. Halleck, 3 May 1863, in *Papers of Ulysses S. Grant*, 8:145–48; Smith, *Grant*, 238.

27. Grant, *Memoirs and Selected Letters*, 1:364–65n.

28. Grant to Halleck, 3 May 1863, 148.

29. *New York World*, 20 February 1863, quoted in Smith, *Grant*, 232; Grant, *Memoirs and Selected Letters*, 1:354.

30. Lincoln quoted in Shelby Foote, *The Civil War: A Narrative* (New York: Random House, 1958–1974), 2:217; Lincoln quoted in Smith, *Grant*, 215.

31. U. S. Grant to General Sherman, 4 July 1863, in War Department, *Official Records*, series 1, vol. 24, pt. 3, p. 473.

32. U. S. Grant to Major General Thomas, 19 October 1863, in War Department, *Official Records*, series 1, vol. 30, pt. 4, p. 479; G. H. Thomas to Major General Grant, 19 October 1863, in ibid.

33. John Rawlins to Mary Hurlbut, 27 October 1863, quoted in Simpson, *Ulysses S. Grant*, 231.

34. Ulysses S. Grant to Ambrose E. Burnside, 17 November 1863, quoted in Bruce Catton, *Grant Takes Command, 1864–1865* (Boston: Little, Brown, 1960), 62.

35. U. S. Grant to H. W. Halleck, 26 October 1863, in War Department, *Official Records*, series 1, vol. 31, pt. 1, p. 740.

36. Grant, *Memoirs and Selected Letters*, 2:445; Smith, *Grant*, 282–83.

37. O. O. Howard to Senator Henry Wilson, 27 December 1863, quoted in Catton, *Grant Takes Command*, 55–56; Colonel L. B. Eaton quoted in ibid., 56.

38. Longstreet quoted in Horace Porter, *Campaigning with Grant* (Lincoln: University of Nebraska Press, 2000), 46–47.

39. William T. Sherman to Ulysses S. Grant, 10 March 1864, quoted in Adam Badeau, *Military History of Ulysses S. Grant* (New York: Appleton, 1868–1881), 1:573–74. Badeau served as military secretary and aide-de-camp to Grant.

40. Ulysses S. Grant to George G. Meade, 9 April 1864, in Grant, *Memoirs and Selected Letters*, 2:482.

41. Grant quoted in Foote, *Civil War*, 3:132; Stanton P. Allen, *Down in Dixie: Life in a Cavalry Regiment in the War Days, from the Wilderness to Appomattox* (Boston: Lothrop, 1892), 188.

42. Ulysses S. Grant to George G. Meade, 5 May 1864, in *Papers of Ulysses S. Grant*, 10:399.

43. Grant quoted in Porter, *Campaigning with Grant*, 70.

44. *All for the Union: The Civil War Diary and Letters of Elisha Hunt Rhodes*, ed. Robert Hunt Rhodes (New York: Orion, 1985), 146; Porter, *Campaigning with Grant*, 79; Sylvanus Cadwallader, *Three Years with Grant*, ed. Benjamin P. Thomas (Lincoln: University of Nebraska Press, 1996), 182; Grant quoted in Smith, *Grant*, 334; William T. Sherman, "The Grand Strategy of the Last Year of the War," in *Battles and Leaders of the Civil War*, 4:248.

45. U. S. Grant to H. W. Halleck, 10 May 1864, in *Papers of Ulysses S. Grant*, 10:418–19; U. S. Grant to E. M. Stanton, 11 May 1864, in ibid., 422; Smith, *Grant*, 364; Porter, *Campaigning with Grant*, 179.

46. Badeau, *Military History*, 2:317–18; James Keleher quoted in Smith, *Grant*, 366; *The Life and Letters of George Gordon Meade* (New York: Scribner, 1913), 2:196.

47. James M. McPherson, *Battle Cry of Freedom: The Civil War Era* (New York: Oxford University Press, 1988), 740–41; Grant, *Memoirs and Selected Letters*, 2:599; Catton, *Grant Takes Command*, 292.

48. Foote, *Civil War*, 3:443; *Diary of Gideon Welles*, ed. Howard K. Beale (New York: Norton, 1960), 2:58.

49. U. S. Grant to H. W. Halleck, 14 July 1864, in *Papers of Ulysses S. Grant*, 11:242–43; U. S. Grant to H. W. Halleck, 8 December 1864, in ibid., 13:83; U. S. Grant to G. H. Thomas, 9 December 1864, in ibid., 96.

50. A. Lincoln to U. S. Grant, 17 August 1864, in Abraham Lincoln, *Collected Works*, ed. Roy P. Basler (New Brunswick, NJ: Rutgers University Press, 1953–1955), 7:499.

51. U. S. Grant to Sheridan, 29 March 1865, in *Papers of Ulysses S. Grant*, 14:253.

52. Sherman quoted in James F. Rusling, *Men and Things I Saw in Civil War Days* (New York: Eaton and Mains, 1899), 146.

3

Institutional Leadership

George C. Marshall

Larry I. Bland

By the end of March 1945, massive Anglo-American formations were streaming across the Rhine River, encircling the key German industrial area of the Ruhr. In the east, the Red Army was less than fifty miles from Berlin. On 30 March, British prime minister Winston Churchill had cabled his representative on the Combined Chiefs of Staff in Washington, DC, "Pray . . . give [General Marshall] my warmest congratulations on the magnificent fighting and conduct of the American and Allied Armies under General Eisenhower, and say what a joy it must be to him to see how the armies he called into being by his own genius have won immortal renown. He is the true 'organizer of victory.'"[1]

"Organizer" was the key to George C. Marshall's triumphant institutional leadership role as U.S. Army chief of staff between September 1939 and November 1945. He was an "organization man" in the best sense of the phrase. He deduced lessons from past events and developed an understanding of the institutional values that affected organizational innovation. A reformer rather than a revolutionary in leading change within the U.S. Army, he successfully raised, modernized, and prepared the army for world war. Marshall directed his extraordinary management skills toward improving relations between the army and the major institutions and leaders that influenced defense and security policy; refining the army's organizational efficiency;

GEORGE C. MARSHALL
(George C. Marshall Foundation, Lexington, VA)

leading the struggle for large, well-equipped, and mobile ground and air forces; seeking ways to reinforce civilian as well as military morale; adhering to a grand strategy compatible with the nation's means and interests; and supporting a strong Anglo-American alliance.

The official history of the U.S. Army's Operations Division—the strategic planning and operations directing group Marshall created in March 1942 to solve organizational problems in the War Department—begins by observing, "Some of the greatest generals of World War II, far from striking the classic posture of the man on horseback, issued their military orders from the quiet of their desks and fought their decisive battles at conference tables."[2] Marshall was the first among them, the ultimate desk general of World War II.

Marshall never led troops in combat, although he could have been supreme Allied commander in Europe—a position subsequently assumed by Dwight D. Eisenhower—if he had wanted the job. At the August 1943 Quebec Conference, Churchill had even agreed that Marshall should take the command, and the decision was leaked to the press.[3] Marshall understood, however, that he was best suited to serve in Washington, DC. His protégé was capable of leading the supreme headquarters of the Allied Expeditionary Forces (AEF), but Eisenhower had little experience at the highest levels of Washington politics and bureaucracy and little familiarity with the U.S. Navy or British members of the Combined Chiefs of Staff.

At the Cairo Conference in December 1943, President Franklin D. Roosevelt asked Marshall if he wished to be named supreme Allied commander in Europe. He would not attempt to estimate his own capabilities for the job, Marshall responded; the president should do that. "I merely wished to make it clear," Marshall recalled, "that whatever the decision, I would go along with it wholeheartedly; that the issue was too great for any personal feelings to be considered. I did not discuss the pros and cons of the matter. As I recall, the President stated in completing our conversation 'I feel that I could not sleep at night with you out of the country.'"[4]

By the time Churchill had sent his 30 March 1945 cable praising the general, the U.S. Army and Army Air Forces numbered 8.2

million people, a remarkable increase of 5,000 percent since Marshall had become army chief of staff in 1939. Moreover, the quality of the personnel, their equipment, and the staffs that managed the war had increased enormously under Marshall's leadership. Historians who have evaluated the performance of the major combatants in World War II award the United States a grade of A in operational performance (highest of all combatants) and a B overall in tactical performance—both improved by two grades over World War I.[5] Undoubtedly Marshall strongly influenced operational performance, and his judicious selection and winnowing of subordinate commanders had considerable impact on the army's tactical performance. For Harry S. Truman, perhaps Marshall's greatest admirer, the general's role in World War II was easily—if somewhat exaggeratedly—described: "He won the war."[6]

The youngest of three children, George Catlett Marshall Jr. was born in Uniontown, Pennsylvania, on the last day of 1880. His father, a prosperous coking coal manufacturer and entrepreneur, was an intellectually curious tinkerer, constantly experimenting with new ways to do things and improve his family's circumstances. Clearly, he communicated these values to his youngest son. The elder Marshall also inculcated his youngest child with a love of the outdoors, particularly of hunting and fishing. But perhaps most important, Marshall's father was interested in the history of the Uniontown region, in which tales of the frontier era and of the French and Indian War abounded. George Washington's Fort Necessity (1754) and the sites of General Edward Braddock's defeat and grave (1755) were located just a few miles east of Uniontown. The Marshalls often visited these and other historically significant places, and such experiences instilled in George Jr. the value of learning from the past.[7] From his mother, young Marshall acquired his taciturn but optimistic and tolerant disposition and his Episcopalian church affiliation. In the 1940s, General Marshall was well known for his response to questions about his political affiliation: "My father was a Democrat, my mother a Republican, and I am an Episcopalian."[8]

In 1890, during the speculative economic boom in western Virginia, Marshall's father sold a large portion of his industrial holdings and invested the funds in land and building facilities around Luray, Virginia. Before long, however, the speculative bubble burst and plunged the family into unaccustomed financial straits. Only his mother's modest income from rental property prevented genteel poverty.

As a young boy, Marshall was educated in private schools, but after the 1891 economic collapse, he matriculated at the local public school. Much to his father's dismay, he demonstrated little academic facility, except in history. Marshall retained his interest in history throughout his life, although his reading was haphazard rather than scholarly. One study of Marshall's thinking notes that he had the habit of "seeing time as a stream": applying a consciousness of past problems, ideas, and solutions to the present rather than seeing every current problem in isolation and thus as new and unique.[9]

Colonel Charles Marshall, a distant relative and former aide to General Robert E. Lee, influenced Marshall's mother to send her sons to the Virginia Military Institute.[10] Marshall's older brother, Stuart, graduated in 1894 and worked in the Uniontown area as an industrial chemist. Stuart opposed George's desire to attend VMI, suspecting that he was inadequately prepared and motivated. Character, physique, and family background were more important for admission than academic achievement, however, and George's mother managed to fund the tuition.

Marshall entered VMI in September 1897. Immediately, he became enthusiastic about the regimen and quickly grasped the keys to being successful at the institution: military achievement and adherence to the honor code. Being of a rather stoic temperament, Marshall was less exercised than most of his peers by the absurdities and irritants of military school life. He accepted adversity as a part of the system to be endured while pursuing higher goals. Tall, slender, hard-working, and ambitious, Marshall pursued promotion as a cadet with vigor, managing to hold the highest office every year. "I tried very hard in all the military affairs," he recalled; "I was very exacting and exact in all my military duties." While his classroom grades were unexceptional, he read "pretty much anything I could get my hands on." Marshall later asserted, "What I learned most at the VMI was self-control, discipline, . . . and the problem of managing men which fell to the cadet noncommissioned officer and cadet officer. He was very severely judged by his classmates if he was slack. They might be willing to try to pull things which would give him the reputation of being slack, but at the same time they would judge you very severely if you proved to be a very slack performer in the business of your military grade." VMI instilled in Marshall the attention to detail that would serve him well in the coming years.[11]

Marshall graduated from college in 1901 without a recorded demerit. He finished fifteenth of thirty-three graduates, fifth of eighteen in civil engineering. The VMI superintendent informed President William McKinley that Marshall was "fully the equal of the best" West Point graduates.[12] Reports of the army's problems and successes in the Spanish-American War (1898) and the Philippine-American War (1899–1902) and the reforms implemented afterward indicated to Marshall that the army was changing from a frontier constabulary to an institution that emphasized modern training and management techniques. Despite the army's recent expansion, however, by the time Marshall was nearing graduation, few officer billets were available for civilian applicants. He obtained permission to take the entrance examination and passed it easily. He received his commission in early 1902.[13]

Marshall's first assignment in the Philippines lasted eighteen months. The isolation of his small command in southern Mindoro made him virtual governor of the area and allowed him to practice his new profession with little oversight. Later, he was transferred to Manila, and after breaking his ankle learning to ride a horse, he volunteered to help the local inspector general organize the paperwork of demobilizing militia units. Marshall had received his introduction to the administrative aspects of a command, and whereas such bureaucratic paper shuffling might have frustrated other junior officers, Marshall recognized the essential nature of this work to unit success. "I became quite an expert on papers," he recalled. "It helped me a great deal in later years."[14]

Following a subsequent tour in the Oklahoma Territory, Marshall was transferred to the Infantry and Cavalry School at Fort Leavenworth, Kansas. Many officers were skeptical of the school's value, but Marshall recognized that its new curriculum was helping to modernize the army. Still a second lieutenant when he arrived at the school, he was the lowest-ranking student; worse, most students were better prepared. His peers did not consider him worthy of the crucial second-year advanced course. Marshall's reaction was to prove his mettle: "I knew I would have to study harder than I ever dreamed of studying before in my life."[15]

Marshall was inspired by one of Leavenworth's new instructors, Major John F. Morrison. Others taught regulations and technique, but Morrison "spoke a tactical language I had never heard from any other officer." He taught his students to recognize the fundamental principles of war in action. "His problems were short and always contained a knockout if you failed to recognize the principle involved in meeting the situation. Simplicity and dispersion became fixed quantities in my mind, never to be forgotten. . . . He taught me all I have ever known of tactics."[16] Although later disparaged by some as the "Leavenworth clique," Marshall and others trained in Kansas would apply these lessons to save the inexperienced U.S. Army from serious embarrassment during World War I.

Through extraordinary effort, Marshall finished at the top of his class in July 1907 and earned a place in the Command and General Staff School, a stepping-stone to the U.S. Army War College and to General Staff assignments. In his second year there, he again led his class, and he was made an instructor for two additional years. During the summers, the best Leavenworth students were assigned to teach at National Guard encampments, a job most regular army officers despised. But Marshall, a natural teacher, thrived in the outdoors, instructing troops who were anxious to learn. Still only a first lieutenant, he commanded units normally led by majors or colonels. Marshall's understanding of the National Guard's problems and limitations, his ability to motivate its men, and his belief in its crucial position as the bedrock of America's ground forces clearly distinguished him from the regular army officers the guard normally encountered. His experience and thinking would prove invaluable as a budding institutional leader in the army. By 1911, the adjutants general of Pennsylvania and Massachusetts were competing for his services.[17]

Marshall's reputation as a premier staff officer attracted the attention of his peers and superiors, but twice—in August 1913, following the maneuvers in Connecticut, and again in February 1914, when he successfully led the "invaders" in maneuvers in the Philippines—overwork brought him to the edge of a nervous breakdown: "I woke . . . to the fact that I was working myself to death, to my superior's advantage, and that I was acquiring the reputation of being merely a pick and shovel man. From that time on I made it a business to avoid, so far as possible, detail work, and to relax as completely as I could manage in a pleasurable fashion. Unfortunately, it was about six years before I could get away from details because they were in my lap."[18]

Marshall had learned a valuable lesson: an organization's effectiveness is dependent on the well-being of its members. In subsequent years, he taught this lesson to subordinates, knowing that overworked leaders were apt to become ineffective. During World War II, he used the Greenbrier Hotel in West Virginia as a place where stressed army leaders could relax. Visiting Algiers in 1943, Marshall enjoined Eisenhower to find time to unwind by playing golf or riding a horse.[19]

The small size of the army's professional officer cadre prior to World War II meant that officers could know or know about nearly every important man in the service. Although it was not a stated value of the organization, mentoring, the close developmental relationship between experienced and less experienced officers, was not uncommon. Between 1914 and 1924, Marshall acquired three mentors who proved instrumental to his development: Hunter Liggett, J. Franklin Bell, and John J. Pershing.

At Fort Leavenworth during the 1908–1909 academic year, Lieutenant Marshall, then a twenty-nine-year-old instructor in the Command and General Staff School, became friends with the fifty-two-year-old Lieutenant Colonel Liggett, who commanded a battalion of the post's Thirteenth Infantry Regiment. Marshall helped

Liggett work his way through the school, which was a key step toward gaining admission to the Army War College. Liggett subsequently attended, taught at, and presided over the college. In 1914, when both men were stationed in the Philippines, Brigadier General Liggett saved Marshall from a routine posting at an isolated fort by making him an aide and introducing him to high-level staff work. Late in World War I, Liggett also sought Marshall's assistance in leading the U.S. First Army.[20]

The second of Marshall's mentors, Major General Bell, was also impressed with the lieutenant's work at the Fort Leavenworth schools. When Marshall returned from the Philippines in May 1916, he expected to join Pershing's punitive expedition into Mexico, but Bell, then commanding the army's Western Department, made him an aide to secure his help with the new citizen-training program. Though he was only a junior captain, Marshall had developed a superb reputation for his abilities in planning, operations, and training. In the Western Department, Bell gave him broad authority to act in his name. When Bell moved east in 1917 to command the Eastern Department's war mobilization, Marshall assumed even more responsibility.[21]

While establishing and managing volunteer officer training camps for General Bell, Marshall favorably impressed Brigadier General William L. Sibert. In the spring of 1917, when Sibert took command of the First Infantry Division, he asked Marshall to join his command in the crucial role of assistant chief of staff for training and operations. Consequently, Marshall was the second man ashore in war-torn France when the first American troop ship docked at Saint-Nazaire on 26 June 1917. Allied and American eyes focused on the division and its leaders. In addition to preparing the First Division for combat, Marshall was directed to establish cantonments for three other divisions that were soon to arrive. The colonels and generals at AEF general headquarters knew Major Marshall and, having no more experience at large-scale war than he, simply instructed him to do what he thought was wise in the way of preparation.[22]

Overcoming the AEF's organizational and training difficulties in France was crucial for Marshall's development as an institutional leader. The fall and winter of 1917, he recalled, were for him "the most depressing, gloomy period of the war"; he and his friends referred to it as their "winter of Valley Forge."[23] Marshall saw firsthand the effects of American overconfidence, inexperience, and unpreparedness. Even with French assistance, the initial U.S. divisions were not ready for combat. Pershing and the AEF General Staff grew increasingly anxious. On 3 October 1917, Pershing and some of his staff arrived at First Division headquarters to inspect a demonstration arranged by Marshall on short notice. After the exercise, Pershing grew furious at what he considered an insufficiently cogent critique by General Sibert and his chief of staff. "He just gave everybody hell," Marshall recalled. "He was very severe with General Sibert . . . in front of all the officers . . . and generally he just scarified us. He didn't give General Sibert a chance to talk at all. . . . So I decided it was about time for me to make my sacrifice play. . . . I went up and started to talk to General [Pershing]. . . . He shrugged his shoulders and turned away from me, and I put my hand on his arm and practically forced him to talk. . . . I was just mad all over," Marshall continued; "I had a rather inspired moment." According to a fellow officer, when Marshall became angry, "his eyes flashed and he talked so rapidly and vehemently no one else could get in a word. He overwhelmed his opponent by a torrent of facts."[24] General Sibert and the other staff officers thought Marshall's actions had ruined his career, but General Pershing was impressed. On subsequent visits, Pershing made a point of seeing Marshall alone and seeking his opinions on the division's progress. In mid-1918, he transferred Marshall to an important post at AEF general headquarters, and in May 1919, he made him an aide-de-camp. Marshall had taken a risk by confronting Pershing, but as a result of his hard work and preparation, he wielded sufficient institutional knowledge to survive the encounter.[25]

Marshall recognized that, as his superior's agent, he must take responsibility both for his own actions and, when appropriate, for the institution. In November 1917, for example, when the first American ground troops were killed in combat, Marshall had no qualms about questioning a French general's orders to the troops and demanding to see the corps commander about them. He recalled, "The idea of a major going to see the corps commander was unheard of. But I was representing the division commander who was a hundred or more kilometers away, so my rank didn't cut any figure with me as far as I could see. My job was to represent him and his interests."[26]

Over the course of his career, Marshall repeatedly demonstrated vigor, confidence, and eloquence in defending his decisions. Moreover, he was never intimidated by the mighty, as Roosevelt, Churchill, Truman, Stalin, and others would learn. On occasion, however, Marshall proved too assertive and outspoken. In December 1917, while he was the acting chief of staff of the First Division, his growing irritation with the staff at AEF general headquarters for their "misunderstanding of our situation" went too far. Nearly all of these men were his friends, and many were his former students at Fort Leavenworth, "but we were wholly out of sympathy with each other, and I felt that they didn't understand what they were doing at all. They had become very severe and they didn't know what they were being severe about. . . . General Pershing was severe, so they modeled their attitude on him. I was so outraged by this that I talked a great deal and I made a great mistake." His attitude cost him the chance to become the division's permanent chief of staff, which would have led to his promotion to brigadier general in 1918 instead of 1936. Marshall's confrontation with the general headquarters staff convinced him that a leader needed to be careful that his staff—who could always "prove" that their ideas were correct—did not become too negative toward outsiders or too prone to be yes-men.[27]

As head of the First Division's operations section, Marshall prepared the report on the first Americans killed, wrote the orders for the first U.S. raid on German lines, and did much of the planning for the first American offensive. On 18 June 1918, Marshall formally requested troop duty. The First Division's commander, Major General Robert L. Bullard, replied that he could not approve the request "because I know that Lieut. Col. Marshall's special fitness is for staff work and because I doubt that in this, whether it be teaching or practice, he has an equal in the Army to-day."[28]

In mid-July 1918, Marshall transferred to AEF general headquarters at Chaumont, where he joined the First Army's operations
section. He found the atmosphere there entirely different. The staff
at Chaumont dealt with ocean tonnages, ports of debarkation, dock
construction, tank manufacture, methods of training divisions, and
the complexities of inter-Allied politics.[29] The leadership lesson he
gleaned there was the danger of "localitis": the unwarranted assumption that one's problems had to be the organization's or the country's key problems. Thereafter, Marshall rarely tolerated displays of
localitis by subordinates. By identifying the problem, he maintained
a proper perspective on the challenges he encountered, a necessary
attribute of institutional leaders.[30]

In the year between Marshall's arrival in France and his transfer to the Chaumont headquarters, the AEF had grown in size and
experience, and Pershing was preparing to launch a full-force attack
against the weakening German army. Marshall's job was to prepare
plans for both the Saint-Mihiel salient offensive, scheduled for 12
September 1918, and the far larger offensive on the Meuse-Argonne
front, scheduled for 25 September. For the latter, Marshall had to
move out 220,000 French and Italian soldiers from one sector and
move in some 600,000 U.S. and French troops, including their supplies and equipment. Despite constricted roads, Marshall succeeded,
and this added to his reputation as a brilliant organizer. His attention to detail, hard work, and commitment to administration helped
maintain the army's effectiveness as its responsibilities increased.[31]

The lessons learned by AEF officers during World War I colored
their thinking in the interwar period. Those officers who arrived
late in the war saw only a weakening German army and a burgeoning AEF. Thus they tended to overestimate the quality of American
ground forces. But Marshall had experienced the AEF's painful and
slow progress toward military competence. Much of this pain was
suffered, he asserted, because too many Americans assumed that infantry training was simply a matter of taking up the trusty hunting
rifle and marching off to rout the enemy. Marshall thought that history textbooks, awash with flag waving but lacking accuracy, encour-

aged and sustained this dangerous myth. Although the nation was again at peace, Marshall understood that World War I had revealed serious shortcomings in the army that had to be addressed for the institution's future effectiveness.[32]

Conscious of the appalling casualty count of the Great War, Marshall, like a number of astute American and European officers, recognized that even in peacetime the army needed to improve troop education, training, and mechanization.[33] Marshall concluded that enlisted recruits required extensive basic training and, perhaps more important, that officers needed rigorous combat leadership training to improve their decision making. Thus, as the Axis powers increasingly threatened American interests between 1939 and 1941, Marshall insisted on ever larger maneuvers. Moreover, he demanded that officers, including colonels and generals, be physically fit. Without stamina, they could weaken or collapse under strain, as many had done in France in 1918. Marshall's rule in World War II was that, to receive a combat command, general officers, regardless of age, had to demonstrate at minimum the physical stamina of a forty-five-year-old in good condition.[34]

Another lesson Marshall derived from his experiences in France was that officer candidates should not be taken exclusively from the narrow class of college students and graduates. His American sense of fairness demanded equal opportunity; moreover, he had seen too many ninety-day-wonder college boys fail disastrously. Marshall wanted all potential combat leaders to go through basic training (or its military school equivalent) and proceed to officer training only if selected. He founded the Officer Candidate School over the opposition of his branch chiefs and defended it vigorously, even to the point of threatening to resign as army chief of staff in March 1941 if it was not implemented. Although it was not a cure-all for the weaknesses resulting from lack of prewar preparedness measures, the school became the main source of junior officers for the wartime army.[35]

During World War I, Marshall had also learned the importance of awarding medals and honors quickly. He was much impressed when French premier Georges Clemenceau appeared at the American front to pin on medals less than a day after the first AEF soldiers were killed. During World War II, Marshall pressed a reluctant Roosevelt to approve various new awards for soldiers, such as the Army Good Conduct Medal, the Bronze Star, infantrymen's badges, unit citations, and campaign and theater service ribbons. Furthermore, to avoid insulting combat soldiers, he generally insisted that commanders in the rear and at headquarters not accept honors until the fighting ceased. Marshall's efforts to implement these reforms demonstrated his commitment to improving the army's future capabilities, an essential element of institutional leadership.[36]

In May 1919, Marshall came under the tutelage of the third of his mentors when he was selected as one of General Pershing's three aides-de-camp, a position he held until mid-1924. During these five years, Pershing placed great trust in Marshall's judgment. Most summers, Pershing would go to France, leaving Marshall in nearly complete control of the War Department. Marshall's association with Pershing, which included traveling around the United States and the world, constituted a postgraduate education in national and War Department politics. One aspect of Pershing's character that impressed Marshall, and that he emulated, was the ability to separate official from private time: on duty, Pershing was formal, focused, and tough; off duty, he was a pleasant companion.[37]

The post–World War I congressional hearings and investigations, the general lack of public interest in army ground forces, and the excessive defense budget cuts taught Marshall important lessons about dealing with Congress, the news media, army public relations, and the National Guard. Former army brigadier general Charles Gates Dawes, head of the new Bureau of the Budget in the Harding administration, liked to talk to Marshall about financial issues. Marshall recalled that Dawes "would sit in my office and talk to me sometimes by the hour, so I was very familiar with these goings on." From such experiences, Marshall developed what a subordinate termed "an uncanny eye for the political angle of every problem."[38] Moreover, Marshall's work in France and in the War Department, where he wrote much of the *Report of the First Army* (1924), greatly enhanced his communication skills. One member of his staff, William W. Bessell Jr., noted, "I served first with him in WWII when I was Army Director of the Joint War Plans Committee. At that time I had completed 23 years of commissioned service and had thought I could compose and write a pretty good staff paper. However, my drafts used to come back from General Marshall with changes which invariably made me wonder why I hadn't thought of his clearer means of expression. I received from him a post-graduate education in staff writing."[39]

The military demobilization after 1918 demonstrated yet again America's tradition of maintaining a small, professional army. Marshall recognized that the army's postwar roles were to be the repository of administrative and technical expertise and the trainer of the citizen-soldier army. The key question was what forms of army reserve components would be most effective. Marshall actively supported the National Guard, the Reserve Officers' Training Corps, and the citizens' military training camps movement.

In 1927 Marshall was given the opportunity to lead the academic department of the Army Infantry School at Fort Benning, Georgia. Since the war, the size of the regular army had shrunk dramatically, promotions had stagnated, command opportunities had evaporated, and equipment had grown scarce and obsolete. Some active duty officers slowly slipped into mental somnolence. Many officers who had seen the AEF only at its peak in late 1918 unfortunately believed that little in the army needed reform. At the Infantry School, Marshall began a long struggle against the intellectual coagulation of the "cast-iron Regulars."[40]

Lieutenant Colonel Marshall made the Infantry School the fountainhead of army ground forces reform. Quietly and gradually, so as not to arouse opposition, he brought into the faculty open-minded officers who had recently returned from troop duty. "We bored from within without cessation during my five years at Benning," Marshall said. He hammered tirelessly on the theme of simplicity: no reading of long lectures on doctrine, no field exercises dependent on elaborate maps, no overly detailed orders from headquarters that stifled local initiative, no overblown intelligence estimates that harried commanders who had no time to read, and no field procedures so complex that tired citizen-soldiers could not adequately perform them. "Get down to the essentials," he directed. "Make clear the real difficulties, and expunge the bunk, complications and ponderosities." He was particularly aggrieved by the "colorless pedantic form" used in army manuals; he insisted on clear, concise language that National Guard and reserve officers, not just regulars, could understand. During Marshall's tenure, some two hundred future generals passed through the Infantry School, either as instructors or students. He had now begun to instill his notions of institutional leadership into the army's rising commanders.[41]

Marshall is not usually remembered for being a teacher, but he was formally employed as a classroom instructor on three occasions. Forrest Pogue, his principal biographer, argues that Marshall would have made a great teacher, that "he himself sometimes regretted that he had not set out on an academic career," and that "a good part of his impact on the Army was actually as a teacher."[42] The teacher's ability to synthesize information and communicate it efficiently was a hallmark of Marshall's role as an institutional leader.

Although he received the assignment shortly after his wife's death in September 1927, the Infantry School period was a happy one for Marshall, and in October 1930, he married Katherine Tupper Brown, a vivacious widow with three young children. Still, he was pleased to return to a troop command in 1932. When the task of organizing and operating the Civilian Conservation Corps was thrust on the army in 1933, many professional officers viewed it as an unwelcome distraction. Marshall, always thinking of the army's future capabilities, saw an opportunity for officers to gain experience in leading masses of raw recruits. He told General Pershing, "The CCC affair has been a major mobilization and a splendid experience for the War Department and the Army. The former has got a lot to learn about decentralization and simplicity."[43]

The Great Depression also determined Marshall's subsequent assignment: orders to report to Chicago to serve as a senior instructor for the Illinois National Guard. Now a colonel, he tried without success to get the assignment changed. The Thirty-third Division's commanding general had demanded from the War Department an outstanding professional officer, because civil unrest seemed likely as the Depression staggered toward another bitter winter. Army Chief of Staff Douglas MacArthur observed that Marshall "has no superior among Infantry Colonels."[44]

Given the numerous dangers to any regular officer's career inherent in service with the highly politicized National Guard, many of them took care to avoid risks.[45] Not Marshall. During his three years in Chicago, he undertook to reform citizen-soldier training in Illinois and to reeducate the guard's officer corps. Marshall also pressed the War Department to assign high-caliber regular officers as instructors and to provide them better support. He worked intensely at improving the Thirty-third Division's morale by stimulating public interest in its activities and ending the guard's relative isolation from the local community. Marshall's successful efforts won him staunch supporters in Illinois and demonstrated his ability to reform and reenergize an organization burdened by politics and outdated methods. These positive relations, along with his history of rapport with reserve components, proved extremely valuable after 1939, when, as army chief of staff, he had to remove large numbers of ineffective National Guard officers, many of whom were replaced with regulars. The political recriminations against the War Department during Marshall's leadership were vigorous; under anyone else they might have seriously disrupted the army's mobilization and modernization. Throughout World War II, Marshall demonstrated his belief in the value of guard officers to army effectiveness, insisting on a sort of affirmative action policy regarding guard officer promotions. After the war, there was no recurrence of the 1918–1920 backlash against the regular army within the National Guard.[46]

In October 1936, Marshall received his long-awaited general's star and took command of the Third Division's Fifth Brigade at Vancouver Barracks, Washington. He would remember this assignment fondly. He was back with troops and leading a huge Civilian Conservation Corps district. This was Marshall's last restful assignment for many years, for in July 1938 the War Department recalled him to head the War Plans Division. Four months later, he became the army's deputy chief of staff, and in July 1939 he became acting chief of staff of the army.

Marshall's commitment to the army's well-being had taken him to the highest levels of command, and once there he continued to seek ways to improve the organization. He had long been interested in the U.S. Army Air Corps and knew many of its leaders. At the Army Infantry School in the early 1930s, he had sought closer relations with the Air Corps Tactical School, but his real education in the air corps began shortly after his 1938 arrival in Washington, DC. Henry H. "Hap" Arnold, chief of the air corps, noted that Marshall "needed plenty of indoctrination about the air facts of life. The difference in George, who presently was to become one of the most potent forces behind the development of a real American air power, was his ability to digest what he saw and make it part of as strong a body of military genius as I have ever known." Marshall understood the military potential of aircraft. He also appreciated the air corps' readiness to innovate and its close relations with the civilian scientific and engineering community in developing airframes, bombsights, navigation instruments, and weaponry. He encouraged a similar approach in the army's ground leaders.[47]

Upon becoming army chief of staff, Marshall required that all General Staff officers be willing to fly as passengers. And despite opposition from groundlings, he brought air officers into positions of power on the General Staff, including Frank M. Andrews as assistant chief of staff for operations (1939–1940) and Joseph T. McNarney as deputy chief of staff (1942–1944). Moreover, as Arnold notes, Marshall used his influence to get the heavy bomber developed over cheaper, medium bomber types. "It is hard to think," Arnold wrote, "how there could have been any American Air Force in World War II without him."[48] Although Marshall was convinced of the value of strategic bombing, he did not believe that air power alone could win wars. Moreover, he did not believe that the air corps (designated the U.S. Army Air Forces after June 1941) was ready for independence from the army. Airmen liked to fly planes, not desks, he reasoned, so they were unprepared to manage an organization. But even as Arnold undertook to suppress agitation for immediate air corps independence, Marshall undertook to develop the future leaders of an independent air force.[49]

Marshall became acting chief of staff on 1 July 1939; five days later, Roosevelt issued an executive order stating that the army chief and the chief of naval operations should report directly to the president on certain issues instead of to their respective civilian departmental heads, the secretaries of war and navy. Marshall was reluctant to go outside the traditional chain of command, but he found it useful to have direct access to the White House. He knew that he would have to earn the president's confidence. Well aware of Roosevelt's affable and manipulative nature, Marshall kept his distance, demonstrated his loyalty, but showed his willingness to disagree with the president's ideas. He never visited the president in Hyde Park, New York, or Warm Springs, Georgia, and he requested that the president cease referring to the navy as "we" and the army as "they."[50] Marshall recognized that too intimate a relationship with even the president could hinder his judgment and ability to head the army.

Marshall was officially sworn in as chief of staff of the U.S. Army on the morning of 1 September 1939, only a few hours after Germany invaded Poland. In the following two years, the American public remained pessimistic about the nation's ability to avoid a Europewide conflict, but there was little desire to get involved. Only the defense of the Western Hemisphere and American possessions was deemed vital. Civilian and military personnel in the War Department were of divided opinions. While military strategists generally agreed that Germany was the most dangerous of the Axis powers, the United States' preparations for war were severely circumscribed, and significant progress in mobilizing American military and economic power began only after the shocking German victories during the spring of 1940.[51]

Given public opinion, Marshall believed that the president's caution was frequently justified. As chief of staff, he was determined to operate apolitically and not to adopt the tradition of circumventing the president's organizational and appropriations decisions by directly engaging friends in Congress.[52] Marshall thought it important to demonstrate his nonpartisan role to the executive and legislative branches. He generally succeeded in maintaining cordial relations between the War Department and Congress, in part by appearing forty-eight times before various House and Senate committees between the summer of 1939 and the autumn of 1941.[53] He was an effective witness, profoundly informed on military matters, better acquainted than most professional soldiers with the political difficulties that beset legislators, and appreciative of the public's anxieties. Many in Congress trusted Marshall over "that man in the White House." In a memorandum to Roosevelt, Secretary of the Treasury Henry Morgenthau Jr. advised, "Let General Marshall, and only General Marshall, do all the testifying in connection with the Bill which you are about to send up for additional appropriations for the Army."[54] Marshall's ability to build bridges between interdependent organizations was a hallmark of his institutional leadership.

Marshall's primary role between late 1939 and late 1941 was to modernize an army that had been traumatized by penury and isolation for nearly a generation, an institutional leadership role for which he had been preparing for most of his career. The U.S. Army counted but 165,000 officers and enlisted personnel as of 1 July 1939, and a year later it was only 50,000 larger. Germany's massive spring 1940 offensive against its western neighbors forced a radical change in American defense policy. Having dragged its feet on ground forces mobilization, a panicky Congress quickly passed legislation for the first peacetime draft in U.S. history and the federalization of the National Guard. Suddenly, green soldiers inundated an ill-prepared regular army. Marshall opposed rushing the army's development, he informed a congressional committee in 1947, "because I knew we could not carry the initial load and we would do ourselves more harm than good."[55] Between the fall of France and the attack on Pearl Harbor, the army's air and ground forces increased 750 percent, and this mammoth shift threatened to overload the whole antiquated system.

Meanwhile, equipment was still only trickling in from manufacturers, and a significant portion had to be diverted to the Allies.[56]

Marshall responded to the mobilization crisis with enormous energy. Not only did he frequently appear before Congress, but he constantly visited cantonments, witnessed new weapons demonstrations, inspected training facilities, observed maneuvers, and searched for effective leaders. He put officers on notice that he expected them to pay close attention to troop morale. In a crisis atmosphere, commanders too often delegated concern over morale issues to junior officers or relied on paper directives. In Marshall's experience, this was potentially disastrous. In mid-1941, he convinced Congress to grant him a special contingency fund of $25 million to underwrite morale-building initiatives.[57]

In the summer of 1940, President Roosevelt appointed Henry L. Stimson as his secretary of war. Given Marshall's respect for Stimson, who had previously served as secretary of state and of war, and his firm belief in civilian control of the military, he and the secretary worked well together. Marshall now held an unassailable position atop the army bureaucracy, precluding the divided authority evident in 1917–1918. His predilection was to pick the best person for a job, then delegate to him tremendous responsibilities and powers, defend him from the vicissitudes of Washington politics and media attention, but remove him quickly if he failed to measure up. Frank McCarthy, who worked closely with Marshall throughout the war and ended his military career as secretary of the General Staff, commented to a friend on this aspect of Marshall's institutional leadership, "I saw him turn over almost the entire high command without regard to sentiment, age, personal friendship, component, branch of the service, or any consideration other than actual productive efficiency, and put into each position the man that he was convinced could do the best job. . . . I think any officer of the General Staff would tell you that General Marshall's first important action, if not his most important action, was to establish as a criterion of command that the man who could best do the job got the job."[58]

Yet Marshall was not a ruthless leader who exploited subordinates for his own benefit. Moreover, he eschewed micromanagement. Having confidence in his subordinates, he was able to focus his thinking six months ahead. At the end of the war, the head of the vitally important Operations Division of the General Staff, John E. Hull, wrote,

> I cannot let the opportunity pass without expressing to you our appreciation for your guidance and loyalty to those of us who have been members of your staff. Loyalty goes both ways, up and down. Loyalty to one's superior is expected and is accepted without question in our service. Loyalty downward is not found in all people. You have demonstrated it to an outstanding degree. By your method of delegating responsibility, encouraging complete freedom of thought, and placing confidence in your subordinates you have made service under you such as to bring out the very best that the officers so serving could produce.[59]

On another aspect of Marshall's institutional leadership, military historian Ray Cline notes that Marshall "retained in his own hands, insofar as it could remain with one man in a coalition war, control of the army's conduct of military operations."[60] Eisenhower had observed early in the war that "General Marshall constantly has officers rotating between him and the very front lines in order to keep himself completely familiar with the problems of the soldier in the field."[61] Marshall understood that, despite the immensity of the war effort, effective leadership demanded that he be as well informed as possible.

A major institutional problem for Marshall was the general unpreparedness of the slow, small, peacetime-oriented War Department organization that he had inherited. On 3 November 1941, Marshall lamented, "This is the poorest command post in the Army and we must do something about it, although I do not yet know what we will do."[62] Too many people asserted their rights to present problems directly to the chief of staff. Central control of plans and operations was weak at best. Lines of communication were slow and lacked adequate oversight. The Japanese attack on Pearl Harbor dramatically exposed the organization's managerial deficiencies.

Marshall restructured the War Department effective 2 March 1942. He took advantage of the president's new emergency powers, of previous recommendations by airmen, and of reassignment of conservative chiefs of cavalry and field artillery. The army air forces received virtual autonomy, and numerous other agencies were subsumed under the army ground and service forces, thus ridding Marshall of directly leading some 40 major and 350 minor commands. While major problems were still channeled directly to Marshall through the deputy chief of staff, general information flowed to the secretary of the General Staff. The newly established Operations Division controlled plans and operations.[63] It is worth noting that in subsequent years, Marshall carried out substantive institutional reforms at the State Department (1947), the American Red Cross (1949), and the Defense Department (1950). He understood that a successful institutional leader had to make difficult decisions to maintain the effectiveness and efficiency of his organization.

The lessons Marshall had learned at AEF general headquarters in World War I and during the interwar period also made him an advocate of international cooperation and of unity of command. Marshall's determination to have all Allied military units in a particular theater under a single commander resulted from his observation of the disorganized command structure on the western front prior to the appointment of Supreme Commander Ferdinand Foch in 1918. Three weeks after Pearl Harbor, Marshall convinced the reluctant British to create the American-British-Dutch-Australian Command in the Pacific under Britain's Sir Archibald Wavell. This short-lived command established the precedent for a single Allied command in the European and Mediterranean theaters. Indeed, one of Marshall's most successful policies during World War II was strengthening the Anglo-American alliance despite members' differing strategic interests.[64]

President Roosevelt's penchant for informal organization, acting essentially as his own secretary of state and dabbling in military strategy, created a particular institutional challenge for Marshall. To the frequent dismay of the British Chiefs of Staff Committee, Churchill did the same, but the well-organized British bureaucracy tended to compensate for the prime minister's behavior. The same could not be said for the American system. Roosevelt, for example, invited Marshall and other military advisors to the August 1941 Atlantic Conference, but only at the last minute, and he forbade them to bring staff assistants. Because of FDR's informal style, American ideas and plans suffered in combined councils until well into 1943.[65]

Marshall was well aware of the president's organizational foibles, and he sought to overcome them. At the Atlantic Conference, he met with Sir John G. Dill, chief of the Imperial General Staff, and despite Marshall's normal reserve, they became quick friends. In early 1942, Marshall insisted, against Churchill's resistance, that Dill become the senior British member of the new Combined Chiefs of Staff in Washington, DC. Early on, Dill instructed Marshall on the intricacies and efficiencies of the British civil-military bureaucracy and kept him informed on secret communications between Roosevelt and Churchill. Dill also conveyed Marshall's ideas and attitudes to his superiors in London. Over the next two years, this relationship attenuated coalition friction, which had undermined previous military alliances.[66]

The British, in fact, were appalled at the Americans' frequent displays of international insensitivity, the number of embarrassing leaks of classified information, and continued injudicious public statements—including disparaging remarks about U.S. allies by senior U.S. military officers. Marshall was sensitive to the negative political and morale effects of such loose-lips tendencies. The "indiscretions of officers in official and unofficial conversations," he stated in an 11 September 1942 memorandum to high-ranking commanders, "have been productive of serious consequences." The commanders were warned to set a good example and to prevent subordinates from making foolish comments that might undermine the war effort. "Considering the fact that we must operate as a team if we are to meet the Germans and Japanese on reasonably equal grounds," Marshall argued, "this state of affairs is extremely critical and must be remedied." Throughout the war, he sought to demonstrate to Americans Britain's sacrifices and contributions to the Allied cause. Marshall knew he must set the tone for the rest to follow.[67]

The United States' highest priorities were to raise a massive military force and to devise plans for its deployment. Strategically, the U.S. military had planned to concentrate on defeating Germany while holding the line against Japan, although after Pearl Harbor, the aggressiveness of U.S. operations in the Pacific increased dramatically. To defeat Germany, the United States Army desired to fight decisive artillery and mechanized battles in the relatively open and well-roaded countryside of northern France and Belgium. Unlike many British leaders, Marshall was reluctant to commit to lengthy and expensive campaigns in the Mediterranean. And while political necessity and military opportunism led to major Allied campaigns in North Africa, Sicily, and mainland Italy, Marshall blocked further investments in what he called the logistics and manpower "suction pump" of the Mediterranean. Instead, he forced a commitment to a spring 1944 invasion of Normandy: Operation Overlord.[68] American planning throughout the war aimed to keep Allied casualties low while raining mass destruction on the enemy from the air. Marshall desired a quick end to the war and supported the use of atomic bombs on Japanese cities, especially after the fierce Japanese resistance on Okinawa and Iwo Jima.[69]

President Harry Truman liked to assert that Army Chief of Staff Marshall won World War II. Churchill was closer to the truth: Marshall was the organizer of the Allied victory. Not simply a management technician but a responsible institutional leader, Marshall fought his decisive battles at desks and conference tables. He was honest, confident, forthright, yet ever humble, never seeking undue credit for institutional accomplishments. He was energetic, hard working, and assertive, always expecting his staff to demonstrate extraordinary commitment. But as a leader, he was also fair and empathetic, consciously providing opportunities for subordinates to relax and reenergize. Intensely prideful, Marshall was acutely sensitive to misperceptions of and slights toward the army, and yet he remained a model of self-discipline in full control of his emotions. Despite working under constant stress and pressure, he also understood the value of mastering the details; he once informed a congressional committee, "It is very important that we be coldly, unemotionally calculating."[70]

As an institutional leader, Marshall understood the importance of communicating effectively, building organizational morale, and developing trusting relationships. In written work especially, he demonstrated and mandated brevity and clarity. As a bureaucratic bridge builder rather than an empire builder, he improved War Department coordination with Congress and the White House. He personally led the establishment of better relations among the branches and departments of the U.S. military and with the Allies and the press. He supported programs that raised organizational morale. He was involved in keeping army personnel informed about both the war and the home front via *Yank*, *Stars and Stripes*, and numerous other publications. He also boosted civilian morale through the *Why We Fight* series and other army motion pictures.[71]

An effective institutional leader, Marshall benefited from his understanding of American history and the army's political and social influence. He learned from personal experience and from his mentors, and he developed an administrative philosophy that emphasized simplicity, efficiency, flexibility, and decentralization. Recognizing that subordinates, too, had careers, Marshall acted as a mentor himself and sought to advance their interests within the army. He disliked the tendency of staffs to develop a yes-man mentality; rather, he encouraged initiative and critical thinking among subordinates and thereby elicited their loyalty, dedication, openness, and superior performance.

Marshall also demonstrated adaptability and was unwilling to permit tradition or entrenched interests to thwart the incorporation of worthwhile ideas. He was, for example, cognizant of the army air force's close relations with civilian engineers and scientists, and he sought to replicate such collaboration with the army ground and service forces. Furthermore, he supported the airmen institutionally, granting them substantial autonomy during World War II.

Similarly, Marshall understood the domestic politics of race and gender. Although he did not propose that the wartime army lead in social reform, he made certain that no group that desired to participate in army operations was excluded. Consequently, he mentored women in the regular army and supported minority military organizations, including the African American Tuskegee airmen and the Japanese American Nisei battalion. In retrospect, it is clear that Marshall's personal character traits, organizational skills, and reform-minded policies made him an exemplar of institutional leadership.[72]

Following a long illness, George Marshall died at Walter Reed Army Hospital on 16 October 1959. He is buried in Arlington National Cemetery. Only a year before his death, Churchill wrote, "In war he was as wise and understanding in counsel as he was resolute in action. In peace he was the architect who planned the restoration of our battered European economy. . . . He has always fought victoriously against defeatism, discouragement, and disillusion. Succeeding generations must not be allowed to forget his achievements and his example."[73]

Notes

1. Winston Churchill to Field Marshal Wilson, 30 March 1945, in Forrest C. Pogue, *George C. Marshall* (New York: Viking, 1963–1987), 3:585.

2. Ray S. Cline, *Washington Command Post: The Operations Division* (Washington, DC: Office of the Chief of Military History, Department of the Army, 1951), 1.

3. *The Papers of George Catlett Marshall*, ed. Larry I. Bland and Sharon Ritenour Stevens (Baltimore: Johns Hopkins University Press, 1981–2003), 4:91, 127–29.

4. Ibid., 103.

5. Allan R. Millett and Williamson Murray, eds., *Military Effectiveness* (Boston: Unwin Hyman, 1988–), 3:321. Overall performance included that by the U.S. Navy.

6. Truman quoted in Eddie Jones to Don Bermingham, 18 December 1948, Frank McNaughton Papers, Harry S. Truman Library, Independence, MO.

7. Pogue, *Marshall*, 1:22–23.

8. *Papers of George Catlett Marshall*, 2:616. See also "By Marshall," *New York Times*, 8 November 1953.

9. Richard E. Neustadt and Ernest R. May, *Thinking in Time: The Uses of History for Decision-Makers* (New York: Free Press, 1986), 247–48.

10. George C. Marshall to Charles A. Marshall (Colonel Marshall's son), 27 February 1948, Secretary of State General Correspondence, George C. Marshall Papers, George C. Marshall Library, Lexington, VA.

11. *George C. Marshall: Interviews and Reminiscences for Forrest C. Pogue*, 3rd ed., ed. Larry I. Bland (Lexington, VA: George C. Marshall Foundation, 1996), 95, 98, 119.

12. *Papers of George Catlett Marshall*, 1:11.

13. Ibid., 11, 18–20.

14. *Marshall: Interviews and Reminiscences*, 142–43.

15. Ibid., 156–57.

16. *Papers of George Catlett Marshall*, 1:45–46.

17. Ibid., 56.

18. Ibid., 2:31.

19. *My Three Years with Eisenhower: The Personal Diary of Captain Henry C. Butcher* (New York: Simon and Schuster, 1946), 247.

20. *Marshall: Interviews and Reminiscences*, 177; Pogue, *Marshall*, 1:127–28; *Papers of George Catlett Marshall*, 1:93, 96–97, 164–65.

21. Pogue, *Marshall*, 1:135–36, 140–43; *Papers of George Catlett Marshall*, 1:97–101.

22. *Papers of George Catlett Marshall*, 1:115–16.

23. *Marshall: Interviews and Reminiscences*, 121.

24. Ibid., 197–98; Benjamin F. Caffey to Forrest C. Pogue, 14 January 1961, Forrest C. Pogue Collection, Marshall Library.

25. *Marshall: Interviews and Reminiscences*, 197–98.

26. Ibid., 206–8.

27. *Papers of George Catlett Marshall*, 1:129.

28. Ibid., 144.

29. Ibid., 152.

30. See Eisenhower's reaction to Marshall's 1944 suggestion that the European theater headquarters was displaying "localitis" in ibid., 4:272.

31. Pogue, *Marshall*, 1:174–79. For Marshall's account of this confused but successful operation, see George C. Marshall, *Memoirs of My Services in the World War, 1917–1918* (Boston: Houghton Mifflin, 1976), 149–56. See also Robert H. Ferrell, *America's Deadliest Battle: Meuse-Argonne, 1918* (Lawrence: University Press of Kansas, 2007), 35–39.

32. See Marshall's speeches on this topic in *Papers of George Catlett Marshall*, 1:219–22 and 2:123–27.

33. Evan Andrew Huelfer, *The "Casualty Issue" in American Military Practice: The Impact of World War I* (Westport, CT: Praeger, 2003).

34. *Papers of George Catlett Marshall*, 3:188, 464.

35. Ibid., 2:512. The Officer Candidate School is examined in detail in Robert R. Palmer, Bell I. Wiley, and William R. Keast, *The Procurement and Training of Ground Combat Troops* (Washington, DC: Historical Division, Department of the Army, 1948), 325–64. The army quickly discovered that the course had to be combined with unit training to be effective, and course duration was extended from twelve to seventeen weeks.

36. *Marshall: Interviews and Reminiscences*, 238–39, 335; *Papers of George Catlett Marshall*, 3:322–23, 369, 419–20, 680–81, 4:61–63, 79, 170–71.

37. Pogue, *Marshall*, 1:218–19, 223, 225.

38. *Marshall: Interviews and Reminiscences*, 108; Paul M. Robinett diary, 30 June 1941, Marshall Library.

39. William W. Bessell Jr. to Fred M. Harris, 9 January 1965, Fred M. Harris Collection, Marshall Library.

40. *Papers of George Catlett Marshall*, 1:339.

41. Ibid., 409–16; Pogue, *Marshall*, 1:249, 269.

42. Pogue, *Marshall*, 1:102–3.

43. *Papers of George Catlett Marshall*, 1:398.

44. Ibid., 399.

45. Ibid., 405.

46. Ibid., 2:655–57, 3:235–36, 251, 313; *Marshall: Interviews and Reminiscences*, 255–57; Jerry Cooper, *The Rise of the National Guard: The Evolution of the American Militia, 1865–1920* (Lincoln: University of Nebraska Press, 1997), 178; Martha Derthick, *The National Guard in Politics* (Cambridge, MA: Harvard University Press, 1965), 59–60, 79.

47. H. H. Arnold, *Global Mission* (New York: Harper, 1949), 163–64, 165–66.

48. Ibid., 195.

49. *Marshall: Interviews and Reminiscences*, 290–91, 297–98, 614–15; Mark S. Watson, *Chief of Staff: Prewar Plans and Preparations* (Washington, DC: Historical Division, Department of the Army, 1950), 286–98.

50. *Papers of George Catlett Marshall*, 2:3; *Marshall: Interviews and Reminiscences*, 610–11.

51. Maurice Matloff and Edwin M. Snell, *Strategic Planning for Coalition Warfare, 1941–1942* (Washington, DC: Office of the Chief of Military History, Department of the Army, 1953), 11–31.

52. *Marshall: Interviews and Reminiscences*, 297.

53. Mark Skinner Watson, *Chief of Staff: Prewar Plans and Preparations* (Washington, DC: Historical Division, Department of the Army, 1950), 8.

54. *Papers of George Catlett Marshall*, 2:214.

55. House Committee on Foreign Relations, *U.S. Information and Educational Exchange Act of 1947: Hearings on H.R. 3342 before the Committee on Foreign Relations*, 80th Cong., 1st sess. (Washington, DC: GPO, 1947), 178.

56. Watson, *Chief of Staff*, 303–9, 321, 327, 329.

57. *Papers of George Catlett Marshall*, 2:505–7.

58. Frank McCarthy to Cliff Miller, 14 August 1945, Frank McCarthy Papers, box 5, folder 18, Marshall Library.

59. *Papers of George Catlett Marshall*, 5:364–65.

60. Cline, *Washington Command Post*, 21–22.

61. Eisenhower to Major General Alexander D. Surles, 15 June 1942, Records of the Office of the Chief of Staff, file 000.7, RG 165, National Archives, College Park, MD.

62. Marshall quoted in Cline, *Washington Command Post*, 73.

63. Ibid., 90–106.

64. *Papers of George Catlett Marshall*, 3:41–42; Matloff and Snell, *Strategic Planning*, 123–26.

65. *Establishing the Anglo-American Alliance: The Second World War Diaries of Brigadier Vivian Dykes*, ed. Alex Danchev (London: Brassey's, 1990), 69, 109; *Papers of George Catlett Marshall*, 2:585, 3:634–35; Watson, *Chief of Staff*, 5–7. Regarding Roosevelt's administrative style, see James MacGregor Burns, *Roosevelt: The Lion and the Fox* (New York: Harcourt, Brace, 1956), 371–73.

66. See Alex Danchev, *Very Special Relationship: Field-Marshall Sir John Dill and the Anglo-American Alliance, 1941–44* (London: Brassey's Defence, 1986).

67. *Papers of George Catlett Marshall*, 3:354–56.

68. Ibid., 516; Maurice Matloff, *Strategic Planning for Coalition Warfare, 1943–1944* (Washington, DC: Office of the Chief of Military History, Department of the Army, 1959), 126–34, 240–43, 303–6, 403–4.

69. *Papers of George Catlett Marshall*, 4:132, 691, 5:70, 75–76; *Marshall: Interviews and Reminiscences*, 423–25.

70. General George C. Marshall, testifying on adding military aid to NATO countries, on 7 June 1950, to the House Committee on Foreign Affairs, *To Amend the Mutual Defense Assistance Act of 1949: Hearings before the Committee on Foreign Affairs*, 81st Cong., 2nd sess. (Washington, DC: GPO, 1950), 93.

71. Pogue, *Marshall*, 3:85–114; Larry I. Bland, "George C. Marshall and the 'Squeekings of Democracy,'" *Documentary Editing* 27 (Summer 2005): 49–57.

72. Arnold, *Global Mission*, 165–66; *Marshall: Interviews and Reminiscences*, 298, 314, 436–39, 470–71; *Papers of George Catlett Marshall*, 2:525–26, 3:135–37, 329, 4:15–16, 153–54, 360–61.
73. Winston Churchill to John C. Hagen Jr., 30 July 1958, William J. Heffner Collection, Marshall Library.

4

Cross-Cultural Leadership

Dwight D. Eisenhower

Kerry E. Irish

Many people have analyzed Dwight D. Eisenhower's leadership as supreme Allied commander in Europe during World War II. Less known are the origins of his leadership principles and the fact that Eisenhower did not relate to other Allied leaders in an impromptu manner, relying on charm and a smile, as much as he endeavored to execute long-held and deeply believed cross-cultural leadership concepts. Indeed, much of Eisenhower's prior military career was a study of coalition leadership. From his tutorial under Brigadier General Fox Conner in Panama to his appointment as chief of staff of the American military mission to the Philippines under Major General Douglas MacArthur, Eisenhower's cross-cultural leadership philosophy had gradually taken form.

The cornerstone of Eisenhower's leadership philosophy was the idea that America's next major war, a second world war, could be won only with allies. He believed that a truly unified allied command, a cross-cultural command, would have to be created. It followed from this premise that nationalist concerns and individual egos would have to be subordinated to the allied team. The coalition commander would have to accept responsibility for allied decisions and share the glory for victories. He must also delegate authority intelligently to the various team members and insist that all personnel prepare to wage war with the highest possible efficiency. Moreover, the commander

DWIGHT D. EISENHOWER
(National Archives, College Park, MD)

would have to show humility, patience, and flexibility to gain the confidence of coalition members. The successful allied commander would have to treat the people of other nations as equals in terms of basic human dignity. Eisenhower demonstrated all of these qualities as supreme Allied commander during World War II.

In early 1922, Eisenhower arrived in Panama at the request of Brigadier General Conner. Conner hoped Ike would help him make the Twentieth Brigade, which was assigned to protect the Panama Canal, an effective fighting force, something it had not been for some time. Conner was an erudite southerner who enjoyed mentoring junior officers, an unusual quality within the interwar American army.[1] Senior officers seldom mentored junior officers with the skill and energy that Conner invested in Eisenhower; and most junior officers would not have responded as well as Ike did. In commenting on the Conner-Eisenhower relationship, Roscoe Woodruff, a classmate of Ike's at West Point who served in Panama in the early 1920s, remarked that had he been Conner's protégé, he would not have regarded it as a great opportunity: "I had little to do with my assignments. In other words, if they told me to do this, I did it. What I am trying to get at is, I didn't look ahead. Very few people do really." Woodruff was "quite sure" that it was Conner who "urged Ike to do certain things," to think about "looking forward to his own career." Woodruff concluded that "Ike was far ahead of most of his contemporaries" in that regard.[2]

Among other things, Conner revived Eisenhower's interest in military history.[3] Ike set up a reading alcove in his ramshackle quarters and made good use of his spare time. Upon finishing a book borrowed from Conner's excellent library, he and the general would discuss it as they rode horses about the post. The years with Conner essentially provided a graduate education in military history and the humanities. Conner provided Ike with key principles of leadership. The general convinced his young scholar that unity of command was essential, that a large campaign must have one commander over all of its forces: air, naval, and ground.[4] Eisenhower later wrote of his education under Conner, "One of the subjects on which he talked

to me most was allied command, its difficulties and its problems.
. . . Again and again General Conner said to me, 'We cannot escape
another great war. When we go into that war it will be in company
with allies. Systems of single command will have to be worked out.
. . . We must insist on individual and single responsibility—leaders
will have to learn how to overcome nationalistic considerations in
the conduct of campaigns.'"[5] In the Great War, Conner had seen
firsthand the arrogance of some of the British and French officers, so
he taught Eisenhower that a commander of allies must lead by "the
art of persuasion," as opposed to relying on peremptory orders.[6] All
the more reason the commander must be a master communicator and
diplomat.

Eisenhower fondly remembered one conversation with Conner:
"Since no foreigner could be given outright administrative command
of troops of another nation . . . they would have to be coordinated
very closely and this needed persuasion. He would even talk about
the types of organization he thought would bring this about with the
least friction. He would certainly get out a book of applied psychology and we would talk it over. . . . How do you get allies of different
nations to march and think as one nation? There is no question of
his molding my thinking on this from the time I was 31."[7] Eisenhower was fully open to Conner's ideas regarding allies and unity of
command. Young Ike had already recognized the validity of highly
coordinated teamwork as a football player at West Point and later
as a coach at various army bases. Conner gave Eisenhower's faith in
teamwork a military application.[8]

Conner also taught Eisenhower the value of preparation and
study. Ike left Panama a dramatically different person.[9] He had a
blueprint for how he might succeed as an army officer—by working
hard, studying, and applying himself to the craft of military leadership. He also had the beginnings of a leadership philosophy. Equally
important, he had a friend and mentor who would open the doors
of opportunity for his young protégé. In the 1920s, Conner guided
Eisenhower's career. The general made sure that Ike attended the
Command and General Staff School at Fort Leavenworth, Kansas.[10]

Eisenhower rewarded his mentor's faith by finishing first in his class. Conner also recommended Eisenhower to General John J. "Black Jack" Pershing.[11] Ike served Pershing during the late 1920s by writing the Great War's battlefield monuments guidebook, a project of great importance to the general. Eisenhower's excellent performance under Pershing led him to the War Department, where he eventually met Chief of Staff Douglas MacArthur.

In the fall of 1935, Major Eisenhower accompanied MacArthur to the Philippines as his chief assistant. Together they were to create a Filipino army capable of self-defense. The task was difficult, perhaps impossible, given the Philippine Commonwealth's meager military budget and the United States' limited support. Eisenhower endured many vicissitudes and tribulations serving under MacArthur. Most of these derived from his deep disagreements with the general over how best to build the Philippine Army and how an American army officer should conduct himself. These often heated clashes compelled Eisenhower to further develop his thoughts on how an American army officer should behave, lead, and relate to allies and fellow officers.[12] For Eisenhower, MacArthur largely served as an anti–role model. General Conner had been a far more positive influence on his development as a cross-cultural leader.

Near the end of his four-year tour, Ike articulated his leadership principles in a commencement address to the graduating Reserve Officers' Training Corps class at the University of the Philippines. Eisenhower's speech revealed his mature thought on the profession of arms and leadership. Preparation and a dedicated work ethic, derived from his years with Conner, were among the ideals that he emphasized. Drawing on the writings of the Prussian military theorist Carl von Clausewitz, Eisenhower counseled that the best young officer prepares himself through study and field exercises: "If, in the greatest of all crises, war, you are to be . . . ready upon your country's call to lead men in battle, it means years of study and self-preparation." The question, then, is, "Will you make of yourselves good officers?"[13] For Eisenhower, it was up to each individual to pursue this focused course. He described the ideal soldier: "On the moral side he must be fair and just, honest and straightforward; he must learn to make firm decisions and to accept responsibility for them without seeking to shift it either to superior or subordinate. He must understand men so that he may lead rather than merely command them; he must achieve self-confidence and courage, and finally, he must be loyal—loyal to his Government, to his superiors, to himself and to his subordinates."[14] If the young Filipino officers did these things, the result would be a formidable military organization, giving the Philippines its best opportunity for self-defense.

One of the keys to Eisenhower's approach to cross-cultural leadership was his belief in social egalitarianism, and this too was reflected in his commencement address. Filipino society was deeply hierarchical.[15] Eisenhower saw these social divisions as detrimental to the team concept he was trying to instill in the Filipinos. He lectured his listeners, many of whom were from the upper class, that no job was beneath them: "Lack of money with which to hire workmen for any task is not serious, provided we are ready, *and able*, to do the job ourselves." He continued, "There is no royal road to this goal [becoming a successful officer]—good blood and breeding may produce an excellent raw material, but only earnest and continued work can transform it into a useful lieutenant, an efficient captain, a capable general."[16]

Eisenhower explained that the Philippines could not hope to defend itself if the entire population did not unite to perform as a team. He quoted Woodrow Wilson: "The highest form of efficiency is the spontaneous cooperation of a free people." He used this idea to remind his young charges that the entire Philippine defense plan depended on teamwork: "The defense of the Philippines is completely dependent upon the spontaneous cooperation of its citizens."[17] Clearly, Eisenhower began forming his views of allied, cross-cultural leadership many years before he became supreme Allied commander. In the Philippines, he had the opportunity to practice and refine those views with Filipino soldiers, and he also worked closely with a mercurial allied political leader—President Manuel Luis Quezon.

While in the Philippines, Eisenhower developed a constructive and trusting relationship with Quezon. The nature of this relationship foreshadowed the principles Eisenhower would employ in his relations with Allied leaders during World War II. First and foremost, Eisenhower generally ignored national, class, and race distinctions and assessed each leader based on his abilities. This practice diverged from the culture of both the U.S. Army and the Philippines, not to mention American social mores. Douglas MacArthur, for example, though he was friendly with Quezon, apparently believed that the Filipino president was somehow beneath him and failed to meet with him as often as the mission required.[18] Out of necessity, Eisenhower substituted for MacArthur and met frequently with Quezon. The two men grew to like and respect each other. They enjoyed playing bridge—Eisenhower described the president as a "peach of a player"—and their personal conversations ranged far beyond military affairs. Eisenhower readily accepted Quezon's advice when possible. Unlike MacArthur, he recognized the value of Quezon's suggestions concerning the Filipino defense plan and frequently implemented them.[19] On one occasion, Eisenhower wrote of the president, "A dozen other related subjects were brought up and the Pres. discussed all in a manner I thought showed a fine, thoughtful mind, and a much keener insight into some things of questionable validity than one would suppose if he listened only to the talk in this office."[20]

Effective cross-cultural leaders must be willing to accept the wise counsel of allied subordinates and political leaders to weld their teams together. Eisenhower was especially adept at this. Not surprisingly, Quezon eventually seemed to prefer Eisenhower's candid but respectful advice over MacArthur's.[21] When Eisenhower left the Philippines in late 1939, Quezon said of him, "Among all of Ike's outstanding qualities, the quality I regard most highly is this: whenever I asked Ike for an opinion I got an answer. It may not have been what I wanted to hear, it may have displeased me, but it was always a straightforward and honest answer."[22] Eisenhower built his relationship with Quezon on trust, communication, respect, and honesty. He was not afraid to express his opinion, and he himself remained open to reasoned advice.

In June 1942, after having distinguished himself in every role

Chief of Staff General George C. Marshall gave him, Eisenhower was given the command of Operation Torch, the Allied invasion of North Africa. His primary task was to build an effective alliance against the enemy. Alliances are inherently unstable, and allies are often prickly partners, as Winston Churchill observed: "There is only one thing worse than fighting with allies, and that is fighting without them."[23] There is no doubt that Eisenhower's greatest contribution to victory in North Africa, and later in Europe, was his leadership in forging an effective international coalition. In this effort, Eisenhower displayed the cross-cultural leadership qualities that he had formed during his interwar career.

Two of Eisenhower's crucial leadership principles were his willingness to make decisions and his willingness to delegate. At first glance, these appear to be contradictory concepts. But Eisenhower knew only he could make some decisions, whereas others were best made by officers closer to the situation. Decisions had to be made at every level of command.[24] His predecessor at the War Plans Division, Leonard T. "Gee" Gerow, had lost that job because of his inability to decide between competing objectives. Gerow too often sent the decisions up to Marshall. Eisenhower once told Gerow, "Gee, you have got to quit bothering the chief with this stuff." Gerow responded, "I can't help it, Ike. These decisions are too important. He's got to make them himself."[25]

Throughout the war, Eisenhower made the most difficult decisions. In North Africa, for example, he chose to work with former Vichy official and Nazi collaborator Admiral Jean François Darlan. The alternative was to use large elements of the Allied armies to govern Vichy North Africa. Such a large deployment would have forced the Allies to abandon their primary goal of quickly taking Tunisia. Only Darlan could compel Vichy forces to cease fighting the Allies.[26] Eisenhower delegated the responsibility for negotiating with Darlan to General Mark Clark, a trusted subordinate. Meanwhile, Eisenhower guided Operation Torch and haggled unsuccessfully with Vichy general Henri Giraud to gain the latter's support of the invasion. Having learned of Clark's success with Darlan, Eisenhower made the final decision to deal with the Vichy admiral. Ike's decision proved enormously controversial, sparking a major political dispute that was played out in the international press, a dispute that almost cost Eisenhower his command.[27] Eisenhower accepted full responsibility, knowing that he had freed his Allied forces to focus on the Nazi and Italian armies and had avoided making any permanent political arrangements.[28] Moreover, he had effectively explained his decision, which won the support of President Franklin D. Roosevelt and Prime Minister Churchill.[29] The latter wrote, "On Eisenhower fell the responsibility of accepting and sustaining what had been done," and his decision was marked by "a high level of courage and good sense."[30] For his part, Eisenhower never attempted to shift the blame for the controversial decision down to Clark or up to Churchill or Roosevelt, who had made it known to Eisenhower that such a compromise was acceptable.[31] In the summer of 1943, Harold Macmillan, the British representative to the Allied headquarters in the Mediterranean, commented on Eisenhower's forceful and deft leadership, "He has a certain independence of thought which is very refreshing, and he is not afraid of taking responsibility for decisions—even when they do not exactly comply with his instructions from home." Macmillan continued, "We are lucky also to have such a loyal and genuine spirit as General Eisenhower."[32] In the Darlan dispute, Eisenhower displayed a firm grasp of what an allied leader could and could not do. Subordinates had to be trusted to do their jobs, and the supreme commander had to accept responsibility for the final decisions.

The question of who would control the Allies' strategic bombers severely tested Eisenhower's commitment to a truly unified command and to the cross-cultural leadership necessary to implement that idea. The specific points of contention were the use and command of the strategic air forces before the invasion of Normandy in June 1944. These forces, American and British, were not under Eisenhower's authority in early 1944. After late January, British bombers focused on German aircraft production in a night bombing campaign, and American bombers hit the same facilities in a daylight campaign (Operation Pointblank). Both strategic forces also attacked other manufacturing plants when opportunities arose.[33]

Heeding Conner's counsel, Eisenhower determined that before, during, and after the Allied invasion of the Normandy coast, he must be able to support the ground forces as he deemed necessary. No one sought to deny Eisenhower such control on D-day, but there was a great dispute over his desire to control the strategic air forces prior to the landings. Ultimately, Ike gained control of these forces, but only after he threatened to resign—the only time he made such a threat.[34] Making this threat was consistent with Ike's commitment to the idea of unity of command when leading a large cross-cultural team.

Eisenhower wanted control of the bombers so that he would not have to worry about securing the cooperation of other Allied leaders in the midst of a crisis.[35] He also sought to use these forces differently in the two months before D-day. Ike was especially concerned that once the invasion began, Adolf Hitler would order massive reinforcements to contain the Allied invasion forces on the Normandy beaches. Eisenhower wanted to make German reinforcement difficult. He planned to use the heavy bombers to cripple the transportation network of northern France by destroying the "nodal points in the railway system—the big centres with repair shops, servicing facilities, marshaling yards, and rail junctions where locomotives congregated—to break the system where its smooth working could most effectively be deranged."[36] This plan, he believed, would achieve immediate results, whereas the alternative plans anticipated a longer time frame than the ground forces might have.[37]

Among those opposed to Eisenhower's plan were strategic air force generals who wanted to retain command independence and Winston Churchill, who feared French casualties as a result of the transportation plan. Churchill was also loath to give up control of British strategic air forces for an invasion he opposed.[38] Consequently, Eisenhower faced a problem rooted not only in cross-cultural allied leadership but in interservice rivalry and opposing air doctrines.[39] Some airmen even believed that the war might be won without the aid of ground forces.[40] Various accounts of this disagreement focus on the dispute over the transportation plan versus the manufacturing plan. But as historian Charles MacDonald points out, "The real issue was Eisenhower's control of the strategic air resources."[41] The great question, a question that went to the heart of Eisenhower's concept of cross-cultural leadership, was: Would the British concede control of their strategic air forces to an American leader?

Eisenhower's primary goal in navigating the controversy was "perfection of team play."[42] Remembering that he had had to implore higher command to provide air forces to support the invasion at Salerno, Italy, Eisenhower was determined to possess complete authority should he need it for Operation Overlord.[43] With the image of the constant arrival of new German containment forces at Salerno burning in his mind, he wrote, "I cannot conceive of enough airpower to prohibit [German] movement."[44] Ultimately, for Eisenhower, the decision regarding the bombing plans came to this: which would best support Overlord? Responding to Churchill's concern for the safety of French civilians, Ike wrote that only "our overpowering air force" made Overlord feasible. Nothing could be allowed to compromise the effective use of strategic air power. He continued, "As a consequence of these considerations I am convinced that while we must do everything possible to avoid loss of life among our friends, I think it would be sheer folly to abstain from doing anything that can increase in any measure our chances of success in Overlord."[45] For Eisenhower, the outcome of the war depended on Overlord's success.[46] He was prepared to sacrifice his career to ensure that victory. Only such high stakes moved him to threaten resignation, a seemingly selfish demand. But the success of the coalition effort depended on focusing all available Allied strength on the invasion. In essence, Eisenhower was seeking from the British a greater commitment to the Allied cause. His determination and ability to get the greatest possible contribution of each team member was essential to his successful cross-cultural leadership.

Amid the bomber dispute in early March 1944, Lieutenant General George Patton went to see Eisenhower at Widewing, England. When Patton entered the room, Ike was on the telephone with his

British deputy commander, Arthur Tedder. He repeated his threat to resign. Patton remembered hearing Ike's side of the conversation: "Now listen, Arthur, I am tired of dealing with a lot of Prima Donnas. By God, you tell that bunch that if they can't get together and stop quarreling like children, I will tell the Prime Minister to get someone else to run this damn war. I'll quit." Patton added, "He talked for sometime longer and repeated that he would 'ask to be relieved and sent home' unless Tedder could get the British and American Air and two Navies to agree. I was quite impressed as he showed more assurance than I have ever seen him display. But he should have had the warring factions in [his office] and jumped them himself."[47]

Patton failed to appreciate Eisenhower's subtle use of the proper emissary to reinforce his position. He had earlier told the prime minister of his intent to resign if command of the strategic air forces were not forthcoming.[48] Tedder, a highly respected airman, was the perfect person to represent Eisenhower's views to other airmen and to his fellow countrymen. Moreover, using Tedder to repeat the resignation threat took some of the personal quality out of it and allowed him to convey Eisenhower's seriousness. Eisenhower himself commented, "I have stuck to my guns because there is no other way in which this tremendous air force can help us, during the preparatory phase, get ashore and stay there."[49] Ike's son John writes of his father's thinking at this moment, "He was sustained by the knowledge that his own prestige had rendered him, as a figure, practically indispensable. He would run the European war, as much as possible, as he saw fit."[50]

The matter came to a head on 25 March 1944 at a meeting of the principals. At this time, British air chief marshal Sir Charles Portal was in an important position to impact the bomber question. He had been made the representative of the Combined Chiefs of Staff (CCS) for this discussion.[51] Tedder and Portal had tested the efficacy of the transportation plan and found the results convincing.[52] Portal changed his mind and supported Eisenhower's plan.[53] All that was left was the actual language of the order giving Eisenhower the control he demanded. Ike wanted the word "command" in the order, but Churchill refused. Eventually a compromise was reached: Tedder, Eisenhower's deputy, would "direct" the strategic air forces.[54] Churchill and his supporters believed they had salvaged something. Nevertheless, Eisenhower had gained command of the crucial forces, thus fully integrating all aspects of the Allied team's military power.

This compromise was classic Eisenhower. It displayed the supreme commander's awareness of cross-cultural issues, his sensitivity to the pride and concerns of another nation and its leaders. But it also demonstrated his strength of mind, cogent analysis, and flexible method. Tedder's directing gave him what he needed: control of all Allied forces available for Overlord. U.S. Navy captain Harry Butcher, Eisenhower's wartime aide and friend, wrote of this accomplishment, "To me this command arrangement represents an achievement of Ike's, obtained by rational and harmonious discussion."[55] This was true to a point, but it seems unlikely that Eisenhower would have gained command of British strategic air forces had he not been willing to sacrifice himself for the principle of unity of command. Even after the issue had been settled, Churchill tried to scuttle the agreement by going over Ike's head to FDR. The American president, however, supported the Allied commander.[56]

Many scholars believe that Eisenhower made the right call.[57] Eisenhower himself believed that his insistence on the transportation plan was his greatest single contribution to Overlord's success.[58] Eisenhower's views regarding the importance of the alliance and of his own role as a cross-cultural leader were also evident in these tumultuous days. Nothing, not even his career, was more important than supporting Overlord with all available coalition forces. The alliance had to be made all-encompassing.

There are no greater examples of Eisenhower's cross-cultural leadership style than in the events surrounding the decision to delay and then launch the Overlord invasion in early June 1944. The manner in which these decisions were reached demonstrated his inclusive approach, his coalition-oriented style, and his insistence on painstaking preparation. His aides, American and British, were routinely consulted on major decisions. Nevertheless, Ike's conception of a truly integrated allied command did not include simply polling his aides on crucial questions and going with the majority. Eisenhower was in command; this meant he accepted responsibility for making the final decisions on the crucial military questions.

While Eisenhower was devoted to building a collaborative allied team, he understood that there could be only one leader, one commander. On the evening of 3 June 1944, he and his British and American lieutenants, a truly allied team, gathered to discuss whether the invasion planned for 5 June should go forth. The weather was worsening, and Group Captain John Stagg, the Allies' chief weatherman, predicted a fierce channel storm for that day.[59] Everyone pondered Stagg's ominous forecast. Air Chief Marshal Sir Trafford Leigh-Mallory spoke first; he recommended the invasion be postponed. Eisenhower polled his commanders. They were of one accord: delay Overlord.[60] Ike knew he had a few more hours. He decided to reconvene early the next morning to review the decision.

The Allied leaders gathered again at 4:00 AM. The weather had not improved. Low clouds precluded any air support. British admiral Bertram H. Ramsey doubted the effectiveness of naval gunfire. General Bernard L. Montgomery, concerned with the enormous logistical problems involved in postponement, wanted to forge ahead. Deputy Commander Tedder argued that Overlord must be delayed. He pointed out that the airborne drop that Lieutenant General Omar N. Bradley deemed essential required calmer conditions. Time was running out. Eisenhower explained that Overlord was dependent on a concert of air, sea, and land forces, but especially airpower. The weather virtually eliminated that arm of the Allied force. Eisenhower deliberated for a moment, then decided to delay.[61] This decision, he later remarked, was "the most agonizing decision of my life."[62] But it was a decision that Eisenhower and his staff were prepared to make. In the months before Overlord, he and Stagg had conducted experiments in weather prediction. They made practice "go" and "delay" decisions and then evaluated them in light of the actual weather.[63] Such careful preparation, along with the collaboration of the multinational team he had assembled, was at the core of Ike's leadership philosophy.

On 5 June, near–hurricane force winds ripped across the English

Channel. Eisenhower, with the advice of his Allied team, had made the correct decision. But could the invasion go forward on 6 June? Eisenhower and his aides met again. Stagg was more optimistic about the weather. Leigh-Mallory remained hesitant, as did Tedder. But Admiral Ramsey favored 6 June. Eisenhower's chief of staff, Lieutenant General Walter Bedell Smith, remarked, "It's a helluva gamble but it's the best possible gamble." Then Montgomery opined, "I would say—go."[64] Eisenhower sat down, folded his hands, and looked at the floor. Ultimately, it was his decision. All the effort of building a team including both Americans and Britons and of consulting air, naval, and infantry experts had been designed to lead to the right decisions and effective execution of those decisions. But still, one man had to decide. Eisenhower did. "The question is," he said, "just how long can you hang this operation on the end of a limb and let it hang there?" No one responded. The supreme commander continued, "I don't like it, but there it is. . . . I don't see how we can do anything else. I am quite positive that the order must be given."[65] Eisenhower confirmed the decision the next morning when he said to his assembled lieutenants, "O.K., we'll go."[66]

The methods Eisenhower used in making decisions in these momentous days before 6 June 1944 epitomized his beliefs concerning leadership and cross-cultural command. He had created an Allied team not for show but for effective collaboration. The team had prepared meticulously for not only the means but also the precise timing of the invasion. Eisenhower did not seek the limelight. He shared credit for success whenever possible. He sought the advice of that team and used it to inform his decisions. But he also knew that he had to lead, and he did not shirk that responsibility. He would take the blame for failure, if it came. As the invasion forces approached the hostile French coasts, Eisenhower wrote, "Our landings in the Cherbourg-Havre area have failed to gain a satisfactory hold and I have withdrawn the troops. My decision to attack at this time and place were based on the best information available. The troops, the air and navy did all that bravery and devotion to duty could do. If any blame attaches to the attempt it is mine alone."[67] Of course, the note was not necessary. Historian John Keegan has written of Eisenhower, "These were the words of a great man and a great soldier; the greatness of Eisenhower as a soldier has indeed yet to be portrayed fully."[68]

While Eisenhower's firmness of mind and purpose were essential in leading the Allied war effort, perhaps his greatest personal qualities were his humility and flexibility. He was committed to listening to the views of others and to his own high notion of fairness in leading subordinates.[69] These qualities, which were essential to maintaining an effective cross-cultural command, were clearly on display in Ike's dealing with the leader of the Free French forces, Charles de Gaulle. Conflicts with the great Frenchman were all too common. Indeed, most Allied leaders found dealing with de Gaulle practically impossible—FDR, for one, despised him.[70] Eisenhower, however, quickly recognized de Gaulle's significance and became the "best friend the FCNL [French Committee of National Liberation] has in London."[71] Still, Eisenhower seldom found de Gaulle, or the French in general, easy to deal with. Quite to the contrary, he wrote, "Next to the weather I think they have caused me more trouble in this war than any other single factor."[72] But Eisenhower refused to allow de Gaulle's prickly personality and hypernationalism to weaken the Allied war effort.[73]

Perhaps no conflict with de Gaulle was more potentially damaging than the dispute over the Allied withdrawal from Strasbourg during the Battle of the Bulge in early January 1945. As the battle raged north of the city of Strasbourg on the Rhine, Eisenhower ordered Lieutenant General Jacob L. Devers, commander of the Sixth Army Group, to withdraw from his exposed positions east of the Vosges mountains. This withdrawal would leave Strasbourg, recently liberated, open to reoccupation by German troops. Eisenhower hoped to transfer two of Devers's divisions north to the Ardennes to combat the German offensive there.[74] Strasbourg, however, was second only to Paris as a bastion of French pride and nationalism. When the city was liberated, de Gaulle had staged a triumphal entry. Frenchmen wept. To give up Strasbourg without a fight was unthinkable to the French people and their leader.[75]

On 1 January de Gaulle wrote to Eisenhower to explain his position. Unbeknownst to Ike at the time, he also wrote to President Roosevelt and Prime Minister Churchill.[76] FDR dismissed de Gaulle's entreaty and supported Ike. Churchill, however, sided with the French and intervened. On 3 January he flew to Versailles to chat with Eisenhower, who was not told that the real purpose of the meeting was to discuss Strasbourg. Still, Eisenhower explained his reasoning to the British prime minister as a matter of courtesy. Churchill then articulated his support of the French position, and he proved persuasive.[77] A few days later, Eisenhower wrote to General Marshall that he had ordered a change in plans to protect Strasbourg before he saw de Gaulle later on 3 January.[78] This was not an easy decision for Ike. He had spent a good part of the morning explaining to his staff why the retreat was necessary.[79] Moreover, no commander likes having major decisions second-guessed. He had previously told de Gaulle that he would not change the order. Then, too, he was acutely aware of the growing criticism back home that he was too often "influenced by intransigent local demands and thus unable to control the situation in Europe."[80]

The meeting with de Gaulle and Churchill on the afternoon of 3 January began badly and degenerated, at least for a while. Somehow Eisenhower's revised plan to protect Strasbourg was either not acceptable or not fully evident before tempers flared.[81] De Gaulle threatened the alliance itself. If Strasbourg were not defended, he would withdraw French forces from Eisenhower's command to defend the city.[82] Eisenhower firmly told de Gaulle that if he did so the French army would receive no supplies.[83] De Gaulle countered that if Strasbourg were surrendered without a fight, or if it were lost because his army was not supplied, he could not be responsible for the behavior of the French underground in the rear areas, where supply lines would be exposed to reprisals.[84] The heated discussion lasted all afternoon. That political considerations often determine strategy was not news to Eisenhower. He had studied Clausewitz's explication of the political-military continuum.[85] In the end, calm and common sense prevailed; a compromise was achieved. Strasbourg would be defended, but not "at all costs," as de Gaulle had hoped.[86] Looking at the map, Eisenhower outlined how Strasbourg might be saved, given that the German offensive in the Ardennes seemed under control and that enemy forces threatening the city were not overwhelming.[87]

Eisenhower recalled that de Gaulle left the meeting in "good humor, alleging unlimited faith in my military judgment." Although Churchill had said little during the exchange, Eisenhower understood that he supported de Gaulle. Afterward, Churchill remarked to Ike, "I think you've done the wise and proper thing."[88] He would later tell de Gaulle, "Eisenhower was not always aware of the political consequences of his decisions, yet for all that he was an excellent supreme commander and he had a heart—as he had just shown."[89]

De Gaulle and Churchill had compelled Eisenhower to consider political issues, including the preservation of the alliance, along with purely military calculations. Ike was not convinced that the loss of Strasbourg was as important as de Gaulle believed, but he took seriously de Gaulle's threat to withdraw his forces from the alliance if the city were not defended.[90] In short, Eisenhower knew that an imperfect political compromise could prevent military disaster. Already short of infantrymen on the front, the Allies could spare none to guard the supply lines in the rear areas. This was how Eisenhower defended his decision to Marshall, on "military grounds."[91] But there was, of course, more to it than that.

Eisenhower always placed the alliance first. It was clear that the United States' two major allies wanted a greater effort made to save Strasbourg. Ike heard the argument, weighed the alternatives, and decided that he possessed some leeway to meet their needs based on the military situation; however, the overriding factor was the need for cooperative relations with the French. In a clear display of his cross-cultural leadership, Eisenhower did not allow his own pride to interfere with a reasoned decision, even though his authority had been challenged and his command of the situation doubted in Washington. Rather, he was flexible. He found grounds for an accommodation that preserved the alliance and allowed the military objectives to remain the focus. In regard to Ike's decision concerning Strasbourg, Charles MacDonald writes, "The credit belonged . . . to a Supreme

Commander who in exercising coalition command saw resilience as a virtue."[92]

In the end, Eisenhower and de Gaulle parted on good terms. Together, they drank hot tea, which helped cool tempers. The supreme commander confided to the French leader that international political considerations from all quarters and interservice rivalries had exponentially complicated his military plans. De Gaulle recalled that as Eisenhower sipped his tea, he specifically lamented his relationship with Field Marshal Bernard "Monty" Montgomery: "At this very moment . . . I am having a lot of trouble with Montgomery, a general of great ability, but a bitter critic and mistrustful subordinate."[93]

To lead effectively, even the best cross-cultural leaders must have subordinates who are willing to follow. In fact, a time may come when a leader must discharge uncooperative followers who are threatening the unity and efficiency of the coalition effort. The problem of insubordinate or reluctant followers is often exacerbated in organizations with people of different nationalities, cultures, and interests. Such was the case in Eisenhower's command during World War II. And although Ike remarked that the French were his greatest problem, Field Marshal Montgomery and General Patton were also troublesome. Indeed, Eisenhower's working relationship with Montgomery almost reached a breaking point in the midst of the Battle of the Bulge.

Montgomery had become Britain's greatest hero of the war by successfully commanding British forces in North Africa at the Battle of el-Alamein. As a result, Churchill chose Monty as commander of the Twenty-first Army Group for Operation Overlord, serving under Eisenhower. Although the two men worked well together during operational planning, problems developed in the weeks of stalemate that followed the Normandy invasion. Montgomery seemed slow to meet his objectives, and he deeply resented Eisenhower's assumption of direct command of ground forces in September 1944, a move that had long been planned. Ike's patience frayed when Montgomery failed to capture the important port of Antwerp in a timely fashion. The British field marshal added to Eisenhower's frustration later in the fall of

1944. He argued incessantly for reinstatement as the ground force commander and for launching a "full-blooded" thrust across the Low Countries into northern Germany, a plan that would have left the balance of the Allied forces in defensive positions.[94] It was primarily Montgomery's harangue on the command issue that brought about a crisis in late December 1944.

Two months earlier, Montgomery, believing Eisenhower an ineffective military strategist, had raised the issue again.[95] Ike responded in writing, using emphatic and clear terms. He opposed Montgomery's idea that a ground commander should be inserted between the supreme commander and the army group commanders. Eisenhower even intimated that should this debate continue, the issue would be given to the CCS for resolution.[96] Montgomery responded, "Dear Ike, I have received your letter of 13 October. You will hear no more on the subject of command from me."[97] Unfortunately, Montgomery did raise the issue in a meeting with Eisenhower in mid-November and again in a letter on 30 November. Eisenhower did not waver even when Montgomery persisted in a meeting at Maastricht, Netherlands, on 7 December.[98] Upset, Monty wrote a bitter lament to Chief of the Imperial General Staff Lord Alan Brooke: "You will have to get his [Eisenhower's] hand taken off the land battle."[99] Events beyond the control of both men soon resurrected the conflict.

On 16 December 1944, Hitler, in the midst of one of the worst Belgian winters on record, launched operation Wacht am Rhein. The subsequent Battle of the Bulge was the Third Reich's last major thrust on the western front. It caught Eisenhower's forces unprepared. Not even the supreme commander had believed that the Germans were capable of such a massive counteroffensive. Eisenhower's mistake reminds one of Julius Caesar's comment as to why the Venellians chose to attack a powerful Roman force: there is a "common tendency of all mankind to wishful thinking."[100] German panzers crashed through the Ardennes Forest—the same path they had taken into France in 1940. Fifteen hundred tanks and six hundred thousand men hammered out a large bulge in Eisenhower's lines and threatened to punch a hole that would turn the panzers loose in the Twenty-first Army Group's rear. Omar N. Bradley's Twelfth Army Group was nearly cut in half. Eisenhower was the first to realize that this offensive was no spoiling attack. He responded quickly.[101] In a controversial but sound move, he placed the northern element of Bradley's army group—Lieutenant General Courtney H. Hodges's First Army—under Montgomery's command to facilitate communication and allow a coordinated response on the northern shoulder of the bulge. This decision, coming so soon after the command dispute, demonstrated Eisenhower's humility and his emphasis on team efficiency. Nevertheless, Bradley seethed while Montgomery, who performed well in the crisis, took Eisenhower's decision as justification of his own views on the command issue.[102]

On 28 December, Eisenhower met with Montgomery at Hasselt, Belgium, to discuss a counterattack on Hitler's exposed forces. Still wanting to launch a single thrust into the Ruhr area of Germany, Monty took the opportunity to press his case for command of Bradley's entire Twelfth Army Group.[103] Again, Eisenhower listened respectfully. It had long been his intention to make the northern thrust the primary, but not the sole, offensive. He informed Montgomery that he would provide Lieutenant General William H. Simpson's Ninth Army to buttress British forces but would not transfer command of the whole Twelfth Army Group. Monty apparently misunderstood Eisenhower and reported to Field Marshal Brooke that the Twelfth would be his for the offensive into Germany. Brooke rightly did not believe Montgomery. Eisenhower had left Hasselt "rubbing his head" and lamenting Montgomery's stubbornness.[104]

Unfortunately, Montgomery did not take orders in the American tradition but negotiated with his superiors in the British custom. However, Montgomery exceeded even the bounds of his own country's norms. He once declared to George Patton that if Patton did not like an order, he should "just ignore it. That's what I do."[105] When, on 29 December, the field marshal wrote Eisenhower another impertinent letter purporting to summarize what had been agreed upon at Hasselt, the command issue once again became an incendiary topic. Chief of Staff George Marshall wrote to Eisenhower expressing his and the president's full support. Under "no circumstances" was Ike to give substantial American forces to Montgomery. Beyond the command issue, Montgomery irritatingly repeated his contention that Ike's fall campaign had been a failure and that the coming offensive would also fail if the British commander were not given his way. He even had the audacity to tell Eisenhower how to write the order he sought.[106] Having read the letter, Eisenhower seethed.[107] Ike voiced his frustrations to his driver and confidant Kay Summersby. She replied, "You must have the patience of an angel." Eisenhower sighed, "If I can keep the team together, anything is worth it."[108] But in the next few hours, Eisenhower realized that his international team, as it was then constituted, was not unified. Ike's "patience was exhausted."[109] A change had to be made.

Eisenhower discussed the situation with his closest advisors, Walter Bedell Smith and Arthur Tedder, and decided to send a letter to the CCS to request that Montgomery be relieved of command.[110] Some have suggested that firing Montgomery would have broken the alliance. Carlo D'Este claims that "the Anglo-American coalition almost came permanently unglued," but this is not convincing.[111] Montgomery would most likely have been replaced with General Harold Alexander, a highly regarded British officer whom Eisenhower respected. Montgomery probably would have been given some ostensibly greater assignment and an exalted title. Sacking Montgomery would have been a problem, but Churchill and Roosevelt would never have allowed one man to derail the international coalition.

Moreover, Ike's decision to replace Monty was not made in a vacuum. There was more to Eisenhower's frustration than Montgomery's persistent rants. During the Battle of the Bulge, Ike had grown irritated with Monty's tardiness in launching the counteroffensive that might trap large numbers of German soldiers in the bulge. Indeed, historian Stephen Ambrose argues that this was the issue that moved Ike against Monty.[112] Eisenhower's view of Montgomery was shared earlier in the war by German field marshal Erwin Rommel, who had taken advantage of the Englishman's caution in

North Africa.[113] In addition, the CCS were considering establishing a ground force commander under Eisenhower. They thought perhaps Alexander could replace Tedder as Eisenhower's deputy and lead the land battle. Eisenhower was not opposed to having Alexander as his deputy if Tedder were promoted, but he would not concede the land commander's role to Alexander or anyone else.[114] Eisenhower's preference was to switch Alexander for Montgomery, not for Tedder. Moreover, Marshall, responding to the clamor for Montgomery from the British chief of staff and the British media, had ordered Eisenhower not to give in to the field marshal.[115] Reflecting his great self-confidence, Eisenhower did not believe that any land commander could better manage the campaign. Nor did he want to complicate matters by lengthening the chain of command.[116]

Montgomery's letter of 29 December was the proverbial final straw, coming as it did after he had promised not to raise the command issue again, after he had been refused his plan in late November, after the same issues had recurred at Maastricht, and after he had been told no in person two days before at Hasselt. Eisenhower concluded that Montgomery could not be led and therefore was endangering the alliance and an efficient victory over Germany. For Ike, Montgomery had seriously weakened the military alliance on the western front. He had refused to follow orders or keep promises. Moreover, Eisenhower had reason to believe that if the team did not function better, the CCS might change the structure of the high command, leaving Montgomery, the problem, in place. Therefore, the impasse with Montgomery had to be resolved.

On 30 December, Eisenhower described the situation in a letter to the CCS, essentially asking the chiefs to choose between him and Montgomery. There is no question that the decision would have been made in Ike's favor. However, before the letter was sent, Montgomery's chief of staff, Francis W. de Guingand, learned of Ike's anger. He rushed to Eisenhower's headquarters to meet with Walter Bedell Smith, and later with Ike, in the hope of saving Monty's job. Eisenhower was not inclined to listen, but he finally agreed to give Monty one last opportunity to apologize and reform. De Guingand returned to his boss and candidly explained the situation. Montgomery asked, "Freddie, what shall I do?" De Guingand produced a letter of apology that Montgomery signed. The British field marshal lived up to the bargain, and in March 1945, when Churchill raised the command issue, Montgomery sided with Ike.[117]

Montgomery never became an exemplary subordinate, nor did Eisenhower always lead as effectively as he might have. Ike probably tolerated Monty too long. Nonetheless, the supreme commander possessed a vision of how the war should be won. He intended to create an effective and efficient allied team; egos, tactics, diplomacy, and sometimes even strategy were subordinate to team unity. Anyone who threatened the collaboration of the team, even the hero of Alamein, was expendable. A year earlier, Ike had written to Lord Louis Mountbatten about the basis of an allied command, "Patience, tolerance, frankness, absolute honesty in all dealings, particularly with all persons of the opposite nationality, and firmness, are absolutely essential."[118]

Dwight Eisenhower possessed a clear vision, which had begun to form during his days with Fox Conner, for how a second world war would be won. A cohesive allied team would be the cornerstone of victory. Everything else—national pride, personal egos, even grand strategy—had to be subordinated to the creation and maintenance of the coalition. Few cross-cultural leaders have so correctly marked the path to victory and steadfastly adhered to it. Other elements of Eisenhower's leadership philosophy flowed logically from this paramount idea. If the team is first, no individual can become more important. The supreme commander must not seek the limelight but take satisfaction in giving credit to others. Perhaps Eisenhower did this to a fault. He also accepted responsibility. He insisted—to the point of threatening resignation—on command of the strategic bomber forces well before D-day, argued for and obtained the crucial transportation plan, and wrote a letter accepting responsibility should the D-day landings fail. As the supreme commander, he did not shirk from making the difficult decisions. His most agonizing moments of the war came in early June 1944, when he decided first to delay

Operation Overlord and then to execute it the following day. These were Eisenhower's heroic hours.

A man who prided himself on accepting responsibility and on making arduous decisions could have tended toward rigidity when it came to considering contrary views. In *The Glorious Cause*, Robert Middlekauff describes how King George III and his mentor John Stuart, the Earl of Bute, fell into this malady: "Master and pupil . . . commonly mistook inflexibility for personal strength and character."[119] This was not one of Eisenhower's faults. Fully realizing that he was the leader of a cross-cultural coalition, a team that was the only means of victory, he listened carefully to the views of his multinational staff and other Allied leaders. When de Gaulle and Churchill impressed on him the political argument for holding Strasbourg, he sacrificed his pride, changed his mind, and found a way to save the city and the alliance itself. As John Keegan writes, Eisenhower's "intellectual flexibility" and "political touch" provided the multinational coalition "a coherent direction."[120]

Preparation was another key to Eisenhower's effective cross-cultural leadership. Few officers had prepared themselves for success as thoroughly as Ike had during the interwar years. From his tutorial under Conner to his study of World War I battlefields, from finishing first in his class at the Command and General Staff School to his experience with Quezon and MacArthur in the Philippines, Eisenhower was always studying and preparing. This intellectual habit paid many dividends during the war, perhaps none so much as when he and Stagg practiced predicting the weather for Operation Overlord. Eisenhower sought to lead, not simply command. For him, this principle was essential for effective cross-cultural leadership. This was why he allowed, at least for a time, Montgomery's challenge to his strategic decisions. All of Eisenhower's leadership principles were undergirded by essential character traits such as honesty, fairness, courage, and even geniality. Almost everyone liked Ike, and this helped him tremendously. In 1938, while he was on leave from the Philippines, the chief of staff of the Philippine Army, Major General Paulino Santos, wrote to Ike,

Our personal and official dealings which have stretched unin-
terruptedly for almost three years have made me realize more
than ever before that ethnological differences do not hinder men from working together for a righteous cause. I have
worked with other Americans before, and in some instances
for longer than I have with you, but I have never formed so
close an attachment as the one obtaining between us. Perhaps it is because neither on your part nor on mine has there
been any selfishness; we gave our best thoughts to the ideals
of my people which in fact are the ideals which your own
people planted here forty years ago.[121]

Santos captured the central elements of Eisenhower's idealism and
cross-cultural leadership philosophy: the subordination of self to the
team and to the ideals of liberty and democracy.

Notes

1. Charles H. Brown, Brown manuscript (unpublished article on Fox
Conner, early 1960s), 2, Dwight D. Eisenhower Papers, composite acces-
sion, fiscal year 1971, box 1 of 1, Dwight D. Eisenhower Library, Abilene,
KS.
2. Roscoe B. Woodruff, interview by Maclyn Burg, 16 March 1972,
oral history no. 404, 4, 15, 16, Eisenhower Library.
3. Dwight D. Eisenhower, *At Ease: Stories I Tell to Friends* (Garden
City, NY: Doubleday, 1967), 185–87.
4. Brown manuscript, 6.
5. Dwight D. Eisenhower, *Crusade in Europe* (Garden City, NY: Doubleday, 1948), 18.
6. Brown manuscript, 6, 7, 8.
7. Eisenhower quoted in ibid., 8.
8. Ibid., 8, 9; William B. Pickett, "Eisenhower as a Student of Clausewitz," *Military Review* 65 (July 1985): 22.
9. Eisenhower, *At Ease*, 184–87.
10. Ibid., 200.
11. Matthew F. Holland, *Eisenhower between the Wars: The Making of a
General and Statesman* (Westport, CT: Praeger, 2001), 104, 105.
12. Dwight D. Eisenhower, diary of the American military mission in

the Philippine Islands, 15 February 1936, 10 November 1938, 12 December 1938, in *Eisenhower: The Prewar Diaries and Selected Papers, 1905–1941*, ed. Daniel D. Holt (Baltimore: Johns Hopkins University Press, 1998), 306–11, 410–12, 412–13.

13. Dwight D. Eisenhower, address (Reserve Officers' Training Corps, 24 March 1939), in *Prewar Diaries and Selected Papers*, 425–29; Pickett, "Eisenhower as a Student," 22–27; Brown manuscript, 12.

14. Eisenhower, address, 427.

15. Richard Connaughton, *MacArthur and Defeat in the Philippines* (New York: Overlook, 2001), 4, 5. Of course, the American army was also very conscious of class and race. Edward M. Coffman, *The Regulars: The American Army, 1898–1941* (Cambridge, MA: Belknap Press of Harvard University Press, 2004), 126, 127, 132, 217–19, 295–99, 409–11.

16. Eisenhower, address, 425–29.

17. Ibid., 428.

18. Connaughton, *MacArthur and Defeat*, 64.

19. Eisenhower, diary, 6 April 1938, 12 December 1938, in *Prewar Diaries and Selected Papers*, 380, 412.

20. Ibid., 5 April 1939, 431.

21. Ibid., 386.

22. Quezon quoted in Kenneth S. Davis, *Dwight Eisenhower: Soldier of Democracy* (New York: Konecky and Konecky, 1945), 252.

23. Churchill quoted in Field Marshal Lord Alanbrooke, diary, 1 April 1945, in *War Diaries, 1939–1945*, ed. Alex Danchev and Daniel Todman (Berkeley: University of California Press, 2001), 680.

24. Alan Axelrod, *Eisenhower on Leadership: Ike's Enduring Lessons in Total Victory Management* (San Francisco: Jossey-Bass, 2006), 232, 233.

25. Quoted in Stephen E. Ambrose, *Eisenhower* (New York: Simon and Schuster, 1983–1984), 1:136.

26. John S. D. Eisenhower, *Allies: Pearl Harbor to D-Day* (Garden City, NY: Doubleday, 1982), 197, 199, 134, 191.

27. Ambrose, *Eisenhower*, 1:208.

28. Winston Churchill, *The Second World War: The Hinge of Fate* (Boston: Houghton Mifflin, 1950), 631; Eisenhower to Combined Chiefs of Staff, 14 November 1942, in *The Papers of Dwight David Eisenhower: The War Years*, ed. Alfred D. Chandler Jr. (Baltimore: Johns Hopkins Press, 1970), 709.

29. Eisenhower to Combined Chiefs of Staff, 707; Ambrose, *Eisenhower*, 1:209.

30. Churchill, *Hinge of Fate*, 629.

31. Robert Murphy, *Diplomat among Warriors* (Garden City, NY: Dou-

bleday, 1964), 118; Michael Beschloss, *The Conquerors: Roosevelt, Truman and the Destruction of Hitler's Germany, 1941–1945* (New York: Simon and Schuster, 2002), 101; Rick Atkinson, *An Army at Dawn: The War in North Africa, 1942–1943* (New York: Holt, 2002), 95; Eisenhower, *Allies*, 183. The Darlan affair was not the finest hour of the two great Allied leaders. Although they did not fire Eisenhower, they did not make it known that the decision had been theirs.

32. Harold Macmillan, diary, 27 August 1943, 15 July 1943, in *War Diaries: Politics and War in the Mediterranean, January 1943–May 1945* (New York: St. Martin's, 1984), 119, 151.

33. W. W. Rostow, *Pre-invasion Bombing Strategy: General Eisenhower's Decision of March 25, 1944* (Austin: University Press of Texas, 1981), 4, 24; Alan J. Levine, *The Strategic Bombing of Germany, 1940–1945* (Westport, CT: Praeger, 1992), 129–31; Gordon A. Harrison, *Cross-Channel Attack* (Washington, DC: Office of the Chief of Military History, Department of the Army, 1951), 208; John Ehrman, *Grand Strategy*, ed. J. R. M. Butler (London: Her Majesty's Stationery Office, 1956–1976), 5:289, 290.

34. Dwight D. Eisenhower, memorandum, 22 March 1944, in *Papers of Dwight David Eisenhower*, 1784, 1785; Eisenhower, *Allies*, 447; Harry C. Butcher, *My Three Years with Eisenhower* (New York: Simon and Schuster, 1946), 498.

35. Dwight D. Eisenhower to George C. Marshall, 21 March 1944, in *Papers of Dwight David Eisenhower*, 1781; Eisenhower, memorandum, 1785.

36. L. F. Ellis, *Victory in the West: The Battle of Normandy* (London: Her Majesty's Stationery Office, 1962–1968), 2:98.

37. Levine, *Strategic Bombing of Germany*, 131; Rostow, *Pre-invasion Bombing Strategy*, 34, 35.

38. Eisenhower, *Allies*, 445, 446.

39. Dwight D. Eisenhower to George C. Marshall, 9 February 1944, in *Papers of Dwight David Eisenhower*, 1717 (see also 1717n2, 1756n, and 1759n); Ambrose, *Eisenhower*, 1:286.

40. Ellis, *Victory in the West*, 98; Ehrman, *Grand Strategy*, 5:289.

41. Charles B. MacDonald, *The Mighty Endeavor: American Armed Forces in the European Theater in World War II* (New York: Oxford University Press, 1969), 254. Eisenhower was as concerned with destroying German air force production as anyone. Destruction of these aircraft manufacturing centers was an important element of the transportation plan. See Ehrman, *Grand Strategy*, 5:291–97, Arthur Tedder, *With Prejudice: The War Memoirs of Marshal of the Royal Air Force Lord Tedder, G.C.B.* (Boston: Little, Brown, 1966), 514, 515.

42. Dwight D. Eisenhower to Winston Churchill, 23 February 1944, in *Papers of Dwight David Eisenhower*, 1748.

43. Dwight D. Eisenhower to Harry Butcher, 14 September 1943, in *Papers of Dwight David Eisenhower*, 1418, 1419; Ambrose, *Eisenhower*, 1:263.

44. Dwight D. Eisenhower to George C. Marshall, 19 February 1944, in *Papers of Dwight David Eisenhower*, 1737.

45. Levine, *Strategic Bombing of Germany*, 131; Rostow, *Pre-invasion Bombing Strategy*, 4; Dwight D. Eisenhower to Winston Churchill, 5 April 1944, in *Papers of Dwight David Eisenhower*, 1809.

46. Rostow, *Pre-invasion Bombing Strategy*, 5; Ehrman, *Grand Strategy*, 5:296.

47. George S. Patton, *The Patton Papers*, ed. Martin Blumenson (Boston: Houghton Mifflin, 1972–1974), 2:422. Patton's observation of Eisenhower's phone call occurred after 6 March. Captain Harry Butcher recorded on 3 March that Eisenhower had threatened to resign in a meeting with Churchill the previous week: he said that he would "simply have to go home" if not given control of the strategic forces. Butcher, *My Three Years*, 498.

48. Ehrman, *Grand Strategy*, 5:296.

49. Dwight D. Eisenhower to George C. Marshall, 29 April 1944, in *Papers of Dwight David Eisenhower*, 1839.

50. Eisenhower, *Allies*, 440.

51. Ehrman, *Grand Strategy*, 5:295–304; Eisenhower, *Allies*, 446.

52. Eisenhower, *Allies*, 446; Tedder, *With Prejudice*, 513, 514.

53. Eisenhower, *Allies*, 446; Ellis, *Victory in the West*, 100; Ehrman, *Grand Strategy*, 5:297.

54. Eisenhower, memorandum, 1784.

55. Butcher, *My Three Years*, 499.

56. Levine, *Strategic Bombing of Germany*, 131.

57. See Harrison, *Cross-Channel Attack*, 224–30; Forrest C. Pogue, *The Supreme Command* (Washington, DC: Office of the Chief of Military History, Department of the Army, 1954), 132, 133; Samuel W. Mitcham Jr., *Retreat to the Reich: The German Defeat in France, 1944* (Westport, CT: Praeger, 2000), 13; Alan J. Levine, *From the Normandy Beaches to the Baltic Sea: The Northwest Europe Campaign, 1944–1945* (Westport, CT: Praeger, 2000), 43, 44, 46; John Keegan, *The Second World War* (New York: Viking, 1990), 415–17; and Ehrman, *Grand Strategy*, 5:286, 287.

58. Ambrose, *Eisenhower*, 1:290; Eisenhower, *Crusade in Europe*, 233.

59. MacDonald, *Mighty Endeavor*, 264, 265; Eisenhower, *Allies*, 468.

60. David Eisenhower, *Eisenhower at War, 1943–1945* (New York: Random House, 1986), 245.

61. Pogue, *Supreme Command*, 167.

62. Eisenhower quoted in Merle Miller, *Ike the Soldier: As They Knew Him* (New York: Putnam, 1987), 612.

63. Pogue, *Supreme Command*, 168.

64. Ambrose, *Eisenhower*, 1:307; Pogue, *Supreme Command*, 169–70; MacDonald, *Mighty Endeavor*, 265.

65. Eisenhower quoted in Miller, *Ike the Soldier*, 613.

66. Eisenhower quoted in Carlo D'Este, *Eisenhower: A Soldier's Life* (New York: Holt, 2002), 526.

67. Dwight D. Eisenhower, note, 5 June 1944, in *Papers of Dwight David Eisenhower*, 1908.

68. John Keegan, *Six Armies in Normandy: From D-Day to the Liberation of Paris, June 6–August 25, 1944* (New York: Viking, 1982), 66.

69. Macmillan, diary, 18 October 1943, in *War Diaries*, 259–60.

70. James MacGregor Burns, *Roosevelt: The Soldier of Freedom* (New York: Harcourt Brace Jovanovich, 1970), 480; Michael Korda, *Ike: An American Hero* (New York: HarperCollins, 2007), 255.

71. Eisenhower, *Allies*, 457.

72. Dwight D. Eisenhower to George C. Marshall, 20 February 1945, in *Papers of Dwight David Eisenhower*, 2491.

73. Axelrod, *Eisenhower on Leadership*, 267.

74. Dwight D. Eisenhower to George C. Marshall, 6 January 1945, in *Papers of Dwight David Eisenhower*, 2399–401.

75. *The War Memoirs of Charles de Gaulle* (New York: Simon and Schuster, 1960), 3:164–71.

76. Eisenhower to Marshall, 6 January 1945, 2399–401 (see also n1); Eisenhower, *Crusade in Europe*, 362; John S. D. Eisenhower, *The Bitter Woods* (New York: Putnam, 1969), 400; *War Memoirs of Charles de Gaulle*, 3:166.

77. Eisenhower, *Bitter Woods*, 400.

78. Eisenhower to Marshall, 6 January 1945, 2399–401; Eisenhower, *Bitter Woods*, 400; Pogue, *Supreme Command*, 401; Don Cook, *Charles de Gaulle* (New York: Putnam, 1983), 269; Alanbrooke, diary, 3 January 1945, in *War Diaries*, 642.

79. Eisenhower, *Bitter Woods*, 400.

80. Eisenhower, *Eisenhower at War*, 603, 604.

81. Cook, *Charles de Gaulle*, 269.

82. *War Memoirs of Charles de Gaulle*, 3:169, 170.

83. Eisenhower, *Crusade in Europe*, 362, 363.

84. *War Memoirs of Charles de Gaulle*, 3:170.

85. Eisenhower, *At Ease*, 186; Pickett, "Eisenhower as a Student," 23; Brown manuscript, 12.

86. Eisenhower to Marshall, 6 January 1945, 2399–401; Eisenhower, *Bitter Woods*, 401; Eisenhower, *Eisenhower at War*, 604.

87. Eisenhower, *Crusade in Europe*, 363; Eisenhower to Marshall, 6 January 1945, 2399–401.

88. Eisenhower, *Crusade in Europe*, 363.

89. Churchill quoted in D'Este, *Eisenhower*, 665–66.

90. Eisenhower, *Eisenhower at War*, 604.

91. Eisenhower to Marshall, 6 January 1945, 2399–401; Butcher, *My Three Years*, 738.

92. MacDonald, *Mighty Endeavor*, 397.

93. *Memoirs of Charles de Gaulle*, 3:171.

94. Bernard L. Montgomery, *Normandy to the Baltic* (London: Hutchinson, 1951), 118.

95. Bernard L. Montgomery, *The Memoirs of Field-Marshal the Viscount Montgomery of Alamein* (Cleveland: World, 1958), 316; D'Este, *Eisenhower*, 635.

96. Dwight D. Eisenhower to Bernard L. Montgomery, 13 October 1944, in *Papers of Dwight David Eisenhower*, 2221–24.

97. Montgomery, *Memoirs*, 317.

98. Bernard L. Montgomery to Dwight D. Eisenhower, 30 November 1944, Eisenhower Papers, pre-presidential, 1916–1952, name series, box 83, Montgomery file (1); Montgomery, *Memoirs*, 303–4; Dwight D. Eisenhower to Bernard L. Montgomery, 1 December 1944, in *Papers of Dwight David Eisenhower*, 2323–25; Tedder, *With Prejudice*, 621; Pogue, *Supreme Command*, 316, 317; D'Este, *Eisenhower*, 635.

99. Montgomery quoted in D'Este, *Eisenhower*, 635.

100. Julius Caesar, *The Gallic Wars* (Norwalk, CT: Easton, 1993), 66, 75.

101. Geoffrey Perret, *Eisenhower* (New York: Random House, 1999), 327.

102. Pogue, *Supreme Command*, 386.

103. Eisenhower, *Crusade in Europe*, 360; Montgomery, *Memoirs*, 317, 318.

104. D'Este, *Eisenhower*, 655; Alanbrooke, diary, 30 December 1944, in *War Diaries*, 638.

105. Montgomery quoted in Omar Bradley, *A Soldier's Story* (New York: Holt, 1951), 138.

106. Forrest C. Pogue, *George C. Marshall* (New York: Viking, 1963–1987), 3:487; Montgomery, *Memoirs*, 318; Arthur Nevins, interview by Maclyn Burg, 15 August 1972, oral history no. 380, 56, 57, 58, Eisenhower Library.

107. John S. D. Eisenhower, *General Ike: A Personal Reminiscence* (New York: Free Press, 2003), 128, 129, 130, 131; Butcher, *My Three Years*, 718; Piers Brendon, *Ike: His Life and Times* (New York: Harper and Row, 1986), 174, 175.

108. Kay Summersby, *Eisenhower Was My Boss* (New York: Prentice Hall, 1948), 205.

109. Eisenhower, *Bitter Woods*, 382.

110. Ibid., 383; Pogue, *Supreme Command*, 386; Cole C. Kingseed, "Education of a Combat Commander," *Military Review* 65 (December 1985): 18.

111. D'Este, *Eisenhower*, 655, 657; Arthur Nevins, interview by Ed Edwin, 23 April 1970, oral history no. 119, 15, Eisenhower Library; Eisenhower, *General Ike*, 129.

112. Ambrose, *Eisenhower*, 1:375.

113. Erwin Rommel, *The Rommel Papers*, ed. B. H. Liddell Hart (Norwalk, CT: Easton, 2003), 280, 360, 361, 395.

114. Pogue, *Supreme Command*, 390.

115. Eisenhower, *Eisenhower at War*, 597, 598; Pogue, *Marshall*, 3:487; Butcher, *My Three Years*, 717.

116. Pogue, *Supreme Command*, 389.

117. Eisenhower, *Bitter Woods*, 381–85; D'Este, *Eisenhower*, 656; Francis de Guingand, *Generals at War* (London: Hodder and Stoughton, 1964), 108–15; Pogue, *Supreme Command*, 391.

118. Dwight D. Eisenhower to Louis Mountbatten, 14 September 1943, in *Papers of Dwight David Eisenhower*, 1420–23.

119. Robert Middlekauff, *The Glorious Cause: The American Revolution, 1763–1789* (Oxford: Oxford University Press, 2005), 20.

120. Keegan, *Six Armies in Normandy*, 22.

121. Paulino Santos to Dwight D. Eisenhower, 22 August 1938, Eisenhower Papers, pre-presidential, 1916–1952, name series, box 101, Sanf–Say (misc.) file.

5

Charismatic Leadership

Lewis B. "Chesty" Puller

Jon T. Hoffman

Lieutenant General Lewis Burwell "Chesty" Puller requires no introduction to an audience of marines. Veterans and partisans of the army, navy, and air force might debate over the preeminent leader in their respective services, but there is absolutely no doubt that Puller is the hero of the U.S. Marine Corps—the very icon of the institution. His larger-than-life image is etched indelibly in every marine almost from the first day at boot camp or Officer Candidate School. His stern, leathery, square-jawed visage stares down from every wall in every building throughout the corps. Countless times every day his name is invoked, like a magical incantation, by officers and noncommissioned officers (NCOs) in every conceivable setting and for every purpose under the sun. His pithy words, daring deeds, and colorful mannerisms are ingrained in the culture of the organization.

Although Puller is often cited as the most decorated man in the history of the corps (a debatable assertion depending on how one ranks the worth of various awards), his valor was only a small component of his legendary status. What most endeared him to his fellow marines was his style of leadership. Like other charismatic commanders, he was able to inspire and influence others on an emotional and often individual level. Whereas some leaders might seem to naturally possess the gift of a magnetic personality, Puller's ability was rooted in actions and attitudes largely developed by years of education and ef-

Lewis B. "Chesty" Puller
(National Archives, College Park, MD)

fort. His approach to the challenge of command, from a small squad to a division, consisted of looking out for the welfare of his subordinates, giving his utmost, leading from the front, and maintaining a genuine connection with those in his charge. These constituted the essential elements of Puller's charismatic leadership.

There is nothing particularly mysterious or magical in this formula, and Chesty certainly was not the first military leader to follow it. Many throughout history have understood and implemented at least parts of it. Baron Friedrich von Steuben, for instance, is said to have counseled in his Revolutionary War drill book that a commander should "gain the love of his men by treating them with every possible kindness and humanity."[1] But Puller was one of those rare individuals who was able to put it all into practice, to include the often difficult aspect of preserving a close relationship with his most junior subordinates even as he rose ever higher in rank. In the corps he came to be most closely associated with charismatic leadership, and thus he remains the best known and most revered of all marines. The example he set has endured as a paramount touchstone in an institution that prizes leadership above all other qualities.

Lewis Burwell Puller was born in the small town of West Point, Virginia, on 26 June 1898. He was the third of four children in a family of modest but comfortable means. Whereas his mother hailed from a distinguished heritage reaching back to the earliest settlers in the state, his paternal forefathers had left no mark until the middle of the nineteenth century. His father's father was a blacksmith, farmer, and budding entrepreneur who achieved a small measure of success as a Confederate cavalry major in the Civil War; he died in battle at the age of thirty.[2]

Lewis was only ten years old when he lost his father, a moderately successful salesman, to cancer. The difficult times that followed and the example set by his mother in dealing with them had a major impact on Lewis's emerging personality. He thought of his mother as a "strong woman" and tried to emulate her, developing his own deep determination and strength of character. He recalled how she maintained discipline in the family without physical punishment: "She treated me like a man and gave me to know she expected me to act like a man."[3] With the constant reminder that he was the elder male in the household, in addition to working part time to help make ends meet, he acquired a keen sense of responsibility at a young age. The predominance of females in his life—his grandmother, mother, and two older sisters—probably accounted for his enduring affection for family and close friends, often expressed in a tender, warmhearted manner.

As a boy, Lewis enjoyed the adventure of the outdoors and the rough and tumble of small-town sports. He was not a gifted athlete and, at five feet eight inches and 144 pounds when full grown, was not physically imposing. His barrel chest, serious square-blocked face, and out-thrust jaw were his most impressive visible features. His voice and manner of speech were also distinctive. He spoke slowly, with a touch of a southern accent, underpinning his own unique and sometimes butchered pronunciations with a deep-throated, gravelly intonation. He was not usually loud, but when the situation warranted it, he could "bark like a howitzer" or "shout commands with all the vigor and carrying power of an angry bull."[4] He developed one other trait that helped create his bulldog-like demeanor. In public or in private, he was neither quiet nor verbose but had a simple, straightforward, "pretty blunt" style in dealing with others. Everyone soon discovered that "you didn't have to guess what Lewie was thinking—he told you, and he did it so simply you could understand."[5] This quality would serve him well in establishing a close connection with his men.

Puller was a mediocre student, even in military schools. His academic performance, coupled with his unpretentious manner and rough speech, "gave the impression of being a little bit illiterate."[6] He encouraged that view, telling friends that in any class he believed there would always be "at least one S.O.B. dumber than I am, so I keep on plugging and have confidence that I will not be at the bottom."[7] But General O. P. Smith, one of the corps' most intellectual officers, knew that Chesty's abiding interest in books had given him a wealth of knowledge. Another officer reached a similar conclusion:

"He was a great student of history. He read every history book he could lay his hands on. Although he talked in a manner which gave you the idea he was not highly educated . . . he actually was."[8] He had a lifelong love for reading, especially in the field of military history. His favorite subject was the Civil War, and the story of his beloved hero Thomas J. "Stonewall" Jackson greatly influenced his own views on tactics and leadership.

For the first half of his military career, Puller diligently pursued every chance for professional education but never was assigned to school beyond the rank of lieutenant. His public attitude toward academic study eventually changed, most likely because he had a sense of inferiority in the one area where he had been unable to match or surpass his contemporaries. He came to wear his lack of advanced training as a badge of honor, becoming an outspoken opponent of military education, arguing that "service in the camp and in the field is the best military school." Behind that public pronouncement, however, he privately believed that education was the key to success and regretted that his own was inadequate.[9]

He had, in fact, started college at the Virginia Military Institute in 1917, after the United States entered World War I. Only in the summer of 1918, when Americans were finally engaging in major combat on the western front, did he quit school to enlist in the Marine Corps—long after most other college students who wanted to fight had done so. It was the only time he did not march immediately toward the sound of the guns, and it ended up costing him any opportunity to see action. From boot camp he went to NCO school, and then quickly into officer training just as the war ended. He earned a commission in June 1919, only to be released from active duty with the postwar reduction in the armed forces. Nevertheless, he was determined to make a career in the military, so he enlisted again in the corps as a private, with the promise of duty as a junior officer in the Gendarmerie d'Haiti.

Created as part of the U.S. effort to put down a rebellion against the Haitian government, the gendarmerie consisted of enlisted Haitians led by marine officers serving in the higher billets and marine

NCOs acting as lieutenants. It was tough duty, even outside combat. In addition to being a soldier, a constabulary officer had to enforce the law, oversee local governments, and supervise public construction projects. The native recruits were almost universally illiterate and were often weak or sick as a result of Haiti's abject poverty. They spoke only Creole, a language few marines had ever heard. Some of the Americans also carried the baggage of racial prejudice, a problem Puller himself did not entirely escape. One marine NCO referred to this combination of challenges as "man-killing work," and Puller himself would later describe it as "a dog's life."[10] It was not surprising then that nearly one-third of the marines who joined the gendarmerie were ultimately transferred out because of their unsatisfactory performance. The process of training Haitian officers had been under way only a short time when Puller joined the force. Here he faced his first significant leadership challenge.

Soon after his arrival, Private Puller, wearing the gold bars of a gendarmerie lieutenant, received command of Provisional Company A. It was an unusual unit, dedicated solely to active patrolling in search of the rebels, as opposed to garrisoning a town or village. His chief assistant was a brand-new Haitian lieutenant promoted from the ranks in part because he could speak English. His native NCOs included one who would later rise to command the constabulary force. Puller could have decided that an American with a year at VMI and a year in the Marine Corps had all the knowledge necessary to tell these men how to fight. Instead, he actively sought and readily accepted the advice of those who had already proven themselves in combat.

Puller never explained his willingness to take counsel from his Haitian subordinates, but one feature of the corps' rapid expansion during World War I—it had drawn almost all its new officers from its own enlisted ranks—had influenced him. He had been struck from boot camp onward by the important role played by these so-called mustangs, who daily demonstrated that they knew how to get things done and often performed better than lieutenants freshly minted from college. That put Puller in a frame of mind to listen to the NCOs in his first command, and their words fell on fertile ground. One sergeant explained his view of leadership, which required the commander to lead his men in battle by example and show no fear. That conformed with the stories Puller had heard from Civil War veterans and what he had learned from studying Jackson and other heroes. He would later say, "In the Confederate Army, an officer was judged by stark courage alone and this made it possible for the Confederacy to live four years."[11] His willingness to listen laid a foundation for a sincere connection with his subordinates and for his future success as a charismatic leader.

Puller took the advice of his Haitian NCOs and implemented their tactics, which immediately proved effective. Operating primarily at night to achieve surprise, his company found and attacked several enemy camps. In the most spectacular of these engagements, he and his Haitian lieutenant scouted ahead of their unit. They succeeded in penetrating undetected into a major rebel leader's bivouac. Their quarry escaped in the ensuing confusion of battle, but Puller would receive his first combat award for this "dangerous and brilliant attack."[12]

Puller spent only four months with this combat command, but during the remainder of his tour in Haiti he had equal success with garrison units in quiet zones. He achieved this in part by demonstrating his regard for his men and for the population he protected. A fellow marine officer noted that Puller, "by his tact, common sense, and dignity of manner, won the confidence and respect of his command of black troops." One of his commanders observed that "he made friends with the Haitians of all classes and by so doing inspired confidence in their minds of our mission." Another senior marine believed that Puller was "liked by the Haitian officials."[13] His own background may have played a role, since he had struggled economically and thus had no pretense of privilege. Whatever the source, his ability to connect with people from a very different culture was another element of his charismatic leadership that made him more successful than many of his compatriots and likely reinforced his conviction that he was on the right path.

In 1921, Puller and sixty-four other marine NCOs earned the opportunity to compete for commissions in the corps at an officer candidate program in Washington DC. Chesty fared poorly in the academic portion, flunking five of the eleven subjects and failing the final qualifying examination. He returned to the Gendarmerie d'Haiti for a year, this time serving as an adjutant in a major headquarters. He performed well enough that his commander, Major Alexander A. Vandegrift (a future commandant of the Marine Corps), interceded on the young marine's behalf and got him another shot at becoming an officer. This time he scraped by in the classroom, and he also benefited from a new ranking system that placed greater weight on one's service record. Overall, he finished fifth of the ten men who made the cut, and on 6 March 1924 he received his permanent commission in the corps. He attended the Basic School for new lieutenants, reverted to form, and graduated twenty-second out of twenty-six. After a stint in artillery, Puller asked for and received orders to flight school in 1926. He finished dead last of sixty-three students in the academic portion and proved only slightly more adept in the air. He managed to fly solo on his second attempt but continued to receive poor marks in subsequent check flights. One of his instructors found him "hardworking but slow."[14] A board of navy and marine pilots dropped him from the class well before the course of instruction was complete. Despite these setbacks, Puller did not lose his enthusiasm for military service.

After five years largely marked by weak performance in formal training programs, Puller found himself in a more congenial setting, leading marines. He received excellent reports for his work with barracks detachments in Hawaii and California. During this time, the United States dispatched a marine force to end the civil war in Nicaragua. After repeated requests, Chesty received orders at the end of 1928 to join the Guardia Nacional de Nicaragua, a marine-led constabulary much like the Gendarmerie d'Haiti. It also experienced the same growing pains, including a high percentage of marines who could not effectively lead local troops. The senior commander felt compelled to issue a series of orders regarding the treatment of Nicaraguan soldiers. One stated that "an officer of the Guardia Nacional must not hold either consciously or subconsciously contempt for the enlisted men."[15]

Puller spent most of his first eighteen months in Nicaragua in staff billets, proving that he could be effective in that realm and making occasional unsuccessful patrols to search for insurgents. Finally, in the middle of May 1930, he received his long-awaited assignment to a real combat billet. In a reprise of his work with Company A in Haiti, he took over the Guardia Nacional's sole dedicated field force, Company M. His second in command was Gunnery Sergeant William A. Lee, who served as a constabulary lieutenant. The company consisted of fewer than three dozen enlisted men. Although it had been in operation for eight months, it had not made any significant contributions in the war.

In a series of actions in June, Puller and his small band quickly established themselves as the most aggressive and effective force in the critical Central Area of Nicaragua. The string of battles began on 6 June, when the patrol encountered a hasty ambush, with the enemy on a ridge overlooking the trail. With barely a pause after firing broke out, Puller dashed up the slope while yelling for his men to charge. They followed him despite the crack of bullets and the explosions of dynamite tossed by defenders. The guerrillas soon scattered, but not before at least seven of them fell to Guardia Nacional fire. Puller and his men remained in the field for most of the remainder of the month, encountering and killing several other rebels. In each of these engagements, Chesty was at the front, leading his men. Meanwhile, other commanders complained that their troops were "footsore and worn out" after only a few days on patrol.[16]

In his report on this operation, Puller argued that Guardia Nacional units made few contacts because they moved too slowly, mainly because they relied on pack mules for supplies and horses for officers. The animals confined the patrols to established trails. By contrast, Company M leaders had begun walking with their men, who were learning to get by with a minimum of supplies and equipment. Puller also made it a habit in his reports to list the name of every Guardia Nacional soldier who participated in each action and to commend those who did well. By setting a positive example, operating under the same conditions as their men, and sharing the credit for success,

Puller and Lee got more out of their subordinates and consequently achieved more.

For the next few months, Company M chased guerrillas all over the Central Area, keeping them on the run and chipping away at their strength. In December, Puller received the Navy Cross (the second-highest award for valor in the corps) for the cumulative efforts of his unit. The citation recognized how he had achieved success: "By his intelligent and forceful leadership without thought of his own personal safety, by great physical exertion and by suffering many hardships, Lieutenant Puller surmounted all obstacles."[17]

During Chesty's remaining months in Nicaragua, his unit stayed aggressive, but the guerrillas apparently chose to avoid them and shifted their operations to the Northern Area. When Puller left the country at the end of his tour in June 1931, local citizens signed a letter asking the Marine Corps to let him stay. His commander told an American reporter that Puller had justly earned the sobriquet "El Tigre," or "Tiger of the Mountains."

After a year as a student in the Army Infantry School at Fort Benning, Georgia, where he finished with average marks, Puller reported back to Nicaragua and retook command of Company M. Within twenty-four hours he had the unit out in the field. During the following month, they fought more than a half-dozen engagements and flushed the rebels from their sanctuary. September 1932 witnessed Company M's biggest battle to date. The unit broke a tough ambush and killed ten of the enemy, but at a cost of two dead. For the first time, Puller saw one of his men die in battle. For his cool leadership under heavy fire, he received a second Navy Cross. In Company M's two toughest fights of this period, the normally aggressive Puller shunned his typical immediate charge and instead relied on rifle grenades to break the enemy. He explained that he did so "mainly in order to save the men of the company."[18] His troops may have been drawn from Nicaragua's chronically poor peasantry, but he was not about to waste their lives needlessly. The welfare of his men remained a top priority.

As the end of 1932 approached, the United States ordered the withdrawal of the few marines still serving with the Guardia Nacional. In late December, in their last combat action, Puller and Lee led a Nicaraguan force that was protecting a trainload of arms. More than 250 rebels ambushed the 70 constabulary soldiers near the town of El Sauce. In an hour-long fight, the government troops drove off the attackers, killing more than 30 of them at a cost of 3 dead and 3 wounded. It was the largest confirmed loss inflicted on the rebels since the Battle of Ocotal in 1927. The engagement cemented Puller's reputation as "probably the outstanding patrol leader of the Marine Corps today."[19] In Haiti he had played a relatively small role, but in the crucible of Nicaragua, Chesty's charismatic battlefield leadership made him a legend.

Puller's next duty station was with the marine legation guard in Peiping (now Beijing), China. There he demonstrated that he was equally interested in the welfare of his men in peacetime. As the post's boxing officer, he arranged intramural bouts with U.S. Army units at their gym. Upon discovering that marine fighters were not getting a fair share of the money from ticket sales, he began sponsoring his own events and distributing the proceeds himself. Soon after, he took charge of the marine detachment of the USS *Augusta*, flagship of the Asiatic Fleet. On his first day aboard, he accompanied his marines and some of the sailors ashore for a scheduled period at the rifle range. Their camp was spartan, and he could do nothing to change that. But after a day of "unappetizing and skimpy" meals, he ordered the navy cook back to the ship. Puller returned a few hours later with a replacement cook and a boatload of provisions. The food immediately improved, as did morale and marksmanship scores. The ship's captain, future Fleet Admiral Chester W. Nimitz, had fired the previous two marine commanders, but he soon praised Chesty for the "excellent results" he obtained with the same manpower.[20] One marine who served in the detachment recalled the high regard that Puller's genuine interest produced in the men and noted that it gave rise to equally high performance: "We would do anything he asked— willingly. In fact, we would go overboard to please him."[21]

In 1936, newly promoted Captain Puller reported to the Basic

School in Philadelphia, where he served as an instructor in drill and tactics. With the recent switch to promotion by selection, the Marine Corps had begun to clean out the deadwood in its leadership ranks. Freshly commissioned officers poured in to replace those who had been forced out. The lieutenants who came under Puller's tutelage during the next three years constituted nearly one-third of the officers in the corps. Since the army was making almost no use of its Reserve Officers' Training Corps graduates during the lean years of the Depression, the marines offered commissions to the top one or two from each school, and many accepted. Along with a select group of NCOs and Naval Academy graduates, the corps skimmed the cream off the top of the available officer candidate pool. Many of these superb young men rose quickly to command battalions and staff divisions during World War II. And their initial taste of leadership training in the corps came from Chesty.

One lieutenant recalled Puller's introductory speech to his group in 1936: "The motto of the Marine Corps is 'Don't let your buddy down!' In the Marine Corps your buddy is not only your classmate or fellow officer, but he also is the Marine under your command. If you don't prepare yourself to properly train him, lead him, and support him on the battlefield, then you're going to let him down. That is unforgivable in the Marine Corps."[22] Chesty was teaching what he had learned; a leader must look after the welfare of his subordinates. Lewis W. Walt, a future four-star general, later told Puller that he credited a large measure of his success to what he had learned from him at Basic School: "You have had a greater influence on my performance as an officer than anyone else, with the possible exception of General [Merritt A.] Edson."[23]

Major General Thomas Holcomb, the commandant of the Marine Corps, spoke to the Basic School class in the spring of 1937. His philosophy of leadership echoed what Puller had practiced since his first days in the corps:

There is one characteristic of enlisted men that I especially want to point out to you, and that is their rapid and accurate appraisal of their officers. You will not for long be able to deceive your men, either with regard to your professional ability or your character. . . . Every military organization, by power of the virtue of example, is like a mirror in which the commander sees himself reflected. Whether consciously or unconsciously, men take their cue from their officers. If the officer is diligent, his men will strive to exceed him in diligence; if he is thorough, they will be thorough; if he is thoughtful of them, they will constantly be seeking opportunities to do something for him.[24]

Chesty's legendary status as a marine would come to rest largely on these two traits of charismatic leadership—his willingness to lead by personal example and his ability to cultivate a deep bond of mutual respect with enlisted men.

Following two more years in China with *Augusta* again and then with the Fourth Marines in Shanghai, Puller returned to the United States in August 1941 to take command of the First Battalion, Seventh Marines. It was a newly organized unit stationed at newly acquired Camp Lejeune on the North Carolina coast. Construction of permanent facilities had just begun, and the entire First Marine Division lived under canvas in difficult conditions that winter. A few months after the Japanese attacked Pearl Harbor, the Seventh Marines deployed to defend the American outpost at Samoa in the Pacific. The weather there was hot, humid, and rainy, and living conditions were even worse.

Most of Puller's men had been in the corps only a short while, but he moved quickly to make his unit one of the best. He confided to his officers and senior NCOs one secret for motivating and connecting with their marines: simply explain the purpose of each task. "Gentlemen, if you want to get the most out of your men give them a break! Don't make them work completely in the dark. If you do, they won't do a bit more than they have to. But if they comprehend they'll work like mad." During one field maneuver, he also gave them a lesson in positive motivation. After both the division commander and the commandant had visited the battalion, Chesty sent a message to his company commanders recounting the compliments handed out by the two generals and ordered that it be read to their men. The battalion surgeon noted how it "peps up an organization when you pass along the good things as well as the bad." Even when a young marine made a mistake, Puller handed down punishment with a touch of empathy. One sergeant recalled "many cases where [Chesty] made a good man out of a bad one, with his strange mixture of understanding, gentleness, and strict discipline."[25]

While Puller's approach was not unique, it was still far from common. His regimental commander, for example, led hikes from a station wagon and secured for himself whatever creature comforts were available in the field. In the spartan conditions of Samoa, this colonel diverted a rare load of cement, intended to provide a proper floor for the dental clinic, to cover the ground in his own tent. One staff officer thought he "simply had no concept of what the conduct of a commanding officer should be in the way of example and guidance and care of his troops."[26] Even some of Chesty's junior officers were slow to learn the importance of demonstrating sincere concern for their men. One captain recorded in his diary that his men had done well on an inspection; "However, I laid them out in fine shape for a lousy [job]."[27]

This was Puller's first big command of American troops in the field. Here he began to earn his corps-wide reputation as a leader who genuinely identified with, and looked out for the welfare of, enlisted men—but he went a step further. In addition to making his officers eat last in the chow line and encouraging them to work alongside their men instead of merely supervising them, he was decidedly "tougher on the officers than the men."[28] Puller's study of Stonewall Jackson likely contributed to this element of his leadership philosophy. Underlined in Chesty's copy of a biography of the Confederate hero was author G. F. R. Henderson's observation on Jackson: "With the officers he was exceedingly strict. He looked to them to set an example of unhesitating obedience and the precise performance of duty. He demanded, too—and in this respect his own conduct was a model—

that the rank and file should be treated with tact and consideration.
. . . His men loved him . . . because he was one of themselves, with no
interest apart from their interest; because he raised them to his own
level, respecting them not merely as soldiers, but as comrades. . . . He
was among the first to recognize the worth of the rank and file."[29]

One story that gained wide circulation in the battalion reflected
that attitude. Puller supposedly came upon a marine who was repeatedly saluting a lieutenant. The young officer explained that the private
had failed to salute and was being taught a lesson by having to do so
one hundred times. Chesty interjected that it was proper for the senior
man to return each salute and then made sure it was done. Whether or
not the incident actually took place, the men of the battalion believed
that it was the kind of thing their commander would do.

In September 1942, the Seventh Marines finally joined the rest of
the First Marine Division on the island of Guadalcanal. Puller's battalion fought its first major battle later that month near the Matanikau
River. In a complicated maneuver dictated by higher headquarters,
Chesty found himself on one side of the waterway with his Company
C while the remainder of the battalion made an amphibious landing
behind enemy lines, well beyond the river. A much larger Japanese
force soon surrounded the latter element. When frontal attacks by
another battalion failed to get across the river, the senior commander
on the scene refused to order another charge, leaving the rump of the
First Battalion cut off. Learning that no plan was in the works to rescue the encircled unit, Puller exclaimed with indignation, "You're not
going to throw those men away."[30] He went to the beach, signaled
a destroyer offshore to pick him up, arranged for amphibious craft
to rendezvous at the site of the landing, then contacted his beleaguered troops and told them to pull back to the coast while the ship
put down covering fire. He personally led the landing craft ashore to
supervise the fighting withdrawal. The hasty rescue showed Chesty's
determination and his commitment to his men when there was no
need to risk their lives.

In the remaining months on Guadalcanal, Puller's battalion
fought more tough battles, suffered its share of losses, and in each

engagement soundly defeated the Japanese. He continued to lead from the front. He circulated along the lines, chatted with the men, washed himself and his clothes in the river alongside them, was always the last one to eat chow, and made sure the chaplains held frequent services. Like many other senior officers on the island, he received an occasional gift of whiskey from friends in the rear. He invariably gave the bottles to the troops, usually with the simple admonition, "Pass it around, just leave a sip for me." The battalion surgeon "noticed as time went on how deeply [Puller] felt the loss of his men, and became more and more thoughtful of them and became almost fanatical in his desire to see that they were properly cared for."[31] This combination of genuine concern for his men and a commitment to leading by example distinguished Puller as a model of charismatic leadership.

After the regiment earned a period of recuperation in Australia, Chesty sought awards for his fighters, just as he had in Nicaragua. He took great pride in the fact that his men received more medals than the other two battalions in the regiment combined. One officer in the division later remarked, "They are passing out the decorations and citations again as only Louie [sic] can do it."[32] Praise for his courage and leadership was almost universal, and one private identified the consequence: "No commander on Guadalcanal was so well endowed with men who fairly worshipped him."[33] An enlisted combat correspondent seconded that opinion, citing Puller as "one of the most highly admired officers in the Marines."[34]

Promoted to lieutenant colonel, Puller became the regimental executive officer in Australia. The First Marine Division also received a new commander, Major General William H. Rupertus, who had a well-deserved reputation as a poor leader. One subordinate aptly described him as "certainly not a hero to his own valet or his own officers. He was an officer of little—if any—loyalty downward and intense loyalty upward." Rupertus had thrived in the corps because he "carried off the externals of soldiering very creditably and looked like a great professional soldier"; moreover, he was "one of the master politicians in the Marine Corps."[35] Another officer believed that Rupertus "didn't give a damn about the people under his command," just as long as he kept "on the good side" of his superiors.[36]

The First Marine Division went into combat under its new commander the day after Christmas in 1943, making an amphibious assault on the western end of New Britain at Cape Gloucester. Just before New Year's Day, the Americans captured their main objective, an airfield complex. The Japanese were not about to admit defeat, however, and the marines continued fighting to defend and expand their perimeter. The battles were not as intense or the casualties as heavy as at Guadalcanal, but nonetheless it was tough combat against an enemy entrenched in a sea of swamp and jungle. Early in January the men of the reinforced Seventh Marines found themselves struggling to fight their way across a stream they soon dubbed "suicide creek." Puller's main responsibility as an executive officer was with the command post in the rear, but a journal clerk noted that, true to form, Chesty was "directing the attack from forward."[37]

On 4 January 1944, the regimental commander relieved the commander of the Third Battalion, Seventh Marines, for lack of aggressiveness. The colonel placed Puller in command of the outfit. With support from tanks, the marines had already broken through, and Chesty continued the advance. That evening as the battalion dug in, an amphibious tractor came forward to resupply the unit. It brought only canned rations, ammunition, and other essentials. One of the crewmen presented a container of hot coffee to Puller, with the compliments of the mess officer, who was obviously trying to curry favor. Chesty, who had endured difficult conditions in the jungle along with the infantrymen, flew into a rage: "If that S.O.B. can get that up here to me, he can get a hot meal up to these troops!" He passed the thermos to a nearby group of enlisted men and backed up his tirade with an order to the battalion's rear echelon to have "plenty of hot coffee and chow" at the front lines in the morning.[38] Chesty's brand of leadership had an immediate impact. A lieutenant noted in his diary two days later, "Puller is really snapping battalion headquarters out of it. Just what they need."[39]

Later in January, the First Marine Division committed a number of detachments from all the regiments to search beyond the main perimeter for the remnants of the Japanese force. Rupertus belatedly decided to merge all of these small units under a single command and chose Puller for the mission. Chesty brought them together at a village, only to discover that the combined force of more than 1,400 men was short on rations and beginning to suffer from malaria and dysentery. While he made arrangements to get more supplies, he ensured that the troops did not sit idle and contemplate their troubles. He assigned each unit a sector of the perimeter and put them to work building defenses. One officer recalled the instructions Puller passed to the junior leaders: "Their place was with their men and he didn't want them coming around the command post. . . . He let everyone know just what he wanted and just where each one stood in relation to the operation so that there would be no question of authority or misunderstanding." Given the confusing composition of the force, that was no small matter. Chesty circulated around the perimeter, sharing in the meager chow and regaling the men with stories about the prewar corps.[40] In word and deed, Puller continued to practice and preach charismatic leadership.

After paring his force to fewer than five hundred men and getting supplies built up via airdrop, Puller set out to link up with a U.S. Army force that had landed on the southern coast of the island. The two-week operation met opposition only from the jungle, rough terrain, and weather. Resupply continued to rely on a tenuous aerial link. The staff at division was surprised at one point by a request for several hundred bottles of mosquito repellent, given Chesty's often expressed contempt for creature comforts in the field. One marine on the patrol later explained the requisition: "The colonel knew what he was about. We were always soaked and everything we owned was likewise. That lotion made the best damn stuff to start a fire that you ever saw."[41]

When Puller and his scratch force returned to the main perimeter on 17 February 1944, he received a pleasant surprise: he had been selected for promotion to full colonel. At the end of the month, he assumed command of the First Marines. In April, his regiment and the rest of the division turned over Cape Gloucester to the army and moved to the island of Pavuvu, where they were supposed to recuperate before the next operation. From afar, the partially palm-covered isle looked like a tropical paradise, but it was little better than the jungle of New Britain. As at Camp Lejeune in 1941, there were no facilities, and the battle-weary marines started from scratch and erected their own tents. Daily downpours, poor food, limited drinking water, and hordes of insects and rats made life miserable.

In the squalor of Pavuvu, Puller's stock among his marines soared even higher. As always, he waited like the lowest private in the long lines to eat chow or buy something from the meager selection at the post exchange. In contrast to Rupertus, who had the division engineers build him a nice house on a hill to catch the breeze, Chesty lived in a dirt-floored tent, as his men did. When a few NCOs jury-rigged a shower for him by placing a fifty-five-gallon drum on top of a small shed, he made it available to everyone and hauled his own five-gallon can of water from the ocean every time he used it. Puller was aware of even the smallest details concerning his men. While pinning a medal on a young marine, the colonel realized that a photographer was focusing on him, not the recipient. Chesty quietly admonished, "If you don't mind, old man, this is the man being decorated."[42] According to his operations officer, Puller was a successful commander because "he personally followed those precepts of leadership which many preached but not everyone followed; the troops came first."[43] While Chesty shared the burdens of life on the island, he did not relax his emphasis on high standards. Still leading from the front, he was out with his regiment early every morning doing calisthenics, and he frequently inspected the camp and the units.

On 15 September 1944, the First Marine Division assaulted the island of Peleliu. The objective was the airfield on the flat southern half of the otherwise rugged island. The Japanese, adapting to the superior firepower of American forces, had dug deep into the coral ridges overlooking the airdrome and emplaced more mortars and artillery pieces than they had previously employed. The First Marines drew the unlucky task of attacking the high ground while the rest of the division secured the primary objective. Rupertus, overestimating the effect of the preliminary bombardment and eager to match the record of the Second Marine Division in seizing the Tarawa atoll in three days, entered the battle with naive expectations: "There is no doubt in my mind as to the outcome—short and swift, without too many casualties."[44] The army's official observer noted, "This expectation was widely circulated among the troops with the resultant belief of all concerned that the landing would be made with practically no opposition."[45]

Despite suffering heavy losses beginning with the first waves fighting to gain the shore, Rupertus pressured his regimental commanders to fulfill his predictions of rapid victory. Puller had not expected the preparation fires to make much difference, but he was as surprised as everyone else at the strength of the Japanese defenses. In the furnace-like heat of Peleliu and the unrelenting physical stress of a desperate battle, an old leg wound Puller had received at Guadalcanal grew badly inflamed, thus restricting his movement and undoubtedly affecting his judgment. He also bore the recent loss of his brother, killed in the invasion of Guam. Chesty brought to bear all the firepower he could in support of his men, but he also passed along the general's unrelenting demands to attack and attack again. The casualty toll mounted alarmingly with precious little ground gained. Asked how his regiment was digging the Japanese out of the ridge, the colonel replied, "By blood, sweat, and hand grenades."[46]

Puller braved the heavy enemy fire right alongside his marines. The commander of a battalion attached from another regiment was amazed when he reported to Chesty: "I was embarrassed to find him operating behind some outcropping of coral, closer to the enemy than [my] command post was. In fact, it was difficult to get out an operations map and read it without exposing ourselves."[47] General O. P. Smith, the assistant division commander, knew that the location "reflected [Puller's] desire to be where he could make his presence felt."[48] Chesty maintained that personal presence was the key to successful command: "I've always believed that no officer's life, regardless of rank, is of such great value to his country that he should seek safety in the rear. . . . Officers should be forward with their men at the point of impact. That is where their character stands out and they can do the most good. . . . Men expect you to, and men look to officers and NCOs for example."[49] A reporter observed after talking to the colonel's marines during the battle, "They will follow him to hell."[50]

After nine days of fighting, the First Marines had captured the southern crests of the ridges, thus protecting the airfield from direct fire and observed indirect fire. The regiment was almost destroyed in the process. After seeing the exhaustion of Puller and his men, the corps commander ordered Rupertus to take them off the front lines. Although the regiment did not depart the island for several more days, its part in the battle was done. It would take the rest of the First Marine Division and most of the army's Eighty-first Division an additional two months to defeat the Japanese forces that the First Marines had faced practically alone for the first several days of the operation.

Losses in Puller's regiment were 311 killed and missing and 1,438 wounded—54 percent of its original strength. Some questioned Chesty's tactical wisdom. One veteran argued that the colonel had "crossed the line that separates courage and wasteful expenditure of lives."[51] Although his aggressiveness may have caused higher casualties in the latter stages, it was crucial to securing the critical flank of the division early in the operation, when a lack of resolve might have resulted in defeat. General Smith had only praise for Puller: "I went over the ground he captured and I don't see how a human being had captured it, but he did. . . . There was no finesse about it, but there was gallantry and there was determination."[52] Certainly, Puller's leadership had been a key factor in motivating his men to go forward despite the odds. One of his riflemen summed it up: "He was one of you. He would go to hell and back with you. He wouldn't ask you to do anything that he wasn't doing with you."[53]

In line with the rotation policy then in effect, Chesty was ordered back to the United States, where he took command of an infantry training regiment at Camp Lejeune. He therefore missed the even bloodier battles of Iwo Jima and Okinawa, where losses per regiment far exceeded those of the First Marines on Peleliu. After the war was over, he commanded a reserve district for two years, then the marine barracks in Pearl Harbor for another two. When the North Koreans invaded the southern half of that peninsula in June 1950, Puller was already slated to rejoin the First Marine Division. General Smith, now the division commander, had assigned Chesty to form and take command of the First Marines, which had ceased to exist in the peacetime corps. In the space of two weeks, the colonel combined three understrength battalions from two regiments of the Second Marine Division, hundreds of individual regulars who were arriving from various posts, and hundreds more reservists who had just been mobilized. They barely had time to draw equipment and test fire weapons before boarding ships bound for Japan. Other than the common designation of marine, there was nothing to turn this disparate group into a cohesive regiment—except for Puller's charisma and leadership. He provided the glue that quickly coalesced the First Marines into a tight-knit fraternity. One sergeant remarked that "the regiment came alive" when everyone realized Chesty was in command. A lieutenant remembered that the colonel "gave us pride in some way I can't describe." In no time at all, there was a common response to questions about unit affiliation: "I'm in Chesty's outfit."[54]

After two weeks on ship, followed by a week in Japan and another week at sea, the First Marines joined with the Fifth Marines, who had already fought in Korea, to spearhead the amphibious assault at Inch'on. The 15 September landing was a daring gamble to outflank the main enemy units that were battering Allied forces along the Pusan Perimeter. The initial fighting was sharp but short, and the First Marine Division seized the port before the day was over. The next day the marines headed for Seoul, the capital and the transportation hub that controlled the flow of logistics to the North Korean army. As they fought their way into the city, Puller's calm demeanor under fire and his penchant for leading from the front provided reassurance to the officers and men who were new to the business of urban warfare. As he and a few subordinate commanders planned the initial assault on Seoul while standing on a ridge, an enemy gun crew fired on the small cluster. An antitank shell whistled past the group, and everyone but Chesty dropped to the ground. As more rounds came their way, he remained standing and carried on the conversation until they were done. He never mentioned the incident. A correspondent with the regiment noted that the colonel was the only one who moved about the battlefield "as if he were killing time on a hunting trip."[55]

After the fall of Seoul, U.S. Army Major General Edward M. Almond invited Puller and other senior marines to dinner at the corps command post. Chesty was amazed that the food was flown in fresh from Japan and served by white-uniformed enlisted men on linen-covered tables resplendent with fine china and silver place settings. During the meal, he inquired about the size of the corps command element. "The answer of over three thousand," Puller later wrote, "left me dumb with astonishment and rage; [it was] enough to form an additional infantry regiment." He found the luxury and waste of manpower unconscionable in a war zone.[56]

As fall turned into a harsh winter, the First Marine Division joined the pursuit into North Korea. In November the outfit pushed up a narrow road leading into the mountains in the northeast corner of the peninsula. Despite the insistence of higher echelons on a rapid advance, General Smith moved cautiously and tried to keep his regiments concentrated as much as possible in the forbidding terrain. After leading the division through much of the previous fighting, the First Marines drew the task of holding key points along the supply line reaching back to the coastal plain. Chesty and one battalion occupied the town of Koto-ri. During the move into the mountains, there had not been enough trucks for all of the regiment's supplies, so Puller had made tents and stoves priorities over ammunition: "I'll take care of my men first. Frozen troops can't fight. If we run out of ammunition we'll go to the bayonet."[57]

On the night of 16 November 1950, the Communist Chinese intervened in the war and launched a coordinated offensive across the breadth of North Korea. Most of the United Nations force reeled in shock and disorder. Smith's earlier caution, however, paid off for the marines, who held on against heavy odds. Soon after, the division began a fighting withdrawal through a gauntlet of ten enemy divisions. The Fifth and Seventh marine regiments bore the brunt of the initial assaults, but the battalions of the First Marines fought their own battles to keep open the road to the coast. Through it all, Puller showed his usual calm demeanor, roaming the undermanned Koto-ri perimeter, chatting with the troops, bucking up their morale, and occasionally providing them with a swig from a whiskey bottle. One machine gunner recalled, "That man made us all feel invincible."[58] In an epic running battle, the marines reached the coast in good order with both their equipment and their casualties. *Time* magazine lauded their effort as a "battle unparalleled in U.S. military history."[59]

As the First Marine Division recuperated in the rear and cleaned up remnants of North Korean forces left behind in the south, Puller was promoted to brigadier general and made the assistant division commander. It was a billet that had few formal duties, and this provided him with the opportunity to visit units in action. By February 1951, the division was on the front lines again, and Chesty briefly served as the division commander. In May 1951, he received orders to return to the United States. He would never again see combat.

Chesty returned home full of bitterness over the conduct of the Korean War. Particularly angry about the ineffectiveness of some U.S. Army units, he poured out his emotions in a series of intemperate interviews that made national headlines. In addition to criticizing soft training, he questioned the nation's will to win: "What the American people want to do is fight a war without getting hurt. You can't do that anymore than you can get into a barroom fight without getting hurt. . . . Unless the American people are willing to send their sons out to fight an aggressor, there just isn't going to be any United States."[60] The blunt declarations created controversy, but the Marine Corps stood by him. After six months in command of the Third Marine Brigade, Puller became the assistant division commander of the newly reactivated Third Marine Division.

As he had done for more than thirty years, Chesty emphasized tough training, believing that readiness for combat was the best form of welfare for the troops. Even after he became a general, no detail was too small to escape his attention. While inspecting a unit, Puller ordered the marines to take off their boots and socks and put on the spares they were supposed to have in their packs. Many had none because they assumed no one would ever check. Chesty drove home the lesson of preparedness by making them march back to their barracks wearing the footgear that had been in their packs. It was not a long walk, even in bare feet, but word of the incident spread and had the desired effect.

In 1952 Puller took command of the unit that was responsible for conducting amphibious training for the U.S. Marine Corps, the U.S. Army, and Allied forces. Two years later, having been promoted to major general, he took over the Second Marine Division. Within a few weeks, however, he suffered a mild stroke that ultimately led to his involuntary retirement from the Marine Corps in 1955. In recognition of his awards for valor, he was promoted to lieutenant general on his last day of active duty. In a final nod to the esteem in which he held enlisted men, a sergeant major pinned on his new insignia.

Puller was a legend long before he left the corps. Many of those outside the institution ascribed his reputation to his five Navy Crosses, the most ever given to a marine. He was indeed a courageous warrior, but that was not the source of his prestige. What endeared him to his fellow marines was his approach to leadership. His decorations only reinforced that fact, since they were not for individual bravery but for leading his units to victory.

That ability to motivate his subordinates went far beyond the battlefield, as evidenced by letters he received in the last years of his career. A master sergeant who had served with him asked for assistance because "I know that you are always mindful of the problems of enlisted men and always a champion for their cause." Even those who had never directly experienced his brand of charismatic leadership knew and revered what he represented. A private with barely a year in the corps wrote for help in getting transferred to a combat unit because, he said, he had been told, "If I ever got [into a] situation that I didn't know who to turn to, that you were the one man in the Marines I could turn to." The respect was not limited to leathernecks or those seeking favors. The chief petty officers of the USS *Mount*

McKinley asked the general to autograph a photo of himself: "With your permission we would like to hang this picture in our Chiefs' Quarters."[61]

Outstanding leadership can come in many forms. Puller's ability to motivate men came from a simple source. His marines knew that he would ask no more of them than he was willing to put forth himself, and that was everything he had. They knew that when they were putting their lives on the line, he would be out front with them. They knew that he would zealously look out for their welfare and shield them as much as possible from daunting hardships and petty troubles. They knew that he saw things from their point of view. He was a lofty figure who was at home among the lowliest of them. Few can rise to greatness and still genuinely retain the common touch. Medals and rank never changed Puller in that respect; he possessed the heart of a private throughout his long career, and his men idolized him for that simplicity. He was indeed the embodiment of charismatic leadership, a commander "who turned the air around him to heroism and romance and selflessness, who could make men act better than they really were."[62]

Notes

1. Quoted in Henry J. Osterhoudt, "The Evolution of U.S. Army Assault Tactics, 1778–1919" (PhD diss., Duke University, 1986), 16.

2. The facts of Puller's life and career are covered in detail in a full-length biography, Jon T. Hoffman, *Chesty: The Story of Lieutenant General Lewis B. Puller, USMC* (New York: Random House, 2001).

3. Lewis B. Puller, interview, notes, Burke Davis Papers, Southern Historical Collection, University of North Carolina at Chapel Hill.

4. Jon Hoffman, "Lieutenant Lewis Burwell Puller," *Marine Corps Gazette*, June 1998, 27.

5. O. P. Smith, interview, 1973, transcript, 333, and Graves Erskine, interview, 1975, transcript, 103, Oral History Collection, General Alfred M. Gray Research Center, Quantico, VA.

6. Smith, interview, transcript, 333.

7. Puller quoted in Thomas G. Pullen to Burke Davis, 1 June, 15 July 1960, Davis Papers.

8. Russell Honsowetz, interview, circa 1972, transcript, 136, Oral History Collection, Gray Research Center.

9. Lewis B. Puller to CMC, 8 March 1946, Personnel Records, Manpower and Reserve Affairs, U.S. Marine Corps Headquarters, Arlington, VA; Hoffman, *Chesty*, 468–69; Lewis B. Puller to Mrs. Puller, 5 October 1950, Lieutenant General Lewis B. "Chesty" Puller Papers, Gray Research Center.

10. Merwin H. Silverthorn, interview, 1973, transcript, 152, Oral History Collection, Gray Research Center; Lewis B. Puller to Thomas G. Pullen Jr., 5 May 1920, Davis Papers.

11. Puller quoted in Hoffman, *Chesty*, 168.

12. Augustin B. Brunot, patrol diary, 30 November 1919, box 25, series 8166, RG 127, National Archives, College Park, MD; Médaille Militaire citation, Personnel Records.

13. J. A. Mixson to Major General Commandant, 25 October 1922, Personnel Records; Joseph A. Rossell to Major General Commandant, 12 October 1922, Personnel Records; Claire S. Christian to gendarmerie, 1 January 1921, box 1, series 176, RG 127, National Archives.

14. Fitness report, January 1926, Personnel Records.

15. Jefe to brigade, 29 July 1929, box 83, Nicaraguan series, RG 127, National Archives; Guardia Det Orders no. 7, 5 September 1929, and no. 8, 15 October 1929, box 1, series 214, RG 127, National Archives.

16. James W. Webb to Central Area, 23 June 1930, box 13, series 202, RG 127, National Archives.

17. Navy Cross citation, Personnel Records.

18. Lewis B. Puller to GN, 18 September 1932, box 1, series 200, RG 127, National Archives.

19. Fitness report, August–September 1932, Personnel Records.

20. Fitness report, October 1934–April 1935, Personnel Records; Lloyd M. Mustin, interview, 1970, transcript, 72, and J. Wilson Leverton Jr., interview, 1969, transcript, 53, Oral History Collection, Operational Archives Branch, Naval Historical Center, Washington, DC.

21. Harry Brandt to author, 30 June 1998.

22. General Lew Walt, "Comments about Chesty Puller" (28 December 1982), copy in the author's possession.

23. Lewis W. Walt to Lewis B. Puller, 28 July 1960, Davis Papers.

24. Thomas Holcomb, "The Major General Commandant's Speech to the Graduating Class, Basic School, 1937," *Marine Corps Gazette*, May 1937, 41.

25. Dr. E. L. Smith, excerpts from letters home, 1941–1942; Ralph M. Briggs to Burke Davis, n.d., Davis Papers.

26. John S. Day to author, 26 January 1999.

27. Joseph H. Griffith, diary, 2 August 1942, Joseph H. Griffith Papers, Gray Research Center.

28. E. L. Smith to Burke Davis, 5 November 1960, Davis Papers.

29. G. F. R. Henderson, *Stonewall Jackson and the American Civil War* (New York: Longman's Green, 1937), 616, 623.

30. Puller interview, notes, Davis Papers.

31. E. L. Smith, diary, 15 November 1942, Davis Papers.

32. Lewis B. Puller to E. L. Smith, 24 October 1943, Davis Papers; Joseph Sasser to E. L. Smith, 28 January 1944, Davis Papers.

33. Private Gerald White to Burke Davis, [1960?], Davis Papers.

34. Sergeant Leopold Jupiter, press release, 17 January 1943, Davis Papers.

35. Colonel Robert Heinl, interview, 1972, transcript, 287–88, Oral History Collection, Gray Research Center.

36. Colonel Peter Negri, interview, 1974, transcript, 37, Oral History Collection, Gray Research Center.

37. Seventh Marines R-1 and R-2 journals, 3 January 1944, box 13, series 65A-5188, RG 127, National Archives.

38. John Nelson to author, 21 December 1994; Seventh Marines R-1 journal, 4 January 1944, box 13, series 65A-5188, RG 127, National Archives.

39. Quoted in Oswald Marrin to author, 7 February 1996.

40. R. A. Evans, "Patrol in New Britain" (unpublished article), Brigadier General R. A. Evans Papers, Gray Research Center.

41. Lieutenant Colonel John Day to Historical Division, 7 March 1952, box 4, series 14051, RG 127, National Archives.

42. Puller quoted in Peter Abdella to Mrs. Puller, 14 October 1971, Puller Papers.

43. Colonel John Day to author, 17 December 1995.

44. William H. Rupertus to Alexander Vandegrift, 7 September 1944, box 9, Alexander Vandegrift Papers, Gray Research Center.

45. Colonel Lloyd Partridge, "Observer's Report on Palau Operation" 6 October 1944, box 24641, RG 407, National Archives.

46. Puller quoted in "Man of War," *Time*, 9 October 1944, 66.

47. Brigadier General Spencer Berger, "Recollections" (address at Peleliu Symposium, Las Cruces, NM, 4 November 1989).

48. "Man of War," 66; General O. P. Smith to Burke Davis, 29 June 1960, Davis Papers.

49. Puller interview, notes, Davis Papers.

50. "Man of War," 66.

51. George McMillan to Burke Davis, 17 October 1960, Davis Papers.

52. Smith, interview, 141.

53. Jim Butterfield, interview by the author, 1995.

54. Harvey Owens, interview, [1960?], Davis Papers; Charles Stiles, interview, [1960?], Davis Papers; Lieutenant Colonel William Koehnlein to author, 12 January 1996.

55. Bruce F. Williams to Eric Hammel, 26 February 1979, Eric Hammel Papers, Gray Research Center; Jimmy Cannon, "The Best Marine of Them All," Lieutenant General Lewis "Chesty" B. Puller biography file, Marine Corps History Division, Quantico, VA.

56. Lewis B. Puller to Mrs. Puller, 11 October 1950, Davis Papers.

57. Puller quoted in Andrew Geer, *The New Breed* (New York: Harper, 1952), 266.

58. Quoted in Hoffman, *Chesty*, 399.

59. *Time*, 18 December 1950, 26–27.

60. Puller quoted in Hoffman, *Chesty*, 438–41.

61. Matthew Jaklewicz to Lewis B. Puller, 24 August 1952, Puller Papers; Walter F. Biggers to Lewis B. Puller, 8 December 1952, Puller Papers; W. C. Reynolds to Lewis B. Puller, 1 December 1952, Puller Papers.

62. Kevin J. Keaney quoted in Hoffman, "Lieutenant Lewis Burwell Puller," 30.

6

Visionary Leadership

Henry H. "Hap" Arnold

François Le Roy and Drew Perkins

In the closing months of World War II, General Henry H. "Hap" Arnold was awarded his fifth star and thus became the only air commander to earn the rank of General of the Army. In May 1949, three years into his retirement, Arnold became the first and only military officer to receive the honorary rank of General of the Air Force. These extraordinary distinctions recognized the instrumental role Arnold played in the development of American air power. His leadership effectiveness resided not only in his ability to foresee the crucial place of air power in modern warfare but also in his unmatched ability to rally others to support and realize this vision. Because of his exemplary leadership, Arnold is rightfully considered the father of the United States Air Force.

"American air power" was little more than an oxymoron when Arnold assumed command of the U.S. Army Air Corps in September 1938. Even with 24,000 airmen and 2,400 aircraft, the force was far from combat ready. Moreover, it was wholly subservient to the strategic priorities and tactical needs of army ground forces. As the country braced for war against Japan and Germany, President Franklin D. Roosevelt tasked Major General Arnold to modernize and greatly expand the nation's air power. A pioneer of military aviation and strategic air doctrine, Arnold rose to the challenge and oversaw the transformation of the army air corps into a war-winning machine. At the

HENRY H. "HAP" ARNOLD
(U.S. Army Military History Institute, Carlisle, PA)

height of World War II, the United States Army Air Forces included more than 2 million airmen and 80,000 aircraft.

General Arnold died in 1950, but he lived long enough to see the realization of his greatest ambition: the air force as a separate, independent branch of the American military establishment. In achieving that goal, he fulfilled a comprehensive leadership vision that included "a symmetry of people, machines, and logistics as the foundation of a balanced air program."[1] He oversaw the development of cutting-edge aircraft technology with tactical capabilities. He created an organizational culture and structure that, to this day, achieves excellence in performance and innovation. He promoted and institutionalized military and civilian collaboration in the academic and industrial arenas. He significantly expanded the breadth and depth of American air power. He developed and executed a strategy for aerial supremacy in World War II and laid the foundation for U.S. air superiority in the cold war and post–cold war eras.

What follows is a documented analysis of Arnold's visionary leadership through the early evolution of American military aviation. Visionary leaders are not starry-eyed dreamers but future-oriented personalities who identify ambitious objectives and provide direction, motivation, and support to reach those goals. An examination of Arnold's career and leadership style reveals that his success came from several key qualities: an early mastery of aeronautical knowledge, a clear articulation of a broad vision, and an unshakable determination to succeed, including persistence in overcoming naysayers and obstructionists. Throughout his career, he proved flexible and adept at leading public relations campaigns, pursuing technological change, and developing strategic and tactical aspects of a fledgling air doctrine. The progression of Arnold's military career parallels closely the first decades of air force history. Coincidentally, Arnold graduated from West Point in 1907, the same year that the army created the aeronautical section of the U.S. Signal Corps. It was hardly an accident, however, that the U.S. Air Force achieved its full independence in 1947, only one year after Arnold retired. For American air power, Arnold was the right man at the right place at the right time.

Henry Harley Arnold was born on 25 June 1886 in Gladwyne, Pennsylvania, the son of a doctor who also served in the National Guard. Little in Arnold's youth suggested future greatness or genius. He was an indifferent student, and though he loved sports and hunting, nothing seemed to destine him to a military career, least of all an outstanding one. His older brother, Thomas, in fact, was slated to continue the family's military tradition. Thomas, however, turned down admission to West Point, leaving Hap to fulfill his father's ambition. In 1903, at seventeen, Hap entered the United States Military Academy, where he again proved a mediocre student. He excelled in horsemanship and athletics, but his reputation was that of an "immature rogue" and prankster. His less than stellar performance at the academy precluded Hap's fulfilling his desire to join the horse cavalry upon graduation. Inasmuch as Arnold would later shape the history of American military aviation, it is also true that aviation gave meaning and focus to his career.[2]

Upon graduating from West Point in 1907, Arnold joined an infantry unit in the Philippines. To escape the drudgery of infantry life, he volunteered for a signal corps detail assigned to map the topography of Luzon and Corregidor. After two years in the Philippines, Arnold was reassigned to Fort Jay at Governors Island, New York. On his way stateside, he stopped over in Paris. On display there was "a queer contraption," the aircraft that Louis Blériot had recently flown across the English Channel. The airplane caught Arnold's interest; he later wrote, "I hadn't any blinding vision of the future of Air Power at this moment, but one thought I did have was . . . : 'If one man could do it once, what if a lot of men did it together at the same time? What happens then to England's Splendid Isolation?'" Desperate to leave the infantry, Arnold seized an opportunity to become an army pilot. In 1911, along with Second Lieutenant Thomas D. Milling, Arnold joined the army's aeronautical section of the signal corps. The pair received flight training at Wilbur and Orville Wright's Simms Station in Dayton, Ohio. Arnold completed his first solo flight on 13 May 1911. The next year, he became an officially sanctioned army pilot when he earned the army's second military aviator certificate.[3]

As America's first two military pilots, Arnold and Milling were uniquely positioned to influence the early development of the air branch. Together, they helped establish the army signal corps' first flight school at College Park, Maryland, where they served as test pilots, mechanics, and instructors. The duo trained new pilots and aircraft mechanics and, in doing so, created the military's airplane nomenclature and maintenance system. By necessity, they also developed preliminary ideas about the future of military aeronautics. They conducted experiments in aerial gunnery and photography as well as reconnaissance and bombing. Arnold and Milling also sought to improve aircraft performance and to spread their early conceptualizations of air power to skeptics. En route to their objectives, they observed and participated in a variety of flying firsts, such as setting altitude records and transporting mail. They also witnessed the accidental deaths of fellow aviators.[4]

By 1912 Arnold was beginning to develop a vision of commercial passenger aircraft, but importantly, he already foresaw the immense potential of military air power. That summer, Arnold befriended a like-minded visionary in Captain William L. "Billy" Mitchell. At thirty-two, Mitchell was the youngest officer ever assigned to the General Staff, and he too had articulated a vision for offensive military air power. In the coming years, he would exercise a profound influence on Arnold as a mentor and confidant. Both men believed that the most effective application of air power would come from an air force organization that was fully independent of the army.[5]

First, however, Arnold became an accomplished pilot. In 1912 he won the Mackay Trophy, an annual award given by *Collier* magazine's publisher, Clarence Mackay, "for the most outstanding military flight of the year." Arnold's experimental flights demonstrated much of the airplane's military potential, especially its value in conducting reconnaissance operations. On 5 November, however, while participating in army ground force exercises in Kansas, Arnold nearly crashed his plane, an experience that left him with a phobia of flying. He could not shake the overwhelming sense of his own mortality, and though he detested administrative work, he took a desk job at the War Department. Nevertheless, because of his pioneering background as a pilot, Arnold was seen as a leading expert in the new field of military aviation. Working directly under the chief officer of the signal corps in Washington, DC, he oversaw the small-scale development, production, and testing of military aircraft. By the time Arnold received orders in 1913 to return to the infantry, first in Kentucky and then in the Philippines, he had developed a firm belief in the war-fighting potential of military airpower. Moreover, he had gained invaluable experience as both a pilot and an aviation administrator, which provided him with critical knowledge and experience to pursue his vision.[6]

In 1916, after an uneventful two-year tour in the Philippines, Arnold was assigned to the Signal Corps Aviation School at Rockwell Field near San Diego, California. He suspected that Billy Mitchell, then the acting chief of the signal corps' aviation section, arranged the assignment, which included promotion to captain. That same year, with Europe at war, Mitchell's grossly underfunded air section received a $13 million appropriation from Congress. In addition to fulfilling his duties as the supply officer for the aviation section at Rockwell Field, Captain Arnold faced his fear of flying and returned to the cockpit. In early 1917, the army gave him command of the new Seventh Aero Squadron in Panama. Through sheer determination, he had overcome the first significant obstacle, albeit a personal one, to his independent air force vision.[7]

Had the United States not entered the Great War, Arnold might have spent the balance of his career in relative obscurity. But from July 1917 forward, he was linked inextricably to the transformation of American air power. Arnold hoped to gain aerial combat experience during the war, but instead of heading for Europe he was stationed again in Washington, DC, where he attained the temporary rank of colonel in the aviation section of the signal corps. As one of the few field-grade army officers with knowledge of military aviation, Arnold assumed major responsibility for the expansion of America's air power capabilities. The challenges he faced were enormous. There were severe shortages of planes, pilots, power plants, and mechanics,

and neither the military nor private industry was prepared to overcome the shortfalls. In the end, American factories manufactured
and shipped approximately 1,200 aircraft to Europe, but only half
of those actually made it to the front. This was woefully short of the
4,500 planes called for by Mitchell, the commander of American aviation units on the western front.[8]

Arnold did seize an opportunity to visit France in late 1918, but
the war had ended when he arrived at the front lines. He longed for
combat duty not because of any misplaced belief in the romance of
war but because he hoped to learn from the experience. Nevertheless, his administrative responsibilities at the War Department had
furthered his commitment to the development of air power and had
sharpened his managerial and organizational skills. He gained invaluable insights into the complexities of logistics and the necessity of
collaboration among the military, industry, and scientific and engineering communities. These were critical lessons for someone seeking the most effective way to apply cutting-edge technologies. Arnold
and Mitchell again recognized that one of the greatest obstacles in
the pursuit of their vision would be short-sighted naysayers who saw
only a limited role for military air power. The two airmen were unable
to convince the General Staff and others that aircraft should be used
for more than reconnaissance and ground force support. They also
faced the challenge of an American aeronautical industry that lagged
behind its European counterparts.[9]

The United States' poor preparation for World War I and its be-
lated and limited involvement in Europe had prevented army aviation
from fulfilling its potential. The signal corps' poor performance in
managing the development of air power led to the creation of the
U.S. Army Air Service in 1918, but the postwar years proved difficult
ones for those who supported a further expansion of U.S. military
aviation. Upon his return from France, Arnold was first reassigned to
Rockwell Field to oversee the downsizing of the post's air elements.
He was soon given the permanent rank of major and remained at
various California posts until August 1924. While on the West Coast,
Arnold rededicated himself to promoting aviation consciousness in

general and military flight in particular, even in the postwar environment of demobilization and military budget cuts.[10]

Arnold, along with Mitchell, the assistant chief of the air service,
pursued an aggressive campaign to educate the public and politicians
on the importance of military aviation and its potential applications
beyond ground support. Arnold, for example, established an aerial
forest fire patrol, while Mitchell began a border patrol program to
assist officials in southern states. Arnold also orchestrated a series of
aerial stunt shows, while Mitchell conducted offensive bombing trials against outdated battleships. Arnold knew that a major impedi-
ment to developing the potential of air power was the lack of research
and development and government support of aircraft manufacturers.
In the postwar era, Congress provided industry with little financial
incentive for aviation development, and this stemmed partly from
the opposition of the hidebound top brass in the army and navy.[11]
Moreover, Arnold and Mitchell's calls for an expanded air force were
undermined by a widespread and general argument that "a country
that had no enemies, that had two great oceans between it and any
conceivable trouble spots in the entire world, did not need an air
force."[12]

After a series of successful assignments in California, during the
summer of 1924 Arnold returned to Washington, DC. He completed
studies at the Army Industrial College and assumed new duties as the
chief of information for the army air service. There he worked closely
with the outspoken Mitchell. The two grew increasingly frustrated
and impatient with those who opposed the expansion of air power.
Their constant and vocal advocacy ultimately led to their professional downfalls, permanently for Mitchell and temporarily for Arnold.
Mitchell became an embarrassment to the army when he harshly
and publicly criticized the ineptitude of the Department of the Navy
and the War Department after the April 1925 crash of the dirigible
Shenandoah. He was court-martialed the next year and forced to
resign. Arnold, ever loyal, testified on Mitchell's behalf at the military proceedings. He also undertook a letter-writing campaign and
pleaded Mitchell's case on the radio and in newspapers even after

the army had ordered him to cease. Rather than conducting a second high-profile court-martial, the army banished Arnold to a remote cavalry outpost at Fort Riley, Kansas. That same year, the U.S. Army Air Service was renamed the U.S. Army Air Corps. Despite a very modest expansion of military aviation in the 1920s, Mitchell and Arnold's objective of an independent air force seemed far-fetched. Mitchell's sacking, however, had taught Arnold the importance of political finesse. As historian Dik Daso notes, "Mitchell's zealous, insubordinate approach to creating an independent air force taught Arnold how not to tackle political problems." It also motivated him to remain in the military rather than accepting a lucrative job offer from Pan American Airways. With his mentor's ousting, Major Arnold became the leading uniformed advocate of expanded air power in the United States, but unlike Mitchell, he would demonstrate the leadership skills needed to realize the vision.[13]

Arnold remained in semi-exile until 1929, but he made the most of his situation. While in Kansas, he devised and tested aerial and ground tactical theories, and he labored to bridge the gap between the army's aviation and infantry elements. He even wrote a book, *Airmen and Aircraft: An Introduction to Aeronautics* (1926). As the commander of the Sixteenth Observation Squadron at Fort Riley, Arnold so impressed his superiors that they sent him to the Command and General Staff College at Fort Leavenworth, Kansas. Afterward, in June 1929, Arnold was appointed to command Fairfield Air Depot Reservation, near Dayton, Ohio, where he remained for two years. During this tour, he simultaneously served as the executive officer for the air corps material division and played a major role in the maintenance and overhauling of the air corps' small fleet of aircraft. In addition, he supervised two extensive aerial maneuvers and became more involved with research and development, which confirmed the need for more extensive collaboration between military and civilian institutions. His reputation as a competent leader continued to rise, and in February 1931, after twenty-three years of service, he was promoted to lieutenant colonel. Even in remote postings, Arnold continued to work toward his vision of expanding army air power.[14]

By the end of the first postwar decade, Arnold's career had survived the Mitchell firestorm; more significant, he had mastered the
essentials of aviation and had learned invaluable lessons in effective
administration. The comprehensiveness of Arnold's vision stood him
apart from other air visionaries. As Dik Daso asserts, he understood
that "air power was a complex system of logistics, procurement,
ground support bases, and operations," and this philosophy "guided his vision for future growth." Indeed, "Arnold's approach to air
power development was actually the first mention of what became the
military-industrial-academic complex after World War II."[15]

In November 1931, Arnold took command of March Field,
near Riverside, California, where he remained through 1935. The
lengthy assignment proved fateful for the development and fulfillment of Arnold's air vision in several respects. By the 1930s, Southern California had become one of the country's leading regions for
aeronautical research and aircraft manufacturing. Pasadena was home
of the Guggenheim Aeronautical Laboratory at the California Institute of Technology, which housed the world's largest wind tunnel.
The laboratory's director was Theodore von Kármán, a preeminent
aeronautical engineer who became a leading civilian proponent of
expanding American air power. Arnold and Kármán first met in
1930, shortly after the latter's arrival at Caltech. They immediately
impressed each other. Despite having profound differences in personality, the two complemented each other and developed a productive
partnership that symbolized Arnold's strategy of increasingly close
relations between the military air force and the scientific and engineering communities. By the mid-1930s, Arnold and Kármán had
developed "a similar vision for military aviation: the United States
needed a cooperative aeronautics establishment which coupled civilian scientific and industrial expertise with the practical needs of the
Army Air Corps."[16]

To further promote military aviation, Arnold also fostered other
critical relationships in California. Robert Millikan, a Nobel Prize
laureate in physics and the president of Caltech, agreed that civilian researchers could play a fundamental role in the development

of military aeronautical technology. Arnold also befriended Donald W. Douglas, the legendary aircraft designer and manufacturer, and the two forged a lasting and fruitful partnership. Arnold developed a keen sense for potential technological improvements in aircraft safety and performance, and he worked with civilian manufacturers to design solutions. Unlike many army officers, Arnold did not possess contempt for civilians or for public opinion. On the contrary, through his calculated diplomacy and personal charm, he, more than anyone, effectively rallied civilians to the cause of military aviation. He did not, for example, dismiss complaints by residents of Riverside about the behavior of boisterous airmen when they were out on the town. Instead, he organized meetings to ease tensions between the townspeople and military personnel. Moreover, taking advantage of his proximity to Hollywood, he forged friendships with celebrities and recruited them to help promote military aviation.[17]

At March Field, Arnold's soldiers conducted public air shows and engaged in a variety of domestic missions that raised the profile of the air corps. During the winter of 1932–1933, for example, blizzards in the western United States stranded Native American settlements without food and other necessities. Arnold's staff created and executed a plan that airdropped relief supplies. Arnold's men orchestrated another rescue mission after the Long Beach earthquake of March 1933. The next year, when the federal postmaster cancelled the government's contract with civilian airmail carriers, Arnold and his airmen transported the mail for four months. The air corps also provided support for many Civilian Conservation Corps projects, including the transportation of food, water, and construction materials for road- and camp-building projects in Death Valley. Finally, while stationed in California, Arnold earned a second Mackay Trophy for his command of ten B-10 bombers that flew some eight thousand miles from the nation's capital to Fairbanks, Alaska, and back. Among other things, the Alaska mission proved the capabilities of the air corps' newest bomber and demonstrated the viability of a tactical squadron's long-range deployment. Each of these missions raised public awareness of the air corps' potential and moved Arnold closer to his visions of strategic bombing and of the air force's institutional autonomy. These visions were based in part on the conviction that long-range heavy bombers were certain to become the decisive weapons of the next major war. These planes, more than the navy's battleships, were capable of projecting America's power around the globe.[18]

By 1935, army aviation was maturing, but air corps champions still battled to increase the organization's autonomy and to secure badly needed funding. In March, the General Staff, which opposed making the air force a separate service equal to the army or navy, established the general headquarters (GHQ) air force as a supplemental organization to the air corps. The GHQ air force consolidated the air corps' tactical combat units, those most directly responsible for providing aerial ground support and coastal defenses. Major General Frank M. Andrews, who led the GHQ air force, promoted Arnold to brigadier general and made him the new organization's operational commander on the West Coast. It was during this time that Arnold worked with Andrews and others to formulate, test, and develop the long-range bomber strategies and tactics that were central to his vision for the air force. Within a year, however, Arnold left the GHQ air force to serve in Washington, DC, as the ranking assistant to the new director of the air corps, Major General Oscar Westover. Despite the creation of the GHQ air force, the "lack of clear-cut thinking" in Washington about the future of American air power disturbed Arnold. In 1936 he published *This Flying Game*, which articulated his comprehensive views on the future of air warfare. He envisioned, for example, offensive bombing campaigns against an enemy's domestic transportation systems. Perhaps even more important, Arnold emphasized the need for the United States to develop a collaborative civilian and military infrastructure that would be capable of building and sustaining an air force second to none. In 1937 Arnold encouraged participants at a planning conference not to "visualize aviation merely as a collection of airplanes. It is broad and far reaching. It combines manufacture, schools, transportation, airdrome, building and management, air munitions and armaments, metallurgy, mills and mines, finance, and banking, and finally, public security—national defense."[19]

This vision was not exclusive to Arnold. It was the American version of a strategic doctrine that had been debated by military staffs around the world and promoted by such military thinkers as Italian colonel Giulio Douhet, author of the influential book *Command of the Air* (1921), Royal Air Force General Hugh Trenchard, and Billy Mitchell, men whose ideas flew in the face of the military dogmas of their time and who suffered much abuse because of them. Arnold belonged to the second generation of air power advocates, the likes of Yamamoto Isoroku, the architect of the Japanese attack on Pearl Harbor; Air Marshal Sir Arthur "Bomber" Harris, head of the Royal Air Force Bomber Command in World War II; and others who adhered to the message of their predecessors and mentors and fashioned their visions into functioning organizations and coherent strategies.

Arnold and Andrews, the commander of the GHQ air force, shared the same vision for air power. They used their positions to advocate for the air arm as a long-range strike force. They established and refined tactical and strategic doctrines based on theories related to large, long-range four-engine bombers. In doing so, they ran up against the army General Staff, which primarily advocated the use of medium twin-engine bombers. Despite the General Staff's differing view, Arnold and Andrews carried on in their efforts to define a clear, practical, and attainable force structure and mission for army aviation.[20]

Andrews and Arnold also attempted to neutralize the short-sighted leadership who wanted to keep the air arm subordinate to ground forces. The consensus held that the navy could defend the coastlines and related waterways and that the United States would not commit to an offensive war in Europe; thus bombers, especially long-range aircraft, were unnecessary. Fighting an uphill bureaucratic battle, the two air proponents lobbied for increased funding for the production of the B-17, a four-engine heavy bomber that later formed the core of the nation's strategic air force.[21]

In September 1938, after the sudden death of Major General Westover, Arnold became the chief of the air corps. Soon the combat-focused GHQ air force and its new commander, Major General Delos

C. Emmons, were placed under his authority. This command allowed Arnold to develop further a greatly expanded but balanced force, one that would combine manpower, machines, and support facilities to create an efficiently lethal air arm.[22] Increasingly anxious about German gains in military air technology, Arnold shifted some of his limited resources to research and development. One of his major talents was the ability to anticipate and recognize technological and mechanical advances demanded by combat and to pursue perfection of those advances. As the commander of the air corps, he organized a meeting of the National Academy of Sciences and invited engineers from the Massachusetts Institute of Technology and the Guggenheim Aeronautical Laboratory at Caltech. Arnold assigned the participants various tasks, including critical projects such as aircraft windshield de-icing and jet-assisted take off. The Caltech laboratory assumed responsibility for the latter, thus continuing the close association between Arnold and Kármán.[23]

The depth of civilian participation in research and development drew the scrutiny of Army Chief of Staff George C. Marshall, who questioned Arnold's methods: "What on earth are you doing with people like that?" Arnold responded that he had recruited the "long hairs" to discover solutions to problems too complex for army engineers.[24] He had no qualms about using jet technology developed by Royal Air Force engineer Frank Whittle to overcome the difficulties experienced by the Guggenheim Aeronautical Laboratory. Arnold intervened to bring the plans of the Whittle jet turbine from Britain, and he assembled a team of researchers from the General Electric Company and Bell Aircraft Corporation to design the first American jet aircraft. Ever the pragmatist, Arnold cared little where solutions came from; the ends, not the means, mattered most.[25]

Beyond directing research and development efforts, Arnold crisscrossed the country, both inspecting civilian and military training and production facilities and giving speeches that advocated joint military-civilian development of air power. He warned his audiences inside and outside the War Department about the dangers of complacency. In February 1939 he stated publicly, "Please bear in mind much time is required to build up an air force. It cannot be done overnight—18 months are required to reach quantity production in planes—note I said reach—2 years are needed to train personnel to make them competent to handle our complicated aircraft. Delay in beginning will make for undue haste to catch up and frenzied haste makes for waste and extravagance."[26] Arnold also pursued the life-blood of the air corps: congressional funding. He hoped to finance more and better planes, improved airfields, and well-trained crews to fly and maintain the air fleet.[27]

Congressional critics, however, argued that a heavily weaponized air force was too expensive and that plans for offensive bombing contradicted the defensive mentality of the army and navy. Arnold did find supporters for his bomber vision outside the air corps, including President Roosevelt, General Marshall, and Henry L. Stimson, who became the secretary of war in 1940. The outbreak of World War II in September 1939 and the fall of France in June 1940 convinced Congress to provide massive funding for American military preparedness. Arnold's air corps received $1.5 billion. Furthermore, upon Arnold's recommendation, Marshall reorganized the army into three distinct branches: the air forces, the ground forces, and the services of supply. The combination of congressional funding and political support had at last provided Arnold and the air corps with the means to develop a national air force second to none. Achieving that objective, however, was fraught with challenges, not the least of which was FDR's decision to divert U.S. military planes to the Royal Air Force under the Lend-Lease Act of 1941.[28]

When the United States entered the war in December 1941, Arnold faced the tasks of expanding American air power while devising and leading a global air strategy to defeat formidable enemies in Europe and the Pacific. Many doubted his ability to meet the challenge set forth by President Roosevelt to build fifty-two thousand aircraft per year and to create an infrastructure to support the operations of a massive air armada. The industrial, scientific, technological, logistical, administrative, and human requirements appeared overwhelming. Arnold, however, was a "possibility thinker," capable of motivating followers by providing a clear vision and a unified sense of direction.[29] Moreover, his decades of experience made him uniquely qualified to steer the transformation of American air power and, in the process, lead the air force to institutional independence. Originally trained by the ultimate problem solvers, the Wright brothers, he had learned the fundamentals of aviation and that "the 'will to do' in many cases may make the impossible, possible."[30] Over his long career, Arnold had maintained an unwavering focus on his objective of a powerful, independent air service. In addition, he acquired and honed management and organizational skills vital to overcoming obstacles and obstructionists.

As commander of the air corps during World War II, Arnold liberally spread his determination to succeed. When he did not have a clear technological or scientific solution to a problem, he drove others to discover the answer. Arnold demanded results from those who worked for him and drove his subordinates hard. Task-oriented, he focused his own energy and channeled that of his assistants toward the fulfillment of specific objectives, always pushing for improved technology and equipment.[31] An engineer at the Douglas Aircraft Company who worked on one of several "Hap-directed" task forces during the war recalled, "You never thought the things [Arnold] asked you to do were possible, but then you went out and did them."[32] Arnold never relented until his goals were met. He was merciless with those who fell short of his expectations, including longtime friends, and he set aside personal sentiment in making organizational decisions. Although it certainly pained him, in January 1944 he relieved his good friend Brigadier General Ira C. Eaker of the command of the Eighth Air Force because the bombing campaign against Germany had not been as effective as he desired. Similarly, he dismissed Major General Haywood S. "Possum" Hansell Jr., another friend, as chief of staff of the Twentieth Air Force because of the limited results against Japan. In both instances, he replaced them with aggressive—if not ruthless—leaders, major generals James H. Doolittle and Curtis E. LeMay, respectively.[33]

Arnold was also determined to resist any force that threatened to disperse aircraft and deplete the air corps. For example, after years of belittling the air service and attempting to undermine its growth, the navy began demanding thousands of airplanes. Arnold feared that the navy's desire for an autonomous air force threatened the principle of unity of command. In addition, the navy's apparent logistical mismanagement in the Pacific theater and its inefficient use of allocated air resources promised to degrade the efficacy of any air element. The navy did not even know the nature of its cargo on some eighty ships sitting in the New Caledonia harbor. Arnold believed that the navy did not possess sufficient airfields to support additional aircraft. Moreover, the inability of army and navy brass to cooperate threatened to further dilute limited air resources and limit their effectiveness.[34]

Rather than relinquishing total control of more planes for antisubmarine duties, Arnold established the Coastal Command for escort and patrol details. Although this had the drawback of diverting assets from the European theater, it delayed naval attempts to control air elements. Army and navy requests for the Pacific did hamper Arnold's quest for sustained efforts against Germany and for Operation Sledgehammer, a planned cross-channel invasion of Europe in 1942. On the other hand, he successfully prevented the dispersion of the new B-29 strategic bombers that, at his insistence, were reserved for the Twentieth Air Force in the Pacific.[35]

Arnold's desire to prevent misallocation of aircraft was driven, at least in part, by his conviction that air power could win the war if resources were properly employed. Such an outcome would likely assure an independent air force. Continued demands from the army and navy and from the British, combined with requests from China for cargo planes, challenged Arnold's plan for concentrated attacks on Germany. To satisfy these many demands, Arnold consolidated the Ferry and Air Service commands into the Air Transport Command to move large numbers of men and materiel to multiple theaters around the globe. In doing so, he achieved unity of purpose and eliminated duplication of work. Arnold's efforts demonstrated the potential for mass transport by air and the viability of a worldwide airline. He did not, however, allow the Air Transport Command to assimilate the commercial airlines, a move that would have impeded their efficiency and independence.[36]

Although Arnold's main objective was winning the war, he maintained his commitment to the army air force. The pursuit of victory in the war was both an end in itself and a means to Arnold's long-held institutional goals. Arnold demonstrated considerable political skill in his advocacy for air power and autonomy, having drawn the right political lessons from the fall of Billy Mitchell. He understood that the cause of the air force would be better served through careful rather than overly aggressive promotion.[37] In addition, he knew that a decisive demonstration of air power's wartime capabilities would prove even more effective than adept political maneuvering. Despite his reputed impatience, Arnold wisely resisted pushing for air force independence during the war. To the dismay of some fellow air officers, Arnold preferred to wait until after victory to press the matter. He possessed an impeccable sense of timing and understood better than most that the requirements of the war precluded the creation of a fully independent air force. He realized that a wartime change would strip the air arm of many services then supplied by the army, services that an independent air force could not yet provide. He nevertheless continued to draw criticism from people like Colonel Hugh Knerr, who believed that complete autonomy was long overdue. Arnold went so far as to establish a committee to suppress sentiments for air autonomy until the conclusion of the war.[38]

The bombing campaigns against Germany and Japan and the ambitious B-29 program were tools to achieve Arnold's two primary goals: victory for the United States and independence for the air force. Arnold and other air power enthusiasts endorsed the doctrine that heavily armored, self-protecting strategic bombers could drive the enemy out of the war through a sustained aerial campaign that targeted manufacturing centers. He was convinced that such an achievement would lend substantial weight to the argument for an independent air force. The heavy losses that bomber crews suffered over Germany, however, shook his optimism. Yet Arnold was slow to admit that bombers needed escorts for the full length of their missions, protection that could be made possible by extending the range of fighters with the use of auxiliary fuel tanks. Apparently, Arnold's offensive mind-set saw the escort fighter, whose mission was defensive, as subordinate to the bomber. In a rare instance of short-sightedness, Arnold clung to prewar doctrine and failed to recognize the vulnerability of unescorted bombers.[39] Additionally, the protracted war forced him to consider that he might have overestimated the ability of air power to determine the outcome of the war.

These realities led Arnold to alter some of his convictions, but as the war progressed, with the Allies outperforming the Axis powers in aircraft production, his B-17s decimated German manufacturing and infrastructure. In the Pacific, the B-29 offered another opportunity to make the case for the significance of air power and therefore an autonomous air force. Arnold argued that the B-29's range and payload could force the Japanese to surrender, a risky assertion that proved at least partially correct.[40] The B-29 conducted firebombing missions against Japan, with the Twentieth Air Force alone destroying more than 2 million homes and killing a reported 240,000 people during conventional raids. The B-29 was also the only plane with the range to make the atomic strikes against Hiroshima and Nagasaki.[41] Still, Arnold's complete faith in air power's ability to win the war was unrealistic, in part because he underestimated the effort required to defeat Germany. Nevertheless, Arnold's war machine contributed much to the defeat of Germany and Japan through the destruction of their ability to wage war, a fact that even detractors of air power acknowledged.

In the postwar era, Arnold understood the importance of cultivating the sympathies of the politicians, the public, and the media to garner support for the air force and to establish it as an independent arm of the military. He devoted considerable attention to public relations, especially once it became apparent in 1944 that the air corps would not be able to win the war on its own and that ground and naval operations were getting increasing press coverage. It was of some concern to him that "the hot pilot [was] being supplanted in national esteem by G.I. Joe," as a staff study warned in August 1944. Arnold knew that public opinion would affect the postwar status of the air force.[42] He did not single-handedly manage the public relations campaigns launched in 1943 and 1944, but he gave them direction.

Starting in late 1944, confident that the war had been decided in favor of the Allies, Arnold began to shift some of his attention to postwar issues. The magnitude of the Air Transport Command demonstrated that the "jet age" would require American military and civilian global air networks and that the air force would play an integral role in postwar geopolitics. Air force challenges would involve determining the future role of air power and integrating advancing technology. To that end, Arnold again contracted the talents of Kármán and his associates and tasked them with the responsibility of devising solutions to such issues. In so doing, he continued the close association between civilian expertise and the military.[43] Arnold and Kármán could take pride in their accomplishments in World War II, but they were concerned that their efforts would go to naught once peace returned. The end of the conflict, they feared, would bring sharp reductions in military budgets and temper the sense of urgency that had driven research and development during the war.

As a consequence, the general and the scientist worked to institutionalize the relationship they had forged to make it a fixture of American air power. Arnold thus created a series of institutions whose purpose was to nurture that vital relationship. In 1944, he established the Scientific Advisory Group (later renamed the Scientific Advisory Board) and appointed Kármán as director. This body of scientists, military engineers, and officers was to address the challenges of long-term technological and scientific planning. In December 1945, Arnold also founded the Office of Scientific Liaison in the Pentagon. Its purpose was to develop and maintain lines of communication between the military and university and industrial scientists. In another stroke of inspiration, he led Congress to endow the Douglas Aircraft Company with $10 million to conduct Project RAND (Research and Development), a one-year study on the future of warfare. The program was renewed and expanded to include scholars from the humanities in recognition that modern war involved more than math and science. This project was borne partly from the industrial and familial ties Arnold had created with Douglas—Arnold's son William had married Douglas's daughter Barbara. The possibility of a conflict of interest required the removal of the RAND Project from the supervision of Douglas and its reestablishment in 1948 as the nonprofit RAND Corporation, today one of the most influential think tanks for military strategy.[44]

With the war won and with an assurance that the air force would be granted its organizational independence, General Arnold left the service in February 1946 following serious health complications. He officially retired from active duty on 30 June 1946. He was succeeded by a protégé, General Carl A. "Tooey" Spaatz, who became the first chief of staff of the United States Air Force on 18 September 1947. Such an event is certain to have brightened Arnold's retirement, as did his promotion in May 1949 to the rank of General of the Air Force, a rank that he alone has held. Living on a ranch near Sonoma, California, he contracted with Harper and Brothers to write his memoirs, in part to supplement his meager government pension. His military responsibilities and work habits, however, had taken an irreversible toll on his health. In January 1948, Arnold suffered a fifth heart attack, and a sixth killed him on 15 January 1950. He was laid to rest at Arlington National Cemetery.[45]

Arnold's career is a testament to effective visionary leadership. His superiors and subordinates alike were struck by his ability to foresee and articulate the present and future needs of American air power to reach the ultimate objectives: winning World War II and securing the independence of the air force. His leadership allowed the United States to achieve air superiority, and often air supremacy, for fifty years and beyond. The general's success as a visionary leader is attributable to his having learned early in his career the essentials of aviation and to his ability to articulate a clear, comprehensive vision. As significant, if not more, was Arnold's persistence in overcoming naysayers and his unwavering determination to succeed. During the interwar years, he was fully aware of the unpopularity of air power theories and of the idea of an independent air force. The military had been divided into land and naval forces for centuries, and each was jealous of the other. Turf-conscious, the army and the navy were steeped in traditions and opposed the creation of a third service that was certain to tax the military budget and shrink their influence. Spreading the gospel of air power and the need for an autonomous air force required the courage and resolve of a missionary. Despite these challenges, Arnold was determined to succeed.

General Arnold was a highly effective visionary leader. In peace and in war, he exceeded the ambitious goals President Roosevelt had set, shaped the American air arm into a war-winning organization, and created the conditions that led to air force independence from the army. To Theodore von Kármán, the general's most trusted civilian colleague, Arnold was "the greatest example of the U.S. military man—a combination of complete logic, mingled with farsightedness and superb dedication."[46]

Notes

1. Dik A. Daso, *Hap Arnold and the Evolution of American Airpower* (Washington, DC: Smithsonian Institution Press, 2000), 5.

2. Ibid., 30.

3. Henry H. Arnold, *Global Mission* (New York: Harper, 1949), 2.

4. Thomas M. Coffey, *Hap: The Story of the U.S. Air Force and the Man Who Built It, General Henry H. "Hap" Arnold* (New York: Viking, 1982), 52.

5. Ibid., 57.

6. Daso, *Hap Arnold*, 59.

7. Ibid., 87.

8. Ibid., 96; Coffey, *Hap*, 91–92.

9. Arnold, *Global Mission*, 71.

10. Dik A. Daso, *Architects of American Air Supremacy* (Honolulu: University Press of the Pacific, 2002), 20.

11. Coffey, *Hap*, 113.

12. James L. Stokesbury, *A Short History of Air Power* (New York: Morrow, 1986), 125.

13. Daso, *Hap Arnold*, 105.

14. Coffey, *Hap*, 140.

15. Daso, *Hap Arnold*, 57.

16. Daso, *Architects*, 4, 27.

17. Coffey, *Hap*, 148–49.

18. Daso, *Architects*, 127–29.

19. Arnold quoted in Daso, *Hap Arnold*, 146.

20. Ibid., 168.

21. Coffey, *Hap*, 166–67.

22. Daso, *Hap Arnold*, 152.

23. Daso, *Architects*, 59.

24. Quoted in ibid., 58–59.

25. Ibid., 59–60, 66.

26. Arnold quoted in Daso, *Hap Arnold*, 60.

27. Ibid., 200–201.

28. Coffey, *Hap*, 225.

29. James M. Kouzes and Barry Z. Posner, *The Leadership Challenge* (San Francisco: Jossey-Bass, 2002), 124.

30. Daso, *Architects*, 3.

31. Michael S. Sherry, *The Rise of American Air Power: The Creation of Armageddon* (New Haven, CT: Yale University Press, 1989), 14.

32. Quoted in ibid., 69.

33. Walter J. Boyne, *The Influence of Air Power upon History* (Gretna, LA: Pelican, 2003), 260–61, 274–76.

34. Ibid., 287, 286, 290.

35. Ibid., 338.

36. Ibid., 282.

37. Sherry, *Rise of American Air Power*, 37.

38. Walter J. Boyne, *Beyond the Wild Blue: A History of the U.S. Air Force* (St. Martin's Griffin, 1997), 9.

39. Coffey, *Hap*, 310.

40. James L. Stokesbury, *A Short History of World War II* (New York: Perennial, 2001), 366.

41. Coffey, *Hap*, 374.

42. Sherry, *Rise of American Air Power*, 183.

43. Coffey, *Hap*, 357.

44. Ibid., 158–59.

45. Daso, *Hap Arnold*, 215–25.

46. Kármán quoted in Sherry, *Rise of American Air Power*, 186.

7

Technology and Leadership

Hyman G. Rickover

Thomas L. "Tim" Foster

In November 1981, two months before the end of his unprecedented sixty-three-year navy career, which included thirty-five years overseeing the U.S. Naval Nuclear Propulsion Program, Admiral Hyman G. Rickover lectured to a Columbia University audience on the components of effective leadership: "What it takes to do a job will not be learned from management courses. It is principally a matter of experience, the proper attitude, and common sense—none of which can be taught in a classroom."[1] In less formal surroundings, he called leadership and management courses "crap." Graduates, he believed, too often came away with the false notion that, by applying a few textbook principles, almost anyone could manage almost anything. To Rickover, academics underemphasized, if not ignored, the importance of determination, innovation, and accountability. Despite his depreciation of leadership studies, an examination of Rickover's extraordinary career, which featured a high degree of excellence, can teach us much about leading people in the field of high technology. Rickover demonstrated, as much as any leader could, the importance of learning lessons from history and personal experience in pursuit of technological excellence. From the perspective of a former senior member of his staff, this chapter explores Rickover's personal characteristics and the leadership practices that inspired the long-term devotion of thousands of people in the Naval Nuclear Propulsion

HYMAN G. RICKOVER
(National Archives, College Park, MD)

Program. It is surprising that Rickover, widely known as a harsh, no-frills taskmaster, was able to attract, retain, and motivate so many talented people to work under austere conditions. Why is it that, even today, so many people, including those who had minimal direct contact with the admiral, still look back fondly on their experiences in his organization, which remains the worldwide standard for nuclear excellence?

Rickover had a paradoxical and unconventional brand of leadership. He was a study in contrasts. He could be serious and funny, brash and humble, harsh and kind, bluntly rude and astutely diplomatic. He was apolitical yet was a master politician. Rickover was clearly in charge, yet he welcomed internal debate and argument. He was intimately involved in organizational details, yet his people managed their departments as if they alone were responsible. He was a strict disciplinarian but also an inspiring cheerleader and enabler. Within the nuclear program, his criticisms of poor performance were pointed and personal. Externally, he assumed full responsibility for the program and its personnel.

The admiral was part engineer, part mechanic, and part liberal arts intellectual. His senior staff, many with far superior academic credentials, admired his engineering genius. Theodore Rockwell, a senior member of his staff in the early years at Naval Nuclear Propulsion Program headquarters, writes in *The Rickover Effect*, "The most memorable interactions with Rickover, the ones that were burned deep into your psyche, were those in which you and everyone else in the room were in violent disagreement with him, and he insisted on doing it his way, and he turned out to be right."[2] When this happened, the standing staff joke was to concede grudgingly that Rickover had been right, but for the wrong reason. Rickover possessed an uncanny ability to anticipate second- and sometimes third-order effects that were often overlooked even by his most experienced staff. This capacity, combined with his courage to invest substantially in precautionary measures, is an important characteristic of effective technological leadership. Rickover's leadership was crucial in establishing the impeccable worldwide reputation of the U.S. Naval Nuclear Propulsion

Program, a record that remains intact and is the envy of other civilian and military nuclear programs.

The admiral's determination, innovative thinking, and accountability, together with his unconventional management techniques, reveal keen insight into human nature and, in particular, into his success in translating principle into practice. This chapter explains why Admiral Rickover, arguably the most significant technical leader in U.S. military history, was so effective and why his people worked so intently and became so loyal not only to what he was trying to accomplish but also to him as their leader.

Born in Russian-occupied Makow, Poland, in 1900, Rickover relocated to America with his Jewish parents five years later. The Rickovers settled in a Chicago immigrant community, where his father, a tailor, set up shop. Young Rickover proved an adequate but unexceptional student. He worked after school as a telegraph messenger to earn spending money and contribute to the family's finances. By pluck and good fortune, Rickover ended up at the Naval Academy in 1918. A U.S. congressman could normally nominate two students for admission to the academy. The raging crisis of World War I, however, temporarily allowed politicians to select up to five nominees. Though he was ranked fourth in his district, Rickover later attributed his nomination to a favor owed to a tenant in the Rickover household. To gain admittance to the academy, Rickover still needed to pass the entrance exam. Ill-prepared in technical subjects, he invested his savings in a private preparatory class in Annapolis, Maryland. He quickly concluded, however, that he was too far behind his peers to benefit from the course. He dropped it, forfeited the money, and designed his own self-study program. He passed the entrance exam, but just barely. One-tenth of a point less on his algebra score, and he would have failed. His ability to quickly assess a situation, his tendency to take self-disciplined action, and his drive to work harder than others would become hallmarks of Rickover's future leadership.[3]

As a midshipman, Rickover realized early on that to succeed at the academy he would be wise to keep a low profile. For example, during his first visit to the mess hall, he found ham on his tray.

Though he had been raised on kosher food, he rationalized, with only a moment's hesitation, that it must be "rare roast beef," not pork. Thereafter, he ate whatever was served.[4] Starting near the bottom of his class, Rickover graduated in the top 20 percent. Still, little of what he had accomplished at the academy and nothing about his physical stature or military bearing hinted of unusual technical ability or impressive leadership potential.[5]

As a junior naval officer, Rickover performed well; his shipboard assignments included deck, gunnery, and engineering duty. He served on a destroyer, two battleships, two submarines, and a minesweeper. From the beginning, Rickover decided to work long hours and spend little time ashore. He was determined to learn all that he could about each ship: how it worked, how crew members approached their tasks, and how best to operate and maintain shipboard equipment. Such intensive practical experience served him well throughout his career. His dedicated work ethic on every assignment, his preoccupation with specifics, and his devotion to self-study help explain his disdain for the notion that one can become an effective technical leader and manager simply by taking courses in these subjects.

Through independent study, Rickover expanded his technical knowledge and his understanding of naval engineering, thus laying the foundation of high technological competency that would be necessary for his future leadership of the nuclear navy. After five years at sea, however, the navy selected him for postgraduate education. In 1929 he earned a master of science degree in electrical engineering from Columbia University, where, by his own account, he began to understand and appreciate the logic and philosophy of engineering.[6]

After Columbia, Lieutenant Rickover won acclaim as an assistant engineering officer on the battleship USS *New Mexico*. When he arrived in 1935, the performance of the ship's engineering department ranked eighth out of fifteen U.S. battleships. His task was to enhance naval effectiveness by minimizing fuel consumption. Although Rickover's efforts were supported by his captain, the crew members did not care for his strict rationing of electricity and water. The most significant fuel conservation stemmed from Rickover's fine-tuning of power plant equipment. After only one year, he led the department to first place, and he maintained that ranking the following year. Rickover demonstrated an important characteristic of a technical leader: finding innovative ways to maximize technology's potential.[7]

From the *New Mexico*, Rickover commanded the USS *Finch*, a minesweeper anchored in Tsingtao, China. After only two months, the navy approved his request for designation as an engineering duty officer. No longer an unrestricted line officer, he was immediately reassigned to duty as engineering planning officer at Cavite Navy Yard in the Philippines. Two years later, in 1939, Rickover, now a lieutenant commander, reported to the U.S. Navy's Bureau of Ships, where he applied his experience with technology and sailors to reshape the navy's electrical section. He disdained unaccountable fiefdoms and assigned individuals cradle-to-grave responsibility for each system and component.

At the bureau, Rickover established the expectation of accountability that would underlie his entire career. In the aftermath of Pearl Harbor, he personally inspected the battle wreckage. What he saw demonstrated unambiguously the need for more combat-survivable shipboard equipment. His civilian defense contractors quickly got the message. One salesman watched Rickover demonstrate how easily he could set fire to the product sample. Another saw him shatter sample equipment by throwing it against a nearby radiator. Rickover announced that the product had failed the "radiator test."[8]

From his superiors at the bureau, Rickover regularly sought more funding and, on occasion, letters from higher authorities that gave him the license he needed to maneuver through the bureaucracy.[9] He rarely sought their advice or guidance. Contrary to his dour reputation, Rickover possessed a good sense of humor together with a delightful irreverence for bureaucracy that encouraged his hardworking staff. When, for example, his people complained to him about their time being wasted preparing a little-read report, he suggested they steal the report's tickler card from the desk of an officer's secretary and forget about it. They did, and no one seemed to miss the report. On another occasion, when an inspector put Rickover's design staff on report for poor productivity, he instructed his staff to "double" production by cutting each of their drawings in half and renumbering them. Rickover believed that many leaders sought refuge in mindless adherence to management directives. "Rules," he once said, "are the lowest common denominator of human behavior . . . a substitute for rational thought."[10] In the end, Rickover found that bureaucratic apathy and ignorance about new technology, if effectively handled, could become an advantage. Some seek to ingratiate themselves with superiors by mindlessly adhering to their directives. Rickover, however, demonstrated initiative and protected his people from bureaucratic red tape, thereby fostering continued productivity, innovation, and high morale. Those of us who worked closely with him valued the much greater freedom we had to act because of his protection from red tape.

Although Rickover was always a maverick, World War II made it even easier for him to find innovative ways to bend, circumvent, or ignore cumbersome bureaucratic rules. Finding it difficult to hire good, draft-exempt engineers, he occasionally prevailed on civilian contractors to supply him draft-exempt engineers as a sort of kickback. In another instance, to provide the British military with urgently needed electrical cable to help protect against German mines, Rickover visited the major U.S. cable manufacturers, quickly assessed their capacities, and directed them to begin round-the-clock production of particular size cables. In other words, he bypassed entirely the U.S. government contracting system, allocated resources for maximum efficiency, and authorized work without a contract. He promised the manufacturers they would be paid, and they were. He disregarded most of the rules, but his determination to find a solution ended the cable shortage—and no doubt saved lives.

By the last year of the war, Rickover had been promoted to captain, and after six years of duty in the Bureau of Ships' electrical section, he became the commanding officer of the new naval repair facility on Okinawa. Rickover labored tirelessly. After five months, the war ended, and Rickover disbanded the facility and returned to the United States.[11] Although his extraordinary leadership in the field of nuclear technology lay in the future, he was forever proud of the contributions his electrical section made to the Allied war effort. From his war experience, he learned and confirmed invaluable lessons regarding how to lead government civilians and contractors in ways that promoted imagination, creativity, technical excellence, action, and accountability.

On 4 June 1946, the chief of the U.S. Navy's Bureau of Ships detailed Rickover to accompany a team of naval officers and several civilians to Oak Ridge, Tennessee. Their purpose was to determine from the Manhattan Project's atomic bomb-making experience whether nuclear propulsion would be viable for naval warships. In making this assignment, the chief had overruled senior officers who considered Captain Rickover too undisciplined and abrasive for the job. He did not, however, despite Rickover's seniority, place him in charge of the team. Rickover, sensing he was being exiled and snubbed, was not eager to participate. Yet, realizing he had little choice, Rickover, as always, applied himself fully to the task in keeping with the adage "Grow where planted." Upon arrival at Oak Ridge, he quickly won the respect of the army officer to whom the group reported. Rickover was assigned to fitness-reporting responsibilities for each team member. He took charge of the group and set in motion the ambitious team study and technical report-writing effort that spawned a revolution in naval warfare. This turning point in his career illustrated several aspects of effective technical leadership: accepting responsibility for assigned tasks, establishing accountability among subordinates, demonstrating determination, and thinking innovatively in crafting a well-thought-out course toward a clear, worthwhile goal.[12]

Nuclear power in submarines completely transformed naval warfare. Diesel electric submarines had proven effective in both world wars; however, they were severely limited in underwater speed and endurance. Nuclear-powered submarines offered the possibility of operating, while submerged, indefinitely and at high speeds. Five years after his team started exploring possibilities at Oak Ridge, Rickover completed the work and persuaded his navy and atomic energy superiors that a nuclear-powered submarine was possible and practical.

Congress gave the Atomic Energy Commission (AEC) sole development and regulatory authority over nuclear power applications, military as well as civilian. For naval nuclear power, Rickover was the bridge between the two agencies, holding simultaneously the navy position of assistant chief of the Bureau of Ships for the Naval Nuclear Propulsion Program and the AEC position of director of the Division of Naval Reactors. This arrangement was instrumental to Rickover's success. It provided a significant measure of autonomy and direct access to senior executive and legislative branch officials. It enabled him to assemble personnel and resources beyond what either agency would otherwise have been willing to provide.[13]

By February 1950, the navy saw sufficient promise in the program to include in its shipbuilding budget the construction of the world's first nuclear-powered submarine, later named *Nautilus*. It helped that the AEC had borne all the nuclear propulsion plant development costs. Support from the navy, however, was not unanimous. Then, as would be the case in subsequent naval nuclear projects, there were always those who were convinced that nuclear power was too expensive. From almost the beginning, Rickover recognized ionizing radiation as the potential Achilles' heel of naval nuclear power. Instead of designing to accepted national standards, he developed more conservative design, manufacturing, and operating procedures to minimize crew and public exposure to ionizing radiation. He wove this philosophy of safety so thoroughly into the fabric of the naval nuclear program that "no civilian or military personnel in the Naval Nuclear Propulsion Program have ever exceeded the Federal lifetime radiation exposure limit or the Federal annual limit in effect at the time."[14]

On 17 January 1955, Rickover delivered the USS *Nautilus*, a spectacular technological achievement. In the eight years since he arrived in Oak Ridge, he had won project approval, recruited and trained a management staff, developed cutting-edge technology with unprecedented design and manufacturing standards, and recruited, advised, and trained industrial manufacturers in the specialty disciplines required for nuclear power. Moreover, he designed, built, integrated, and tested the multitude of mechanical, electrical, and steam propulsion systems and components required for naval nuclear application. He selected and trained nuclear propulsion plant operators and ship commanders and established special safety maintenance procedures and protocols. Rickover developed and delivered this revolutionary warship in a fraction of the time that the AEC experts had predicted.[15]

The traditional, conservative approach to the project would have been to build and test equipment and systems in the shop, without regard to space limitations; to prove concepts; and then to redesign the systems to scale. To save time and money, however, Rickover opted for the often risky concurrent development approach. He was convinced that by exercising close headquarters technical control over all aspects of the project, he would be able to successfully design, build, and test shock-resistant and maintainable equipment and systems in exact shipboard configurations. He ordered reactor, propulsion plant, and ship designers to design and build a land-based prototype propulsion plant exactly to the configuration needed for ship construction. This allowed time for problems to surface in prototype construction that could be avoided in ship construction. Rickover's insistence on building as a design tool a full-scale, wooden mockup of the submarine's nuclear propulsion plant turned out to be brilliant. Designers, construction teams, testers, operators, and maintenance crews used this mockup and mockups for the designs that followed to critique and refine designs, shipboard arrangements, and operating and maintenance procedures. The full-scale wooden mockup and the land-based prototype were important Rickover innovations in technological development, and he gave credit for them to navy skepticism. In July 1958 Rickover noted, "One of the most wonderful things that happened in our *Nautilus* development was that everybody knew it was going to fail—so they left us completely alone so we were able to do the job."[16]

The *Nautilus* performed well in sea trials. Rickover himself led the trials from onboard, a practice of responsibility that he continued during the initial sea trials for the many ships he subsequently built. Rickover's presence on initial sea trials demonstrated his personal commitment to making sure that they were conducted properly and, should something go wrong, that he was there to make decisions and accept responsibility. His presence also showed the crews the significance he attached to the events and his confidence both in them and in the ships. The *Nautilus* would log more than a half-million nautical miles before being officially decommissioned in 1980. The revolutionary ship won Rickover worldwide recognition as the father of the nuclear submarine. Indeed, with his subsequent development of nuclear-powered surface cruisers, destroyers, and aircraft carriers, he became the father of the nuclear navy. Rickover's brand of technical leadership showed the importance of accountability—of personally participating in critical events to demonstrate concern for crew safety and to show his supreme confidence in both product and crew.

While Rickover was developing the world's first nuclear-powered submarine, two successive navy flag selection boards, in 1951 and 1952, passed him over for promotion. By his own account, Rickover had "stepped on many toes." Biographer Francis Duncan explained it this way: "Often scathing in his comments about others and contemptuous of social niceties required in official life, he could be cutting and abrasive, leaving behind him resentment for remarks that were burned into memory."[17] By law, his failure to be selected for flag rank meant he would have to retire in June 1953.

Rickover's senior staff brought the problem to Congressman Sidney Yates, who enlisted the support of newly elected senator Henry "Scoop" Jackson. The senator, who knew and admired Rickover, was a member of the Senate Armed Services Committee. The navy needed the committee to confirm all navy promotions to flag rank. With behind-the-scenes support from Rickover's staff, these two members of Congress rallied congressional and press support. His plight became big news nationally, with articles and editorials in *Time*, *Life*, the *Washington Post*, and the *New York Times Magazine* that protested the navy's unwillingness to promote the service's leading technology officer.[18] As a consequence, the Senate delayed the promotion of thirty-nine admirals. To break the impasse, the secretary of the navy instructed the selection board on the need for a nuclear-experienced flag officer, a position that uniquely fit Rickover. The line officers, who composed the majority of the selection board, voted to promote Rickover, whereas the engineering duty officers voted against him.[19] In the end, Rickover won. Determined to rid its ranks of an abrasive, contentious, and unconventional officer, the navy had instead made him a national hero. Moreover, all of the fanfare built for Rickover a reliable base of congressional support that grew with his subsequent accomplishments. Although no one knew it then, his navy career would be extended by three decades, during which he was largely immune from executive branch bureaucracy.[20]

The success of the *Nautilus* was dramatic confirmation of Rickover's stellar technological leadership. But he did not stop there. He continued with the development of nuclear-powered aircraft carriers, a cruiser, and destroyers. He developed ever faster, quieter submarine propulsion plants, eventually reaching his goal of building "life of the ship" reactor cores that never had to be replaced. The Soviet Union, which relied almost entirely on its submarines to counter enemy surface ship and submarine threats and to disrupt seagoing commerce, possessed a formidable and numerically superior submarine fleet. The Soviets built faster, deeper-diving submarines. Their ballistic missile subs could hide beneath the Arctic ice and then surface if necessary to launch missiles against U.S. cities. However, the superior quieting and more sophisticated acoustic sensors of American submarines gave U.S. skippers a substantial tactical advantage over their Soviet counterparts, who had to assume that they were being followed and targeted by enemy submarines whether they were or not. The Soviets' noisier ballistic missile submarines had to be escorted by attack submarines, whereas U.S. ballistic missile subs could simply rely on their superior quieting for self-defense. The Soviet Union spent lavishly trying to overcome U.S. technological superiority in submarines. Although the reasons for the demise of the Soviet Union remain subject to academic debate, straining the Soviet economy through massive defense spending was part of the Reagan-era strategy.[21] Intimately aware of the situation, Rickover and his people were certain that they had contributed significantly to the end of the cold war.

The admiral's leadership and technological achievements extended beyond nuclear-powered warships. He also designed, developed, and constructed America's first civilian nuclear-powered electrical power plant at Shippingport, Pennsylvania. The U.S. government made the related technology, design, and operating procedures available to the public, and the plant's design became the world's model for pressurized water nuclear reactor electric power generation.[22]

Central to Rickover's success were an extraordinary determination and an insatiable appetite for work. The navy, especially the nuclear navy, was his life's passion. At work, his desk was his command center. From there, he managed voluminous paperwork and engaged in countless telephone calls and personal visits from staffers. He avoided social lunches, preferring to eat soup and fruit in his office while continuing to work. Often, this was a time for Rickover to philosophize with senior members of his staff. Day in, day out, the admiral was easily accessible. Section heads typically enjoyed immediate access. When Rickover was not available, the caller could ask to be put on "the list," which the admiral usually cleared within a couple of hours. By day's end, he ensured his "in" basket was empty. For hard work, Rickover often said, there is no substitute. He labored six long days per week and did not hesitate to make work-related telephone calls on the seventh.

A hallmark of Rickover's effective technological leadership was his determination to stay abreast of the current situation and to actively support his subordinates. As he remarked, "Capable people will not work for long where they cannot get prompt decisions and actions from their superior."[23] For this reason, Rickover tried to minimize his time away from his office. When traveling short distances to evening meetings, he preferred to leave in the late afternoon, sleep at his destination, and return directly to his office early the next morning. On longer, cross-country jaunts, he had his mail couriered to him. He remained always in charge; no one sat in for him in his absence. On-site meetings were highly efficient. Rickover's staff arrived early to meet with local officials, and together they crafted a clear, purposeful agenda for the session with the admiral that focused on current status, problems, and actions taken and recommended. Before a meeting adjourned, each senior representative was required to sign a summary of any agreements made, which included who would take action and when. As a technology leader, Rickover insisted on formal documentation of technical and programmatic decisions. He required written agendas prior to approving staff travel. His office kept a tracer system to ensure the traveler issued a timely, formal trip report. He viewed trips and meetings without signed agreements and commitments as frivolous wastes of time and money.

Rickover was totally committed to his profession. Convinced that leading by example was important, he wanted to be visible and available, and thus he rarely took personal leave. Section heads had to obtain his signature on their leave requests. The author cannot recall an instance in which Rickover did not approve anyone's leave request, but the practice deterred most from asking for more than a two-week vacation. Getting the admiral to sign one's leave chit also was a powerful incentive to be sure one's work was completed. Rickover joined no private clubs or organizations. He avoided movies and parties. His social life consisted primarily of evenings and Sundays with his wife—and reading. The admiral played no sports, but on doctor's orders he walked a brisk mile every day. In bad weather, he walked his mile around the hallways of his Washington headquarters, often discussing business with a section head who was forced to keep pace. Rickover was not involved in youth sporting leagues, the Boy Scouts, theater groups, or charitable events. He turned down suggestions that he use his prominence to promote Jewish causes.

Rickover, uninterested in material possessions, lived simply. An office yeoman paid his bills, deposited his paychecks, withdrew cash for him, and balanced his checkbook. He did not own a car. For more than thirty years, he and his wife lived in the same modest one-bedroom apartment on Connecticut Avenue in Washington, DC.[24] He was a focused man, determined to drive himself and others toward significant accomplishments. He did this for the good of the nation but also for individual fulfillment. Rickover once described it this way: "The essence of a purpose in life [is] to work, to create, to excel, and to be concerned about the world and its affairs."[25]

In his limited spare time, Rickover broadened his intellect by reading history, biographies, and autobiographies. He approached even this favorite recreation with sensitivity to its possible application to his work. Ever disciplined, he recorded ideas and thoughts about the readings and had them transcribed and tabulated so that he could draw on them for speeches and testimony. Audiences were often surprised to discover that this highly respected engineer who operated at the forefront of technology was so well read in other fields and able to place his work and other contemporary events into historical and philosophical contexts. His revolutionary accomplishments in nuclear power, together with his candor, wit, erudite observations, and humor, provided welcome relief for legislators. Attendance at his hearings before Congress was usually very good, and people rarely left disappointed. By the 1960s Rickover was a living legend who usually provided an entertaining respite from the drudgery that budget hearings often entailed.

Rickover thrived on hard work. An uncommon leadership trait was his ability to move easily from problem to problem without getting bogged down in any one. Even for potentially serious problems, he would focus, size up the situation with key staff, determine a course of action, and then shift his attention while others worked on the problem. He found great meaning and satisfaction in what he did. He was accomplishing something important in association with highly intelligent people who shared his passion. He took pleasure in seeing subordinates develop and in using his prestige and personal network to support them. He once stated, "I have accumulated over the years a considerable amount of 'grease.' For equipment, grease in the can is of no value; it must be applied. Use me." The navy taxed Rickover's mind and talents and provided him intellectual and social stimulation.

Demonstrating his commitment to technological leadership, Rickover wrote books and gave speeches on wide-ranging topics that often seemed only remotely related to his job. He published three books on improving American public schools, including his most popular work, *Education and Freedom* (1960). These books helped to focus public attention on the need for improved technical education in the post-*Sputnik* era. He championed national educational standards and testing long before the ideas became widely accepted. Rickover's strong sense of civic responsibility was another unconventional aspect of his leadership style that motivated his subordinates. Members of Congress sought Rickover's advice on public policy issues ranging from education and environmental protection to defense acquisition policies and practices. Over vigorous objections by some of the nation's most powerful lobbying groups, Rickover persuaded Congress to require cost accounting standards for government contracts and defense contractor certifications of claims made under government contracts. Historians, too, were influenced by Rickover's ideas. His 1976 book *How* the *Battleship "Maine" Was Destroyed* provided convincing evidence that a shipboard malfunction—not foreign mischief—had sunk the USS *Maine* in a Cuban port and triggered the Spanish-American War. One of Rickover's greatest leadership legacies, however, was the lasting culture of nuclear safety, environmental responsibility, and performance excellence, all of which stemmed from his skill in selecting, training, and leading people.

Asked to divulge the secret of his leadership success, Rickover often responded that "a boss should hire only people smarter than he is, then listen to them and do what they say." Just as he had developed a personal philosophy characterized by determination, innovation, and accountability, the admiral invested much of his career instilling those same qualities in his subordinates. Throughout his career with the Naval Nuclear Propulsion Program, the admiral maneuvered to secure the best, not the least threatening, personnel. To a class of aspiring navy technical leaders, he said, "Recruiting people who are more competent, or potentially more competent, than the head of the organization . . . is the single most important responsibility of the administrator, and he cannot delegate it."[26] The absolute importance of nuclear safety convinced the navy brass to give him dibs on hiring the brightest newly commissioned officers. No officer, however, was accepted into the nuclear program without being carefully screened by Rickover's senior staff and interviewed by the admiral himself.

No efforts were made to sell candidates on the importance or prestige of the nuclear program. To the contrary, Rickover wanted to see how determined each applicant was to join the program. Before the interview, candidates were required to sign commitments to serve five years in the program if selected. Prior to entering the admiral's office, each candidate had been interviewed by two or three of his senior headquarters staff members. The interviewers provided their personal written assessments and recommendations, but no matter how positive or negative their recommendations to the admiral, he personally interviewed each candidate. For each interview, Rickover had before him the recommendations from these staff interviews as well as summaries of the candidate's background, education, grades, and accomplishments. His interview was the final, crucial step. Often, Rickover tested the promise of candidates by subjecting them to intense interrogation. He was a master in turning almost any answer against the candidate. He was convinced that this was the best, most efficient way to distinguish between those who could think on their feet and those who were accustomed to getting by with mindless platitudes. The interview process also served as a crash introduction to the world of the Naval Nuclear Propulsion Program. For most, their Rickover interview was memorable, if not pleasant. Years afterward, many were still able to recount the exchange in detail. The tenor of the interview was not always a reliable bellwether: many who left his office dispirited were surprised to learn they had been selected.

Rickover's interview process was time consuming, but he was convinced of its importance, and he enjoyed it. The interviews provided a break from routine and a welcome encounter with bright young minds. What he learned from candidates sometimes fed his outspoken public criticism of American schools, including the Naval Academy. Rickover acknowledged that his selection process was imperfect. Those he rejected were not necessarily failures, and not everyone he hired became a star performer. In his words, "I have never accepted an officer without an interview. The batting average based on performance is about 60 percent. This is much greater than is usually found in industry for similar important jobs. Twenty-five percent would be considered very good."[27] Nevertheless, the pains he took to seek out the right people for the job underscore how important it was to managing sophisticated technology. It was inconceivable to him that a program leader would delegate the all-important responsibility of hiring to subordinates.

Rickover preferred newly commissioned officers. More experienced officers might have developed poor attitudes and work habits. Prospective nuclear reactor operators, both officers and enlisted men, spent six months in classroom training. This was followed by six months of practical, land-based reactor training. Rickover forbade the use of simulators in training. "Simulators are not an acceptable training device for naval operators," he testified. Using actual nuclear reactors, he believed, best ensured that trainees took their responsibilities seriously. Today, naval reactor operators still train and qualify on real reactors, but they also receive supplementary training on sophisticated simulators that can simulate accident conditions that are impossible to replicate safely on real reactors. After successful shore-based training, operator graduates report for sea duty, where they train and requalify to operate the particular shipboard reactor.[28]

One-time qualification was not enough in Rickover's day, either. To maintain technical proficiency throughout the nuclear fleet, he required continued training and requalification for nuclear operators through each sea duty tour. Every year, a special team of experienced officers tested crews on their knowledge and execution of operating and maintenance procedures. To qualify as an engineering department head, junior officers had to pass rigorous written and oral examinations at Rickover's headquarters. Those who failed the exam were dropped from the program. Prospective commanding officers for nuclear ships had to take an intensive, three-month course in which they studied under and were extensively tested by senior reactor experts. Throughout their careers, nuclear-trained officers had to demonstrate their technical competence. Admiral Kinnard R. McKee, Rickover's successor, often underscored the point by suggesting that one might ask a brain surgeon when he or she last had to requalify. Central to Rickover's technical leadership was the conviction that "the training of our people goes on forever."[29] Rickover recognized that technological proficiency does not end with rollout. Management continuity and effective and continual training of the appropriate personnel is as necessary as quality engineering.

Because naval nuclear engineers designed but did not operate reactors, their formal training started with a year of practical engineering duty within one of the technical sections of the program's headquarters. This was followed by six months of formal postgraduate education in naval nuclear propulsion engineering under senior engineers at the Bettis Atomic Power Laboratory. In the early years of the program, Rickover sent selected engineers to the Massachusetts Institute of Technology for postgraduate nuclear education. Later, he developed within the program suitable education and training abilities, and he generally discouraged his people from pursuing advanced degrees after hours, considering them an unnecessary distraction.

Whereas nuclear personnel were engaged in continuous training, Rickover sometimes joked that his two main jobs in the program were "mail-router and training officer." He said, "I probably spend about 99 percent of my time on what others may call 'petty details.' But if the person in charge does not . . . concern himself with details . . . neither will his subordinates."[30] Rickover's legendary attention to detail, however, did not stifle staff initiative and accountability as one might expect. He believed that "everything in this world is done by or through people."[31] His entire approach to technical leadership was predicated on this proposition, and he executed it superbly.[32] He charged his staff with the responsibility for all aspects of their jobs; it was up to them to determine and accomplish their tasks. He applied the same principles to his field representatives, defense contractors, and nuclear-powered ship commanders. "When doing a job—any job," he said, "one must feel that he *owns* it and act as if he will stay in the job 'forever.'"[33]

In leading his staff, Rickover expected not deference but innovation and action. He encouraged people to argue about issues on the merits of their positions and without regard to one's rank or position. "Free discussion," he said, "requires an atmosphere unembarrassed by any suggestion of authority or even respect."[34] His objective was to determine the best course of action, not to achieve consensus. The maximum benefits of intellectual debate, he believed, would arise only from an atmosphere that was free from deference to authority. A sycophantic subordinate was useless to him. As a result, loud, spirited exchanges were common. Only in the Pentagon, Rickover liked to say, was intelligence measured by the gold on one's uniform. Both the military personnel who were assigned to his headquarters staff and his military representatives in the field were required to wear civilian clothes. The initiative, creativity, and free exchange of ideas Rickover encouraged kept his command at the forefront of technological innovation.

Rickover encouraged open discussion, but he demanded accountability. On all documents submitted for his approval, every section head affected by the decision had to initial his support or explain his objections in writing. There were no Lone Rangers bypassing colleagues to cut special deals with the boss. Disagreements were settled in the admiral's office. At these meetings, Rickover often acted not as a moderator or judge but rather as an advocate for one side or the other. Wanting unvarnished conviction from his staff, he had no patience for those who sought to mask their own views by contending they were only playing the devil's advocate. If he thought a subordinate's argument stupid, he would say so, but subordinates could and did rebut him. Once the admiral documented his decision, he expected his staff to collaborate in its execution. Sometimes one or more staff members would come back the following day with a memorandum recommending and justifying reconsideration. Rickover did not exactly welcome these epistles with open arms. But whether or not he changed his decision, he accepted the appeal as an act of loyalty and conviction, not a challenge to his authority.

Rickover rarely reversed a major decision, even an imperfect one. This principle provided invaluable organizational stability, allowing his people to act with confidence. He never expected perfect decisions. Nevertheless, he knew that a technology leader must be accountable, have the courage to face unpleasant facts, recognize when he has made a serious mistake, and, if warranted, change course: "Don't defend past actions; what is right today may be wrong tomorrow. . . . Consistency is the refuge of fools."[35] In April 1965, after conducting a meticulous assessment of technical problems in developing the civilian seed-blanket light water breeder reactor that he had agreed to develop to pump water for California, he promptly reported to the AEC, to the governor of California, and to Congress that the project would take far more time than California could afford. He terminated the project. Instead of recriminations, he earned respect for his promptness and candor.[36]

To promote personal accountability and streamline the decision-making process, Rickover employed a flat organizational structure that purposefully minimized hierarchy. He had no executive officer or technical director to delay, filter, or distort information coming from or going to more than twenty headquarters section heads and a large number of field representatives, ship commanders, and contractors who reported directly to him. Rickover dismissed the conventional management theory that a leader could generally supervise effectively only five to seven subordinates. "What would I do with the rest of my day?" he asked. "How would I stay interested?" Rickover did employ a deputy on whom he relied heavily for a wide variety of matters, including managing personnel and training program-wide. But all section heads and field representatives reported directly to Rickover.

Rickover did not use organization charts, administrative manuals, or mission statements. Instead, he made the organization's broad objectives sufficiently simple that they did not need to be formalized. Each person's job, in brief, was to ensure the safe, reliable application of nuclear power and to spend government money as if it were his own. Rickover believed charts and job descriptions tended to limit individual responsibility, whereas his leadership philosophy emphasized innovation and accountability. Rank, position, and title had little relevance within Rickover's headquarters organization, although everyone there knew which people he relied on most. The admiral called all personnel by their last names. The sections that reported to him were commonly known throughout the program by the section head's name, not by function or code number. There was no break-down of section code number or telephone listing from which others might figure out the hierarchy of Rickover's staff. Age was no indica-tor of status, either. Some of his top people were very young by gov-ernment standards. Outsiders found it safest to assume that everyone they dealt with from the admiral's staff had his ear, which gave even relatively junior personnel considerable influence they would not have enjoyed elsewhere. But it was also true that important information that came even to the lowest levels of Rickover's staff tended to get to him quickly. More than once, the author, as a very junior navy lieutenant, met with some navy captain or admiral and reported the results to Rickover, and within ten minutes, the admiral was on the phone with that person expressing his appreciation or condemnation.

Throughout his headquarters, Rickover applied the same ac-countability precept he previously used so effectively in the Bureau of Ships' electrical section. Each section head possessed full cradle-to-grave responsibility for his area, including planning, budgeting, contracting, and logistical support. It was each section leader's job to coordinate his work formally with all other sections that could be affected, including project officers, systems engineers, radiation and environmental specialists, and the business section, which co-ordinated budgeting, contracting, and logistical support. A group of experienced, nuclear-qualified naval officers known as the "Line Locker" managed the nuclear training program, liaised with the fleet operators, and provided the sections with valuable fleet operator in-put. Before a section could spend money, approve a design, modify equipment, approve contract placement, or launch a new initiative, it had to have a prime contractor recommendation, including technical justification and associated contract, schedule, and cost ramifications, and the formal concurrence of all affected parties. The project of-ficers helped ensure the input and approval of all affected parties. In essence, the program operated with a self-regulating structure, one that allowed Rickover to engage issues selectively without usurping section head responsibilities. His emphasis on individual accountabil-ity made this possible.

Beyond stressing personal responsibility, Rickover used daily correspondence, telephone calls, and face-to-face conversations to establish discipline, to motivate, and to teach important principles. By working twenty-four hours a day, he quipped, one person might do the work of three. By training others and allowing them to assume more work, one could accomplish much more.[37] The admiral did more than just train and supervise his people. He willingly shared information and acted promptly on their requests. He obtained appropriations to support their work and made himself readily available. Moreover, with help from several trusted section heads, he fended off outside distractions so that the rest of the staff could focus on their work. In return, Rickover expected his subordinates to think, to initiate, to communicate, to identify problems, to act responsibly, and to request help when needed.

In Rickover's Naval Nuclear Propulsion Program, all problems, whether related to technology, scheduling, finances, or other factors, were opportunities for improvement; however, responsibility had to be assigned. Aware that most people were not conditioned to freely criticize colleagues—particularly close associates—Rickover made problem reporting a virtue. The price of suppressing bad news, or being oblivious of problems, could be as high as losing Rickover's respect and confidence or even being removed from the job, if not from the program. Candid problem reporting became so ingrained throughout the Naval Nuclear Propulsion Program that it lost much of its stigma. Problem identification and reporting, together with action planning to correct the course, are essential for leaders seeking to push technological change.

Rickover also held subordinates accountable by requiring continuous reporting in the form of "Dear Admiral" letters from all field representatives and weekly phone calls from those at critical work sites. Prime contractors and commanding officers frequently wrote letters. These candid and detailed briefs reported on problems, new or ongoing, and on corrective actions taken. Each letter had to state clearly whether assistance was needed from Rickover or from his staff. "Share good news with your spouse," he counseled. "All I care about are the problems." Rickover knew that the requirement to write weekly letters pressured people to think constantly about their jobs and to investigate and resolve problems. Without this impetus, even good subordinates, when isolated from headquarters, often settled into comfortable routines and succumbed to overly friendly relations with those they were supposed to monitor. Rickover knew from practical experience that even in well-run operations, problems abounded. Those who reported no problems, he believed, were either lazy or oblivious of reality. The "Dear Admiral" letters kept Rickover informed but also reinforced the importance of each person's accountability. They gave field representatives clout, not only with the site managers they oversaw but also with the section heads at headquarters. Field representatives had the same direct access to the boss as did section heads. Rickover emphasized that the duty of a navy field representative was to represent the government to the contractor, not the contractor to the government.

There was no doubt that Rickover read the "Dear Admiral" letters as well as the mountain of reports and correspondence that daily crossed his desk. He almost always reacted quickly, and sometimes dramatically. He might call to encourage or seek clarification from an author; on the other hand, he might bypass the author and take direct action with senior contractor management. In just a few moments, the admiral could focus senior management on the need to fix a problem immediately. In the process, he dramatically validated the importance of the incoming correspondence and greatly strengthened the hands of his field representatives in their future dealings with site management. Rickover saw his job as that of a demanding customer dealing from strength, not as an affable contractor teammate.

Rickover often scribbled comments on the "Dear Admiral" letters and other documents. Sometimes the commentary consisted only of question marks, exclamation points, or slashes. Other times, "Nuts!" "No!" "See so-and-so!" On the latter occasions, he would also write a large J (a code to his secretary) and the initials of the section head from whom he wanted a response. To clear these so-called J notes, section heads had to persuade the admiral by written response that proper action had been taken. The J note system required little of Rickover's time but had far-reaching impact on the organization. The notes held individuals accountable and reminded recipients of the admiral's commitment to success.

Rickover rarely set time limits for responses to his queries, but sooner was always better than later. His questions became more difficult to answer with the passage of time. On occasion, Rickover sent J notes simply because he sensed problems. His staff then struggled to figure out what was bothering him by determining the facts, assessing the situation, and reporting back—either persuading him that all was OK or that they had taken appropriate corrective action. Rarely did they ask him for clarification. It was their job, not Rickover's, to determine what, if anything, needed doing and to supply the admiral with answers.

Lower-level subordinates who staffed the J notes and drafted responses learned from the experience, but the admiral's "pinks" system probably was even more effective in maintaining accountability. Typists at headquarters, under threat of expulsion, had to make a pink copy of every document they typed, which they carried to the mailroom without review by their superiors. Every few hours, the mailroom delivered the pinks to the admiral, who proceeded to comment on them in a fashion similar to the manner in which he responded to the J notes. He tabbed pinks that he questioned. A section head could clear a pink only by returning to Rickover with his personal folder of tabbed pinks in hand, show him the tabbed pink, explain the issue and how it had been resolved, and persuade him to "pull the tab," which meant he could release the letter. The pinks reinforced Rickover's leadership ideal of personal accountability and training, and under his system, even the most recent hires' performance was exposed. The pinks provided opportunities for subordinates at every level to demonstrate innovative problem solving—or to learn memorable lessons. They made individuals at all levels feel personally responsible and provided them opportunities to articulate their own ideas rather than simply parroting the views of their immediate bosses. Whatever Rickover's reaction to a pink, it demonstrated that the quality of each person's work was important to him. It was his way of avoiding complacency, and most of those on the receiving end of a Rickover tirade did not take it personally. Learning from one's mistakes could be uncomfortable but was not often job threatening. Deception or dishonesty, however, was never tolerated. Nuclear safety demanded candor and integrity.

Rickover, as a technology leader, emphasized the importance of personal integrity. Never was this trait more manifest than in his battles against corruption in the defense industry. To him the issue was not just money, although he believed government officials should be good stewards of public funds. Business and technical integrity, he was convinced, went hand in hand. He believed people who were crooked in financial matters would also be crooked in technical matters. Through congressional testimony, he exposed a variety of problems on this front, and he was always careful to make specific recommendations. During the 1960s, as corporate mergers and acquisitions became fashionable, Rickover warned against a growing preoccupation with stock prices at the expense of quality, sound engineering, and manufacturing efficiency. To Congress, he testified, "They don't care if they are manufacturing ships or horse turds—as long as they make a profit."[38] Business schools, he was convinced, fostered this dangerous attitude by unduly emphasizing data manipulation, particularly financial data. Seven years after Rickover began testifying about cost-charging irregularities, Congress established the Cost Accounting Standards Board, which prescribes standards to which government contractors must adhere. This battle was won despite objections from the American Institute of Certified Public Accountants, defense industry lobbyists, the Department of Defense, and the General Accounting Office. At Rickover's urging, Congress also mandated that contractors certify their claims under government contracts. The coupling of honest business dealings with technical excellence was but another example of the accountability and responsibility that were at the core of the admiral's leadership.

During the 1970s, Rickover launched a campaign against the nation's three largest shipbuilders, which had collectively filed $3 billion in phony claims against the navy. He showed navy and congressional officials how corporations could use false claims to postpone reporting large losses that, if disclosed, would depress stock prices. The admiral cared nothing about stockholders. Large corporations were using these phony claims to pressure government officials to make what he called horse-trade settlements independent of the amount the navy actually owed. This, he complained, corrupted the contracting process. It diverted technical and management attention from serious national security work and poisoned day-to-day working relations, to the detriment of efficient, quality production. As backlogs of unsettled claims grew, pressure mounted to settle the claims quickly and move forward. Rickover was the bottleneck; he used letters and public testimony to make it as difficult as he could for government contractors and government officials to enter into claim settlements independent of claim merits. Bailout claim settlements, he reasoned, would undermine the concept of competitive bidding. With large programs and billions of dollars in future revenue at stake, bidders in subsequent programs would be more tempted than ever to submit lowball bids, capture the military's business, and then use work-stoppage threats to force government bailouts to avoid delay in urgent defense programs.

Rickover well understood the risks of challenging senior defense officials and large, influential defense contractors. Regardless, he continued to speak out. The navy, eventually succumbing to congressional pressure brought by Rickover through the crusading U.S. Senator William Proxmire, referred the claims to the Justice Department for investigation of possible fraud. The Justice Department launched investigations, which resulted in the recommended prosecution of the contractor General Dynamics under the False Claims Act. While senior Justice Department officials were reviewing that recommendation, Admiral Rickover arrived at his home on the evening of 9 November 1981 from initial sea trials of the USS *Boston*. His wife, Eleanore, greeted him with the news she had heard on the radio: the Reagan administration had decided to retire Rickover from active duty at the end of January 1982. That same week, the Justice

Department's fraud division chief called him to report that it would not prosecute General Dynamics. The rationale was that the navy had not been misled and that it had already settled the claims for more than it legally owed.[39] Rickover and his staff were convinced that his retirement and the administration's decision not to prosecute the shipbuilding claims were connected.

Over his six decades of service in the navy, Admiral Rickover adhered to a set of core leadership principles that he applied consistently. He was a unique individual, a true character who, as a leader, eagerly seized opportunities. Rickover was a gifted technician, an engineer who benefited from both academic and practical training. He respected nature's limits and emphasized attention to technical detail. He recognized the need for leadership continuity in complex technical programs, and toward that end, he sought to hire and develop people who were smarter than he was, not those most likely to agree with him. He trained his people through hands-on, day-to-day efforts throughout their careers and inspired them to perform at exceptional levels. In decision making, he nearly always sought the counsel of his subordinates and generally heeded their advice. He instilled a strong sense of urgency and promoted individual responsibility, which made every job seem valuable. He often led by example. His work ethic, integrity, and commitment to public service were legendary. He delivered impressive results that revolutionized naval warfare. President Richard Nixon remarked, "The greatness of the American military service, and particularly the greatness of the Navy, is . . . because this man, who is controversial, this man, who comes up with unorthodox ideas, did not become submerged by the bureaucracy; because once genius is submerged by bureaucracy, a nation is doomed to mediocrity."[40]

Not everyone has the opportunity to capitalize on military urgency to lead effectively. Crisis situations are not requisite. Determination, innovation, and accountability—all hallmarks of Rickover's approach—are keys. The admiral demonstrated a keen ability to recognize and seize opportunities. Most important, he understood people and how to inspire them to do their best. Perhaps what made

Rickover such a leadership icon in the technological realm was his ability to recognize, nurture, and employ natural human desire to pursue excellence. He summed it up this way: "Happiness comes from the full use of one's power to achieve excellence. Life is potentially an empty hole. There are few more satisfying ways of filling it than by achieving and exercising excellence."[41]

Notes

1. Hyman G. Rickover, "Doing a Job" (speech at Columbia University, New York, 5 November 1981).

2. Theodore Rockwell, *The Rickover Effect: How One Man Made a Difference* (Annapolis, MD: Naval Institute Press, 1992), 323.

3. Francis Duncan, *Rickover: The Struggle for Excellence* (Annapolis, MD: Naval Institute Press, 2001), 10–11.

4. Unless otherwise noted, quotations of and information about Rickover are from the author's personal observations and experiences.

5. Rockwell, *Rickover Effect*, 22.

6. Duncan, *Struggle for Excellence*, 27.

7. Ibid., 55.

8. Rockwell, *Rickover Effect*, 72.

9. Hyman G. Rickover, "Comments to the Navy Postgraduate School" (Monterey, CA, 16 March 1954).

10. Ibid.

11. Duncan, *Struggle for Excellence*, 83–88.

12. Ibid., 96–99.

13. Richard G. Hewlett and Francis Duncan, *Nuclear Navy, 1946–1962* (Chicago: University of Chicago Press, 1974), 92.

14. *The United States Naval Nuclear Propulsion Program* (Department of Energy and Department of the Navy, March 2007).

15. Francis Duncan, *Rickover and the Nuclear Navy: The Discipline of Technology* (Annapolis, MD: Naval Institute Press, 1990), 246–47; Rockwell, *Rickover Effect*, 59, 87, 146.

16. Gary E. Weir and Walter J. Boyne, *Rising Tide: The Untold Story of the Russian Submarines That Fought the Cold War* (New York: Basic Books, 2003), 62.

17. Duncan, *Rickover and the Nuclear Navy*, 14.

18. See ibid., 13.

19. Rockwell, *Rickover Effect*, 144–57.

20. Rickover commented to the author on several occasions, "If the damn fools had just promoted me the first time, they could have ordered me elsewhere for a few years and retired me. Instead, look what they got."

21. Sherry Sontag and Christopher Drew with Annette Lawrence Drew, *Blind Man's Bluff: The Untold Story of American Submarine Espionage* (New York: Public Affairs, 1998), 275.

22. Rockwell, *Rickover Effect*, 294–95.

23. Rickover, "Doing a Job."

24. Duncan, *Struggle for Excellence*, 71.

25. Hyman G. Rickover, "Thoughts on Man's Purpose in Life" (speech, Rotary Club of San Diego, CA, 2 October 1977).

26. Rickover, "Comments to the Navy Postgraduate School."

27. Ibid.

28. Joint Economic Committee, *Economics of Defense Policy: Adm. H. G. Rickover*, 97th Cong., 2nd sess., pt. 1, 28 January 1982, 74.

29. Rickover, "Comments to the Navy Postgraduate School."

30. Rickover, "Doing a Job."

31. Rickover, "Comments to the Navy Postgraduate School."

32. Rickover, "Doing a Job."

33. Ibid.

34. Rickover, "Comments to the Navy Postgraduate School."

35. Ibid.

36. Duncan, *Rickover and the Nuclear Navy*, 217–19.

37. Rickover, "Comments to the Navy Postgraduate School."

38. Rickover quoted in *Time*, "Rebellion Rampant in the Yards," 26 July 1976.

39. Patrick Tyler, *Running Critical: The Silent War, Rickover, and General Dynamics* (New York: Harper and Row, 1986), 321–22.

40. Richard Nixon, "Remarks at a Promotion Ceremony for Admiral Hyman G. Rickover" (3 December 1973), The American Presidency Project, University of California, Santa Barbara, http://www.presidency.ucsb.edu/ws/print.php?pid=4058.

41. Rickover, "Thoughts on Man's Purpose."

8

Adaptive Leadership

Harold G. "Hal" Moore

H. R. McMaster

In *Command in War*, Martin van Creveld notes that "the history of command in war consists of an endless quest for certainty."[1] In the 1990s, consistent with van Creveld's observation, initiatives under the auspices of "defense transformation" sought to achieve "dominant battlespace knowledge" to permit commanders to make the right decisions, target the enemy with precision munitions, and even anticipate enemy reactions. In 1995, Admiral William A. Owens, the vice chairman of the Joint Chiefs of Staff, predicted that it would soon be possible to "see and understand everything on the battlefield."[2] The vision of future war as lying in the realm of certainty rather than uncertainty, however, is ahistorical, neglecting the complexity of combat and ignoring factors that place certainty in war beyond the reach of emerging technologies. Recent combat operations in Afghanistan and Iraq have exposed flaws in the conceptual foundation for defense transformation. Moreover, they have focused attention on the political, human, psychological, and cultural dimensions of armed conflict, all of which make and keep combat unpredictable.

Indeed, philosopher of war Carl von Clausewitz's observation that the uncertainty and complexity of combat demanded leaders who possessed "military genius" seems as relevant today as it did nearly two centuries ago. Clausewitz argued that commanders needed intellect, courage, and determination—the three principal com-

HAROLD G. "HAL" MOORE
(courtesy of Harold G. Moore)

ponents of military genius—to penetrate "the fog of greater or lesser uncertainty" that surrounds combat.[3] Effectively demonstrating these three traits would enable a leader to adapt when confronted with the unpredictable environment of combat.

Lieutenant General Harold G. "Hal" Moore possessed the characteristics of Clausewitz's military genius, and as a lieutenant colonel he demonstrated superior adaptability during one of the most storied battles in American military history, the Battle of Ia Drang Valley, 14–16 November 1965.

The First Battalion, Seventh Cavalry's heroic performance at landing zone X-ray in the Ia Drang Valley, chronicled in Moore and Joseph L. Galloway's classic book *We Were Soldiers Once . . . and Young* and in the movie *We Were Soldiers*, revealed the lieutenant colonel's extraordinary ability to adapt to the uncertainties of battle against a vastly larger and very determined enemy. In the ensuing action, the First Battalion killed over six hundred North Vietnamese Army soldiers while losing seventy-nine of its own troopers. Moore's preparation for command, especially his development of the ability to evaluate his environment and make appropriate adjustments, was consistent with Clausewitz's charge that commanders must gain a broad understanding of the nature of combat "to illuminate all phases of warfare through critical inquiry and guide him in his self-inquiry."[4] Moore's career-long preparation, combined with his intellect, courage, and determination, enabled him and his battalion to achieve an improbable victory under uncertain conditions.

As a seventeen-year-old pursuing an appointment to West Point in 1940, Moore already showed signs of determination and adaptability. Believing his chances of success would be better in Washington, DC, than in his native Kentucky, Moore moved to the capital, where he found a job in a Senate office. Two years later, a Kentucky congressman did offer Moore an academy appointment, but to the Naval Academy at Annapolis instead of the Military Academy at West Point. Unwilling to give up, Moore offered an alternative to the representative: if Moore could find a West Point appointee willing to go to the Naval Academy, would the congressman appoint Moore to the West Point opening? The two Kentuckians agreed, and soon after, Moore donned a uniform of cadet gray. Through tenacity and creative thinking, Moore found a way to reach his objective.[5]

After graduating from West Point, Moore continued to develop his intellect as a soldier and leader, taking advantage of every opportunity to study the art of war. In addition to operations assignments, his career provided him with opportunities to read and think about the profession of arms. In various assignments he developed operational concepts for future war, taught tactics at West Point, and attended the staff and war colleges. He recognized what British historian Sir Michael E. Howard observed was one of the principal difficulties with which a military professional must contend: "His profession is almost unique in that he may have to exercise it only once in a lifetime, if indeed that often." Moore studied military history as Howard recommended—in width, in depth, and in context.[6] Moore encouraged fellow officers to "read military history" and to consider broadly how warfare had changed over time, as well as to study particular battles in detail to gain an appreciation for the complex causality of events and outcomes. He advocated "visiting battlefields with maps and texts in hand" for that purpose. Indeed, soon after his arrival in Vietnam, having recently read Bernard Fall's *Street without Joy*, an account of French failures in Indochina, Moore and Sergeant Major Basil Plumley visited the site of the June 1954 Viet Minh ambush that destroyed the French army's Mobile Group One Hundred along Route 19 west of An Khe and Pleiku. After visiting the battleground, Moore vowed that he would never underestimate the enemy that his battalion would soon face.[7] Decades later, reflecting on the Battle of Ia Drang Valley, Moore acknowledged the importance of his earlier preparation: "Everything I'd learned at West Point, my service in the Korean War and the study of leadership in battle, I put into action."[8]

Moore's study of military history permitted him to place his own experiences in context to appreciate both their value and their limitations and therefore to better adapt to change. For example, he recognized that the mainly static defensive operations he experienced during the Korean War were largely the result of the war's political context and the lengthy armistice negotiations. After Korea, Moore taught infantry tactics at West Point, attended the Command and General Staff College at Fort Leavenworth, and served at the Pentagon as "a one-man air mobility branch." In the latter assignment, Moore developed innovative ideas about future conflict that he would put into practice in Vietnam. He had one-on-one discussions with some of the most visionary and experienced senior officers in the army, including generals James M. Gavin and Hamilton H. Howze. Moore helped to develop air mobility concepts designed to increase the tempo of operations and strike the enemy from unexpected angles, all to seize and retain the initiative in battle. Even before experiencing the mainly defensive battles in the latter stage of the Korean War, Moore had experimented with air mobile operations following World War II. As a young lieutenant serving as an assistant operations officer for an airborne regiment, he planned a series of airborne operations on the Japanese island of Hokkaido to confirm that the Japanese military was no longer using airfields and other military facilities.[9] Moore bridged theory and practice in the fall of 1964, soon after assuming command of the First Battalion, Seventh Cavalry, at Fort Benning, Georgia. The battalion performed with great distinction during the air mobile tests in the Carolinas. After the Carolina exercises, the army chief of staff asked Moore to teach other officers about the emerging tactics. Moore's early commitment to intellectual development enabled him to earn a reputation as one of the most innovative tacticians in the army.[10]

Although Moore adapted tactics to technological advances, he was perhaps even more aware of how human nature and psychology contributed to the uncertainties of combat.[11] Moore's view of the human dimension of war was consistent with military historian John Keegan's conclusions on the phenomenon of battle:

What battles have in common is human: the behavior of men struggling to reconcile their instinct for self-preservation, their sense of honor and the achievement of some aim over which other men are ready to kill them. The study of battle is therefore always a study of fear and usually of courage; always of leadership, usually of obedience; always of compulsion, sometimes of insubordination; always of anxiety, sometimes of elation or catharsis; always of uncertainty and doubt, misinformation and misapprehension, usually of faith and sometimes of vision; always of violence, sometimes also of cruelty, self-sacrifice, compassion; above all, it is always a study of solidarity and usually also of disintegration—for it is toward the disintegration of human groups that battle is directed.[12]

Moore's close reading of military history as well as his combat experience convinced him that "the personality of a big battle is often formed by small unit actions."[13] He also knew that, in battle, soldiers fought primarily for one another.[14] He believed that determination, discipline, competent leadership, confidence, and cohesion served as bulwarks against fear and unit disintegration. Given the inherent uncertainty of battle, Moore recognized that these traits would enable a unit to adapt to any contingency. He therefore set out to develop those qualities in every unit he commanded, including the First Battalion, Seventh Cavalry.

Through extensive training, a continuous emphasis on discipline, and dedication to excellence, Moore consciously built an agile unit capable of adapting to unforeseen and difficult conditions. He challenged his soldiers and units to meet high standards. He used physical training, guard mount, and weekly parades to instill discipline and a commitment to excellence. He fostered competition between units and did not permit the display of second-place trophies; in combat, second place is equivalent to losing. Moore even forbade soldiers to faint during parades and held leaders responsible if their soldiers did collapse.[15]

Moore set the highest standards for leaders under his command. He removed officers who were unable to meet his expectations but trusted those who proved themselves. Moore spread his adaptive leadership philosophy by decentralizing, or "powering down" authority to subordinates. He taught and practiced "mission orders" and encouraged his junior officers to adjust to the unexpected by making independent decisions. In 1964, just prior to departing for Vietnam, the First Battalion received an influx of green lieutenants. Moore adjusted by developing a specialized training program to ensure that the new platoon leaders had the basic knowledge, skills, and ability to lead their soldiers in battle. Because of the emphasis on air mobility operations, he ensured that all new leaders received capabilities briefings from experienced helicopter pilots. In training, new platoon leaders often found themselves in command of four helicopters when conducting decentralized operations.[16]

Moore especially understood the critical role of sergeants in his organization. He told the battalion that Sergeant Major Basil Plumley worked directly for him and him only and charged the sergeant major with developing the noncommissioned officers. Moore urged his new lieutenants to respect the experience and knowledge of their sergeants and to learn from them.[17]

Historian Michael Howard observes that many commanders fail at the beginning of a war because they "take too long to adjust themselves to reality, through a lack of hard preliminary thinking about what war would really be like."[18] Moore, however, developed a vision for combat operations in Vietnam that established a basis for adaptation; his battalion's training reflected his forward thinking. During the fourteen months before sailing for Vietnam, his battalion conducted extensive field training exercises, emphasizing helicopter-borne air assault operations and the integration of artillery and air support. Moore designed training scenarios to include unpredictable situations, casualties, and extraordinary physical exertion. During the exercises, Moore occasionally declared that a leader had been killed, pulled the man aside, and evaluated the unit's response. He believed that "a squad leader must be ready to command a platoon or the company." While in transit to Vietnam, Moore continued to conduct classes and chalk talks with his officers. His new lieutenants conducted training with their platoons to ensure that they understood how the battalion would fight as a team.[19]

Moore designed his training regimen to prepare soldiers and units for the physical and psychological uncertainties of combat in Vietnam. He understood that battle confidence derived from soldiers' trust in their own abilities, in their weapons, in their leaders, and in their unit's ability to fight together and to successfully adapt to the perilous and unpredictable conditions of battle. In short, Moore endeavored to build a "family of fighters."[20] He strived to develop and preserve a high degree of cohesion in the battalion. Just prior to departing for Vietnam, in addition to gaining many new lieutenants, the battalion lost nearly one hundred men because of expiring enlistments. With combat imminent, Moore and his commanders worked diligently to maintain unit cohesion despite the disruption of losing team members. Colonel John D. Herren, who as a captain commanded B Company in Moore's battalion, recalled that the "unit personality" and high degree of cohesion developed in training enabled the battalion to overcome the loss of key personnel.[21] Still, the ramifications were significant, affecting the unit from captains down to riflemen.[22]

As the battalion was deploying to Vietnam, Moore and his staff continued their "hard thinking" about overcoming the unpredictability of battle. Unsure about the specifics of their mission, he and his officers planned a contingent combat operation designed to secure territory for a primary base. Although never executed, the plan permitted Moore to develop a fundamental understanding of the terrain and the enemy. He held long discussions with then-captain Tony Nadal, who had already served a one-year tour in Vietnam as an advisor to the Army of the Republic of Vietnam. Nadal, who became the battalion intelligence officer and later commanded A Company, discussed with Moore the concept of small, helicopter-borne insertions to conduct reconnaissance. They agreed that when contact had been made with the enemy, additional forces would rapidly move in to reinforce the effort and envelop the enemy. Such thoughtful preparation would enable them to exploit opportunities and adapt tactics to developments on the ground.[23]

Moore possessed an uncanny ability to visualize operations, an ability he worked to develop throughout his career. As a young captain during the Korean War, he served as a regimental operations officer and an assistant division operations officer, positions usually reserved for the most talented majors in the organization. During that time, he seized the opportunity to observe regimental and battalion commanders. He learned many lessons, including the importance of deliberately studying terrain and conducting continuous reconnaissance. He also learned to form an accurate estimate of the situation from thorough terrain analysis, an understanding of his own force's capability, and an appreciation of the enemy's abilities. Moore came to believe that a commander must continuously think ahead and ask questions. An adaptive leader must anticipate problems and plan countermeasures to preempt them. He must also absorb detailed intelligence indicators and revise his estimate of the situation to anticipate enemy actions. Later Moore would give the following advice to commanders: "When there is nothing wrong—there's nothing wrong except—there's nothing wrong! That's exactly when a leader must be most alert."[24]

As the First Battalion sailed toward Vietnam, Moore continued to read and think broadly about combat. Captain Nadal brought with him a footlocker of books on Vietnam and counterinsurgency operations. Moore read a third of those books while in transit and held discussions with his officers on a wide range of subjects relevant to their mission.[25] Although those readings did not provide specific tactical solutions, they did inform him on the broad aspects of the mission and the nature of the enemy his battalion would face in Vietnam. Such self-education was consistent with Clausewitz's philosophy. Reading and study do not provide a leader with a "manual for action" but rather a means to "light his way, . . . train his judgment, and help him to avoid pitfalls."[26] In preparation for Vietnam, and across his career, Moore consciously built an intellectual foundation for command. His experience and thinking about war drove his commitment to extensive training, informed the decisions he made in battle, and prepared him to cope with the uncertainties of combat.

After emphasizing the "great role intellectual powers play in the higher forms of military genius," Clausewitz turned his attention to courage, which he described as the "soldier's first requirement." He further defined two types of courage: physical "courage in the face of personal danger" and moral "courage to accept responsibility." With advances in communications and transportation technology, an argument often emerges that it is advantageous for leaders to command from locations remote from the battlefield. Advocates of command from the rear believe that physical courage is no longer a vital quality for a commander; distance from the front provides a dispassionate and more comprehensive view for decision making. Moreover, they contend, reduced personal danger is an advantage because of the demoralizing effect a commander's loss might have on his soldiers. Moore staunchly opposed the practice of command from the rear. He agreed with British major general J. F. C. Fuller's assessment of "chateau generals" in World War I:

> A fallacy, which may be largely traced to the telephone, is that the further a commander is in the rear of his men, the more general a view can he obtain, because he will be less influenced by local considerations. It is a fallacy because, within certain limits, the further he is away from moral actualities, and unless he can sense them he will seldom be able fully to reason things out correctly. . . . But supposing him to be a man who cannot control his emotions, and one so influenced by local conditions that they obliterate his intelligence, that is supposing him to be a thoroughly bad general, he will not avoid bird's eye views twenty miles to the rear. For if he does so, on account of his limited self control he will be as strongly influenced by the rear atmosphere and all it will convey to him, as he would have been by the forward atmosphere had he remained forward to breathe it.[27]

Moore recalled that the single most important lesson he learned from studying effective commanders could be summarized in four words: "Lead from the front!"[28] At a time when many commanders believed that the helicopter was the ideal command platform because it afforded a broad view of the battlefield, Moore argued that his duty as commander required him to be forward with his men. He needed to set the example, to share the hardships and dangers, and to assess the situation before making decisions. He explained, "Some commanders used a helicopter as their personal mount. I never believed in that. You had to get on the ground with your troops to see and hear what was happening. You have to soak up firsthand information for your instincts to operate accurately. Besides, it's too easy to be crisp, cool, and detached at 1,500 feet; too easy to demand the impossible of your troops; too easy to make mistakes that are fatal only to those souls far below in the mud, the blood, and the confusion."[29] Moore accepted the personal risk. He believed that "any officer or any soldier for that matter, who worries that he will be hit, is a nuisance. The task and your duty come first."[30] Moore typically went into battle with his radio operator on the first helicopter lift. He told his commanders and staff that he needed to be forward "to get the smell of the fight."[31]

In the Ia Drang Valley, Moore organized his staff to maintain a comprehensive estimate even as he remained forward. Captain Gregory "Matt" Dillon operated a tactical command post, often from a helicopter with other critical officers, including the fire support officer, the forward air controller, and a liaison officer from the helicopter lift unit.[32] While Dillon and others of the command post ran the operation, issuing orders and coordinating fires and logistics, Moore focused on command. His commanders and staff knew to provide candid assessments and recommendations to inform his estimates and decisions. An effective commander, Moore believed, needed at least "one or two people under you who are totally trustworthy—who will be honest with you when you are going off track on an issue or situation." Indeed, Moore considered respectful dissent "the essence of loyalty."[33] For candid advice as a battalion and later brigade commander in Vietnam, Moore relied most heavily on Captain Dillon, his operations officer, and Sergeant Major Plumley.[34]

Even in intense combat, Moore remained calm and made time to evaluate the situation. He recalled that "in battle, I periodically detached myself mentally for a few seconds from the noise, the screams of the wounded, the explosions, the yelling, the smoke and dust, the intensity of it all and asked myself what am I doing that I should not be doing and what am I not doing that I should be doing to influence the situation in my favor?"[35] Sergeant Major Plumley described "the old man" as a "thinker" who was "always thinking about what was going to happen."[36] As Major General Fuller declared, "A man who cannot think clearly in a bullet zone is more suited for a monastery than the battlefield."[37] Moore was suited for the battlefield. Courage, and the self-composure that it produces, is an essential trait of adaptive leadership.

Clausewitz's third quality of military genius, determination, derives from, "first, an intellect that, even in the darkest hour, retains some glimmerings of the inner light which leads to truth; and second, the courage to follow this faint light wherever it might lead."[38] This combination of intellect and courage gives great commanders the coup d'oeil that allows "the quick recognition of a truth that the mind would ordinarily miss or would perceive only after long study and reflection." This ability to assess rapidly and accurately a given situation is the essence of adaptability. Captain Nadal believed that Moore was able to sense the appropriate course of action because he recognized the "truth" of a situation; "he knew the nature of a fight."[39] Moore knew that, no matter how long he took to contemplate decisions, he would never have all the information or time to remove uncertainty and risk from command in battle. He considered the initial plan for an operation as merely a "springboard into action," after which interaction with the enemy and unanticipated conditions would demand quick decision making and flexibility to seize and retain the initiative.[40] Moore would later advise commanders to "trust your instincts. In a critical, fast-moving battlefield situation, instincts and intuition amount to an instant estimate of the situation. Your instincts are the product of your education, training, reading, personality, and experience."[41] Clausewitz believed that determination was necessary to "limit the agonies of doubt and the perils of hesitation when the motives for action are inadequate."[42] Similarly, Moore declared that "if my head tells me one thing and my gut tells me something else, I always go with my gut."[43] Moore's performance as commander revealed that he indeed possessed the fortitude of mind and character to permit the First Battalion, Seventh Cavalry to defeat a much larger, well-trained, and determined enemy.

Although it is beyond the scope of this essay to recount the Battle of the Ia Drang Valley in its entirety, a brief analysis will demonstrate how Moore's preparation of the battalion paid off under fire and how Moore's military genius—his intellect, courage, and determination—manifested itself in his and his battalion's ability to adapt to the exigencies of battle.

Moore's anticipation of the mission in Ia Drang Valley and his preliminary commander's estimate of the situation served as the foundation for his adaptive decision making during the battle. On 12 November 1965, the assistant division commander, Brigadier General Richard Knowles, visited Moore and mentioned that he would not object to a battalion-sized operation in the Ia Drang Valley near the Cambodian border. Moore and his staff immediately initiated a map study of the area. Moore recalled that he "ran an endless string of 'what ifs' through my mind," including "what I could do to influence the action if the worst case scenario came to pass." He concluded that he would have to be forward to assess the situation and make rapid decisions. Moore would be the first soldier on the landing zone.[44]

At 5:00 PM on 13 November, Moore received a warning order. The battalion responded immediately by consolidating forces in preparation for the operation. Within five hours the battalion completed all necessary preparations. Meanwhile, Moore and his staff formulated a tentative battle plan and arranged for an aerial reconnaissance. Early the next morning, Moore himself conducted the reconnaissance as artillery batteries moved into supporting positions. Moore returned to his command post after selecting the site for landing zone X-ray. He issued only a brief verbal order: the landings would begin at 10:30 AM.[45] Moore recognized that this large, complex operation would be different from the smaller, company-sized operations the battalion had been conducting. The battalion's ability to adjust effectively on short notice to a new mission was a product of its intense air mobility training conducted at Fort Benning and in the Carolinas. The battalion's officers and sergeants knew how to prepare for the operation and how to fight. A lengthy written order was unnecessary.[46]

Preliminary intelligence indicated that the battalion was headed for battle with a substantial North Vietnamese force. The aerial reconnaissance Moore ordered identified communications wire crossing a trail just north of the planned landing zone. Intelligence collectors also intercepted a radio transmission emanating from the Chu Pong massif, a large mountain located just west of the landing zone. The transmission, in Mandarin, indicated a large, well-organized force.[47] Moore used those scraps of intelligence to revise his estimate of the situation. Upon arriving at the landing zone, he immediately made adjustments to the plan. He carefully surveyed the terrain. His attention was drawn south and west, where the enemy could use concealed routes to approach the landing zone. He ordered a shift in B Company's mission—an intensification of its reconnaissance to the west of the landing zone on the far side of a creek bed. Shortly after moving out, B Company captured a prisoner who indicated that approximately 1,600 North Vietnamese soldiers were located on the Chu Pong massif and they "very much wanted to kill Americans." At the outset of the fight, the 160 U.S. soldiers who had arrived at the landing zone faced an enemy force ten times that size.[48]

Soon B Company was in contact with the vanguard of an enemy force moving toward the landing zone. B Company's mission was to establish contact with the enemy and "hit him before he could hit us." Moore understood the criticality of the terrain. He also had a sense of time and timing. He needed to get the rest of the battalion into the landing zone and control enough ground to establish an effective defense. "Only if we brought the enemy to battle deep in the trees and brush," he recalled, "would we stand even a slim chance of holding on to the clearing and getting the rest of the battalion landed."[49] The commander of B Company, Captain Herren, believed that if Moore had not adapted his tactics and ordered the reconnaissance mission on the far side of the creek bed, and if B Company had not "hit the enemy head-on," the North Vietnamese would have moved unimpeded to the landing zone and might have overwhelmed the battalion's lead elements.[50]

Moore made other critical decisions as the fight developed, analyzing and then prioritizing actions. He knew that the landing zone was key terrain that had to be defended. He told A Company commander Captain Nadal that "the original plan was out the window." Instead of conducting reconnaissance to the west, Nadal's company would establish defensive positions to block the attacking enemy. Nadal thought that Moore's early decision to send B Company to make contact with the enemy and his subsequent decision to employ A Company in defensive positions "combined aggressiveness with sound judgment."[51] When Moore received word that one of B Company's platoons had been cut off, he resisted the temptation to organize an immediate relief effort. Captain Herren maintained that if Moore had committed the remaining companies piecemeal into an offensive relief operation, "the LZ [landing zone] would have been overrun and the integrity of the battalion threatened."[52]

Moore's forward location and his ability to make decisions under uncertain conditions were paramount to the battalion's survival. Captain Nadal's A Company soldiers were in heavy contact with the enemy as soon as they occupied defensive positions. The operations officer, Captain Dillon, who was in a helicopter command post, recalled that none of the factors on which Moore based his early decisions were discernible from the air.[53]

Moore knew that in rapidly changing circumstances, a commander had to "be ahead of the game, be proactive not reactive, see the trends and have confidence in [his] vision."[54] Over the next two days, he made a series of decisions that anticipated enemy actions. Benefiting from his Korean War experience, Moore strengthened defensive positions where he believed the enemy perceived weakness. Unable to be strong everywhere, he accepted risks elsewhere. He applied artillery and aerial fires at critical times and locations. On the second morning of the battle, he formed a reserve and employed it at the critical place and time to defeat a determined enemy attack.[55]

Moore also understood that under intense battle conditions he had to do more than make the right decisions; he had to project a calm, positive presence before his soldiers. A desperate fight was developing, and Moore's forward location and the calmness with which he commanded inspired confidence among his soldiers. When Herren's platoons were cut off, Moore deliberately organized artillery and air support. At the most trying moments—when casualties mounted, when the enemy penetrated the defenses, when friendly fire impacted inside the perimeter—Moore remained calm.[56] For Moore, an adaptive commander must

> exhibit his determination to prevail no matter what the odds or how desperate the situation . . . [and] display the WILL TO WIN by his actions, his words, his tone of voice on the radio and face to face, his appearance, his demeanor, his countenance, the look in his eyes. He must remain calm and cool. NO fear. [He] must ignore the noise, dust, smoke, explosions, screams of the wounded, the yells, the dead lying around him. That is all NORMAL!
>
> [He] must never give off any hint or evidence that he is uncertain about a positive outcome, even in the most desperate of situations.
>
> Again, the principle which must be driven into your own head and the heads of your men is: *Three strikes and you're NOT out!*
>
> . . . There is always one more thing you can do to influence any situation in your favor.[57]

In other words, the commander must be determined to identify alternatives and adapt. Moore was confident that "training and dogged determination, tenacity, and willpower can turn the tide of battle." He believed that "if you think you might lose, you have already lost, in whatever enterprise you are involved in."[58] During a lull in the battle, Moore walked the perimeter to look every soldier in the eye, to assess their morale, and to steel their resolve.[59]

Moore struck a balance between the desire to be directly involved in the fight and the need to think clearly and anticipate the next action. He decided, for example, against moving with B Company deep into the forest lest he "get pinned down and become simply another rifleman." His operations officer managed the fight, but when necessary, Moore intervened. He later recalled that "until the LZ went hot, Matt Dillon and Mickey Parrish had controlled all the flights into X-Ray from the command chopper overhead. No more. I took control because only I knew where my men were, where the enemy ground fire was coming from, and where the safest spot to land was at any given moment. From this point forward, every helicopter coming into X-Ray would radio me for landing instructions."[60] Just as he developed a sense for the next enemy action, he also knew when to intervene.

In retrospect it is clear that Moore's personal preparation for command and his preparation of the battalion were keys to the unit's success in the Ia Drang Valley. His soldiers and leaders took initiative and demonstrated the courage, determination, confidence, and adaptability necessary to overcome the confusion and fear of battle. As they had done in training, soldiers assumed the responsibilities of those who fell. For example, leadership of B Company's "lost platoon" passed from the platoon leader to the platoon sergeant, to a squad leader, and ultimately to Sergeant Ernie Savage.[61] During those three November days, there were countless other instances of extraordinary heroism and leadership.

While Moore displayed the adaptability inherent in the intellect, courage, and determination of Clausewitz's military genius, it is clear that Moore possessed another quality: love for his fellow soldiers. Although he remained calm and unemotional during the battle, Moore showed emotion when he talked after the battle about his deep respect and affection for his troopers. He had vowed never to leave a fallen trooper behind, and he made good on that promise. He and his wife, Julie, did all they could to comfort the families of those who fell in battle. Moore, along with battlefield reporter Joe Galloway, honored the courageous troopers who fought in the Ia Drang Valley by telling their story in *We Were Soldiers Once*, one of the most compelling and moving accounts of men in battle ever written.

Moore's performance as an adaptive leader was brilliant. He later commanded his own brigade in Vietnam with great distinction and led his soldiers in highly successful operations. After the war he continued to set the standard by building disciplined and effective units as the commander of the Seventh Infantry Division in Korea and the commander of Fort Ord, California. As the army deputy chief of staff for personnel, his last position in the army, and in retirement, he remained a great teacher who inspired future generations of officers and soldiers. He communicated his message of "good, simple leadership" as well as his love for the American soldier.[62] He lived his own advice: "No matter how high in rank you go, never forget to keep instructing and talking with officers where the rubber meets the road."[63] It is impossible to gauge the influence of a man who was such a successful field commander and a great inspiration to so many. His influence spanned generations in the U.S. Army. Tony Nadal testified to Moore's integrity, his professionalism, his dedication to his family, and his genuine concern for others. He called Moore his "role model for life."[64] Ernie Savage described Moore as a man of "personal, moral, and spiritual courage."[65] After Moore spoke to the senior class at the U.S. Military Academy in 2002, one cadet remarked that Moore made him "feel proud [of] becoming an officer and entering into the Army as a profession."[66]

Notes

1. Martin van Creveld, *Command in War* (Cambridge, MA: Harvard University Press, 1985), 264.

2. Owens quoted in Williamson Murray, "Clausewitz Out, Computers In: Military Culture and Technological Hubris," *National Interest*, 1 June 1997, http://www.clausewitz.com/CWZHOME/Clause&Computers.html.

3. To review what Clausewitz identified as causes of uncertainty in war, see Carl von Clausewitz, *On War*, ed. and trans. Michael Howard and Peter Paret (Princeton, NJ: Princeton University Press, 1976), 80–90, 101, 113–14, 117–18, 119–21, 136–40, 148–50, 161, 184–91, 198–203, 577–78, 585, 605–10.

4. Ibid., 141.

5. Christy Truitt, "An American Soldier," *East Alabama Living*, Spring 2005, 61–62.

6. See Michael Howard, "The Use and Abuse of Military History," in *The Causes of War and Other Essays* (Cambridge, MA: Harvard University Press, 1983), 195–97.

7. Harold G. Moore, interview by the author, 8 February 2007. See Bernard Fall, *Street without Joy: The French Debacle in Indochina* (New York: Stackpole, 1994), 209–50.

8. Moore quoted in Truitt, "American Soldier," 63.

9. Moore, interview.

10. John D. Herren, interview by the author, 12 January 2007; Colonel John D. Herren, letter of support for the Distinguished Graduate Award, 31 October 2005, in the author's possession. See also Harold G. Moore and Joseph L. Galloway, *We Were Soldiers Once . . . and Young* (New York: Random House, 1992), 22–23.

11. Gregory P. Dillon, interview by the author, 11 January 2007.

12. John Keegan, *The Face of Battle: A Study of Agincourt, Waterloo, and the Somme* (London: Penguin, 1978), 303.

13. Moore quoted in Owen Connelly, *On War and Leadership: The Words of Combat Commanders from Frederick the Great to Norman Schwarzkopf* (Princeton, NJ: Princeton University Press, 2002), 214. See also Harold G. Moore, "Battlefield Leadership," 16 December 2003, http://www.au.af .mil/au/awc/awcgate/documents/moore.htm.

14. Harold G. Moore, lecture (United States Military Academy at West Point, NY, 22 April 2005).

15. Moore, "Battlefield Leadership"; Dillon, interview; Tony Nadal, interview by the author, 12 January 2007; Herren, interview; Moore and Galloway, *We Were Soldiers Once*, 18–19.

16. Moore, interview; Moore, lecture; Nadal, interview; Herren, interview; Dillon, interview. See also Moore and Galloway, *We Were Soldiers Once*, 24.

17. Basil Plumley, interview by the author, 9 February 2007; Moore and Galloway, *We Were Soldiers Once*, 22; Moore, lecture; Dillon, interview.

18. Howard, "Use and Abuse," 194.

19. Moore, interview; Moore, "Battlefield Leadership"; Moore, lecture. See also Moore and Galloway, *We Were Soldiers Once*, 23.

20. Harold G. Moore, "Hal Moore on Leadership in War and Peace," *Armchair General*, September 2004, 7.

21. Herren, interview.

22. William F. Jasper, "The Real Hal Moore," *New American*, 25 March 2002.

23. Nadal, interview; Moore, interview.

24. Moore, interview; Moore, "Battlefield Leadership"; Moore, lecture.

25. Nadal, interview; Dillon, interview; Moore and Galloway, *We Were Soldiers Once*, 22.

26. Clausewitz, *On War*, 141.

27. J. F. C. Fuller, *Generalship, Its Diseases and Their Cure: A Study of the Personal Factor in Command* (Harrisburg, PA: Military Service, 1936), 61–63.

28. Moore, interview.

29. Moore and Galloway, *We Were Soldiers Once*, 40.

30. Moore quoted in Brian M. Sobel, "Hal G. Moore: The Legacy and Lessons of an American Warrior," *Armchair General*, September 2004, 50.

31. Moore quoted in Nadal, interview.

32. Harold G. Moore, "After Action Report, Ia Drang Valley Operation 1st Battalion, 7th Cavalry, 14–16 November 1965," 9 December 1965, http://www.au.af.mil/au/awc/awcgate/vietnam/ia_drang.pdf.

33. Moore, "Leadership in War and Peace," 7.

34. Moore, interview.

35. Moore quoted in Cole Kingseed, "Beyond the Ia Drang Valley," *Army Magazine*, 1 November 2002, http://www.ausa.org/webpub/DeptArmyMagazine.nsf/byid/CCRN-6CCS62.

36. Plumley, interview.

37. Fuller, *Generalship*, 61–63.

38. Clausewitz, *On War*, 102.

39. Nadal, interview.

40. Dillon, interview.

41. Connelly, *On War and Leadership*, 215; Moore, lecture.

42. Clausewitz, *On War*, 102–3.

43. Moore, "Leadership in War and Peace," 7.

44. Moore and Galloway, *We Were Soldiers Once*, 40.

45. Moore, "After Action Report."

46. Moore, interview; Nadal, interview.

47. Dillon, interview; Moore, "After Action Report." See also Moore and Galloway, *We Were Soldiers Once*, 57.

48. Moore and Galloway, *We Were Soldiers Once*, 63–64.

49. Ibid., 64.

50. Herren, interview.

51. Moore and Galloway, *We Were Soldiers Once*, 64; Nadal, interview.

52. Herren, interview.

53. Dillon, interview.

54. Moore, interview.

55. Herren, interview; Dillon, interview.

56. Dillon, interview.

57. Moore, "Battlefield Leadership."

58. Moore quoted in Sobel, "Hal G. Moore," 53.

59. Moore and Galloway, *We Were Soldiers Once*, 131.

60. Ibid., 73, 108.

61. Ibid., 91.

62. Joseph L. Galloway, interview by the author, 8 December 2006.

63. Moore, interview.

64. Nadal, interview.

65. Savage quoted in Sobel, "Hal G. Moore," 56.

66. Quoted in Kingseed, "Beyond the Ia Drang Valley."

9

Exemplary Followership

Colin L. Powell

Jeffrey J. Matthews

Nine days before Christmas Day in 1989, General Colin L. Powell received word that an American marine lieutenant had been shot near a roadblock manned by the Panamanian Defense Forces. Powell also learned that a U.S. Navy lieutenant and his wife who had witnessed the shooting had been physically assaulted by Panamanian interrogators. On 20 December, these provocations, combined with Panama's increasingly volatile political situation under dictator Manuel Noriega, contributed to President George H. W. Bush's decision to launch a military invasion code-named Operation Just Cause. These events represented the first major foreign policy crisis not only for the Bush administration but also for Powell as the newly confirmed chairman of the Joint Chiefs of Staff (JCS).

After a stellar thirty-year career in the U.S. Army, the fifty-two-year-old Powell was the youngest person ever elevated to the chairmanship. He was also the first Reserve Officers' Training Corps graduate and the first African American to serve as chairman. Moreover, the Goldwater-Nichols Department of Defense Reorganization Act of 1986 had significantly enhanced the chairman's power, a transformation that Powell relished. Historically, the six members of the JCS had operated by watered-down consensus, but the chairman alone would now act as the senior military counselor to the president and to the secretary of defense. "I was no longer limited to a messenger

COLIN L. POWELL
(National Archives, College Park, MD)

role," Powell later wrote. "Now, I was the principal military advisor." As chairman, Powell was the highest-ranking uniformed member of the U.S. military, and he oversaw a JCS staff of 1,600 people. In addition, President Bush's secretary of defense, Richard "Dick" Cheney, inserted Powell directly into the chain of command by stipulating that all civilian orders to the military be channeled through the chairman. In spite of Powell's awesome power as the uniformed leader of America's armed forces, his primary professional duty as head of the JCS was that of a follower, providing expert counsel to his civilian leaders and overseeing the execution of their visions and decisions.[1]

Powell's entire military career, in fact, illustrates the all-important role of exemplary followership in the leadership process. Most people in positions of substantive organizational authority must also follow someone else in the hierarchy, which requires them to assume the complicated dual roles of follower and leader. There is little doubt that Powell emerged as an extraordinary leader during the first Bush administration. Indeed, in the afterglow of American military successes in Panama and the Persian Gulf War, Senator John S. McCain proclaimed Powell "the greatest military leader this country has produced since World War II."[2] But throughout Powell's tenure as a senior military officer—serving at the rank of colonel and higher—most of his job titles actually signaled the persistence of his follower status rather than his growing leadership authority. For example, he held the following key positions: executive assistant to the special assistant to the secretary and the deputy secretary of defense, military assistant to the deputy secretary of defense, executive assistant to the secretary of energy, senior military assistant to the deputy secretary of defense, assistant division commander for operations and training, deputy commanding general of combined arms combat development activity, senior military assistant to the secretary of defense, and deputy assistant to the president for national security affairs.[3]

In December 1987, when the U.S. Senate confirmed Powell as President Ronald W. Reagan's national security advisor, the general was rightfully elated for having reached a uniquely powerful position in the federal government. "I was no longer someone's aide or number two," he wrote. "I had become a 'principal,' with cabinet-level status, if not the rank." Clearly, Powell's position entailed tremendous responsibility and gave him potentially significant influence on government policy. In the end, however, his status was still more that of a follower than of a leader. He oversaw only a small staff, and his primary directive was to provide counsel in service of his boss's worldview. Again, his secondary role was plainly evident in his official title: assistant to the president for national security affairs. In his 1995 autobiography, even Powell admitted that his responsibilities were primarily supportive and administrative: "the guy who made the NSC [National Security Council] trains run."[4]

In tracing Powell's remarkably successful military career, we can examine the unsung yet pivotal role of exemplary followership. Among the most important attributes of highly effective followers are honesty, dependability, competence, courage, enthusiasm, assertiveness, and independent critical judgment. Until recently, the concept of followership has been given short shrift by leadership scholars, practitioners, and students. Preoccupation with leaders has come at the expense of appreciation for the crucial influence of followers, even though leadership success (or failure) has always been directly connected to both leaders and the led, not to mention the powerful forces of environmental factors. Furthermore, this analysis highlights the undeniable truths that most organizational leaders concurrently play the part of follower and that effective followership contributes to successful leadership development. Rare is the leadership position that is not simultaneously a position of followership.[5]

Colin Powell's potential as an exemplary follower and leader did not emerge clearly until he attended City College of New York in 1954. Nevertheless, in the years prior to university, his working-class, immigrant parents shaped the personality traits and moral values that became the foundation of his future successes in the military. Young Powell gleaned from his parents' example a dedicated work ethic, self-discipline, and high standards. His role model parents also instilled a lasting appreciation for formal education and a stringent moral code of selflessness, respect, honesty, and loyalty. They expected him to earn a college degree, and given the ten-dollar annual tuition, City College seemed the logical place for their obedient son to begin his life's journey.

Neither a gifted student nor a gifted athlete, Powell entered college as a teenager lacking intrinsic motivation and direction, both attributes of an exemplary follower. His eventual pursuit of a geology degree stemmed less from natural curiosity then from a sense of ease and convenience. The turning point of his young life came with his decision to enroll in the U.S. Army ROTC. Powell befriended fellow cadet Ronnie Brooks, the first in a long line of military role models and mentors who would help him develop into a highly skilled follower and leader. A year ahead of Powell, the tall and intelligent Brooks rose rapidly from cadet sergeant to battalion commander to drillmaster and to cadet colonel. Powell immersed himself in the military regimen and followed Brooks up the chain of command. Early on, Powell learned that dedicated and effective followership was instrumental to earning recognition and promotion and that the more he excelled as an accomplished and agreeable follower, the more other cadets turned to him as a model and mentor.[6]

Despite earning a dismal C– cumulative grade point average, Powell excelled in his ROTC courses and thus completed college as a distinguished military graduate in 1958. More important to him than academic grades, he had found his calling: soldiering. At twenty-one, Powell was still very much his parents' child: obedient, respectful, friendly, and conscientious. And though he was far from a deep, critical thinker, he had demonstrated at college independence, initiative, and competence, and he had calibrated a direction for his life. Much to his delight, his uncommon success within the ROTC program earned him a regular rather than reserve officer commission in the U.S. Army.[7]

After completing rigorous airborne and ranger training at Fort Benning, Georgia, Lieutenant Powell was stationed at Gelnhausen, West Germany, where he completed his initial apprenticeship as a professional leader and follower. Powell served as a platoon leader with the Forty-eighth Infantry. At twenty-one, the ROTC graduate was younger than many of the forty-five men under his command. An inexperienced leader, he found it challenging to promote group morale and to motivate his diverse followers, a mixture of volunteers and draftees. Wisely, he observed a highly respected subordinate, his seasoned platoon sergeant, who led effectively through a delicate balance of hard-nosed coercion and sincere concern for his troops. Learning from this example, Powell frequently adopted an open and compassionate approach, but he was less inclined to use coercive power. Instead, he sought to inspire quality performance by organizing professional competitions, which allowed him to evaluate and reward individual soldiers. Powell also learned valuable lessons from senior ranking role models. Captain William C. Louisell Jr., for example, reprimanded Powell for loudly berating a fellow soldier because of the tirade's demeaning effect. On another occasion, when Powell misplaced his sidearm, Captain Wilfred C. Morse chose not to file an official report. Instead, he confronted his green lieutenant, "scared the bejeezus out of him," and then dropped the matter. In the end, however, as evidenced by the following excerpt from his 1960 efficiency report, Powell's first tour of duty proved extraordinarily successful, revealing him to be both an effective follower and a burgeoning leader: "Lt. Powell is one of the most outstanding young Lieutenants I have seen. He is an original thinker, and his ideas are good. He is a driver and accepts responsibility willingly. He expresses his opinions quietly and convincingly. If his recommendation is not accepted, then he cheerfully and promptly executes the decision. He is calm and unexcitable. He is well liked by both superiors and subordinates. He has high standards and he demands and gets high standards. . . . [He is] one of the few exceptional officers who should be considered for more rapid promotion than his contemporaries."[8]

Powell's practical training as a follower and leader continued at Fort Devens, Massachusetts, where he served in the First Battle Group, Fourth Infantry for twenty months before heading to South Vietnam. While stateside, Powell received a first-rate education in followership from his superiors, including the astute Major Richard D. Ellison, who taught him "how to push the smart proposals, derail the dumb ones, and strangle the most embarrassing in the cradle, all the while keeping our superiors happy."[9] As a junior leader, Powell absorbed information and ideas from other young officers, and he again engaged his own soldiers in countless competitions to boost morale, confidence, and self-esteem. Fully committed to the U.S. Army, Powell proved a quick study, an intellectual trait that was not lost on his superiors. One leader described him as an ideal follower who possessed "keen insight and professional knowledge" and who "time and time again has gone beyond what was normally expected of him."[10]

By the time Powell arrived in Saigon on Christmas Day in 1962, he could draw on four and a half years of active duty experience. Recently promoted to captain, he served as a battalion advisor to the Third Infantry Regiment of the Army of the Republic of Vietnam, which was responsible for patrolling a stretch of the Laotian border. During this tour, Powell advised three very different Vietnamese commanders. Their varying leadership styles and levels of experience forced Powell to adjust carefully between following and leading. He developed a close personal bond with Captain Vo Cong Hieu, a well-respected and capable commander who often accepted Powell's counsel. Under Hieu, Powell learned the absolute importance of building trust and loyalty among one's followers. On one occasion, a U.S. marine gunner accidentally killed two South Vietnamese soldiers in Powell's unit. "I had trouble erasing the look of betrayal on the Vietnamese soldiers' faces," he recalled. But Powell's credibility rebounded when a Vietnamese private on lead patrol was saved by a protective vest. The American advisor had insisted that it be worn. Thereafter, the soldiers hailed Powell as "a leader of wisdom and foresight." Unfortunately, Hieu's replacement, Captain Kheim, was the antithesis of a good leader: egotistical, brash, and—most damning of all—disrespectful of his men. In contrast to Kheim, Powell delighted in developing personal bonds with the soldiers and was even known to lead them in song on Saturday nights. The Vietnamese regiment's third commander during Powell's tour, Captain Quang, was the least experienced, and he recognized that he lacked battlefield credibility among his four hundred followers. As a result, Powell, who enjoyed the full confidence of the combat unit, began acting as the de facto commander. "I was supposed to be an advisor, not the leader," he wrote in his memoir. "Nevertheless, the two of us were in quiet collusion. Leadership, like nature, abhors a vacuum. And I had been drawn in to fill the void." Powell's unofficial command of the Third Infantry Regiment ended in July 1963, when he stepped on a potentially lethal *punji* spike that pierced his right foot. A helicopter evacuated him from the A Shau Valley. He received a Purple Heart and served the remainder of his tour as an assistant operations advisor to the First Division of the Army of the Republic of Vietnam. His experience "in country" had demonstrated his professional competence and physical courage and had taught him much about balancing the complicated dual roles of follower and leader.[11]

In the four years before Powell returned to Vietnam for a second tour, he spent much of his time as a student or teacher, and both roles enriched his capacity to lead and follow. First, he furthered his martial expertise by completing pathfinder training and the Infantry Officer Advanced Course at Fort Benning. In 1966, Powell received early promotion to major and became a faculty member at the Army Infantry School. As an instructor, he improved his communication skills, learning how to project with authority, use physical gestures, and otherwise "hold center stage." Powell believed that the communication techniques he developed at Fort Benning were integral to his development as a professional soldier. The next year found Powell again seated in the student's chair, this time at the Command and General Staff College at Fort Leavenworth, Kansas. The purpose of the storied military school was to broaden the command perspectives of rising officers from platoon- and company-level leadership to the division level and beyond. One of the many benefits for Powell was gaining clearer insights into his own decision-making style. War gaming at Leavenworth, Powell would later write, "revealed a natural inclination to be prudent until I have enough information. Then I am ready to move boldly, even intuitively. . . . For me, it comes down simply to Stop, Look, Listen—then strike hard and fast with all the power you need."[12]

Major Powell graduated second in his class from the Command and General Staff College in spring 1968, and by July he had been assigned to the Third Battalion, First Infantry, Eleventh Infantry Brigade in Duc Pho, South Vietnam. During this tour, he did not serve in a battlefield advisory or pseudocommand position but rather as a staff administrator, first as the executive officer for the Third Battalion and then as a planning and operations officer at brigade headquarters. Nevertheless, while in Vietnam he performed his follower duties exceptionally well and further honed his already impressive communication skills through the "performing art" of military briefings.[13]

Although he was not in a direct combat role, Powell frequently visited infantry units in the field and returned to headquarters with dead and wounded aboard his helicopter. He himself demonstrated considerable heroism in November 1968 when he accompanied Major General Charles M. Gettys, the division commander, on an inspection of a recently captured North Vietnamese base camp. Their UH-1H helicopter crashed while attempting a difficult jungle landing, and Powell, though hampered by a broken ankle, managed to pull Gettys from the smoking wreckage. With the help of others at the scene, he also rescued the general's aide, his chief of staff, and one of the pilots. For his calm, decisive action, he earned the prestigious Soldier's Medal. In May 1969, as Powell approached the end of his tour, General Gettys offered effusive praise for his follower's analytical intelligence, professional competence, and agreeable temperament: "His broad knowledge of the military, spirit of cooperation, and unique ability to rapidly sift through voluminous information, extract and analyze pertinent data, and reach a sound decision was immediately recognized. . . . His ability, knowledge and helpful cooperative attitude were . . . widely known. . . . In fact, he earned the respect and admiration of his superiors and subordinates alike."[14]

After more than a decade in the U.S. Army, Powell had demonstrated to his superior officers many attributes of an exemplary follower: enthusiasm, confidence, competence, courage, collegiality, loyalty, determination, and dependability. There was no doubting his intelligence, but even Powell would later admit that he had not yet developed a proclivity for independent critical thought or a willingness to question the ideas of his superiors. The most valuable followers possess these traits. Over the years, Powell had witnessed a pervasiveness of "poor management practices" within the army, ones that often promoted style over substance. This mode of operation was referred to as "breaking starch." Powell explained, "Rather than blowing the whistle, senior officers went along with the game and junior officers concluded this was how it was played." He openly confessed that he "broke starch with the best of them."[15]

In regard to Vietnam, Powell also admitted his unquestioning support for President Lyndon B. Johnson's foreign policy and the military's strategies and tactics. "I had no penetrating political insights into what was happening," he wrote. "I thought like a soldier who knew his perimeter, and not much more." Serving in Vietnam, he never thought twice about setting ablaze local villages and ransacking food stores. After chronicling such activities in his 1995 memoir, Powell wrote, "However chilling this destruction of homes and crops reads in cold print today, as a young officer, I had been conditioned to believe in the wisdom of my superiors, and to obey." Beyond the conformist culture of the army, Powell's intellectual submissiveness in the 1960s was also driven by his personal ambition. He admitted to the dominance of "the career lobe of my brain. And, for a long time, I allowed myself to think only on that side, an officer answering the call, doing his best, 'content to fill a soldier's grave.' But as time passed and my perspective enlarged, another part of my brain began examining the experience more penetratingly. . . . A corrosive careerism had infected the Army; and I was part of it."[16]

After Powell returned to the United States in the summer of 1969, he received promotion to lieutenant colonel and earned an MBA at George Washington University. He subsequently served in the Pentagon in the office of Lieutenant General William E. DePuy, a visionary commander who was intent on reforming the army. Among other things, Powell learned from the fiery general the importance of imaginative, independent, and bold thinking by leaders and followers alike. "DePuy taught me something invaluable," he wrote, "about holding on to one's core of individuality in a profession marked by uniformity and the subordination of self." Powell's successful stint at the Pentagon led him to a one-year hitch as a White House Fellow, part of a program designed to provide promising young leaders, military and civilian, with a practical education in public policy development. As a self-described "fledgling student of power," Powell gained first-rate schooling on the "messy, disappointing, even shocking" processes of a functioning democracy by working as a special assistant to Fred Malek, the deputy director of the Office of Management and Budget. Malek, like DePuy before him, proved an influential role model who demonstrated to his army protégé the value of initiative, risk taking, and assertiveness. "Out of that experience," Powell declared, "emerged one of my rules: you don't know what you can get away with until you try." To Malek, Powell possessed the ideal traits of an effective follower, "very smart . . . very good with people, and . . . very well organized."[17]

In 1973 Powell was transferred to South Korea, where he assumed command of the Eighth Army's First Battalion, Thirty-second Infantry, Second Infantry Division. Working under the legendary Major General Henry E. "Gunfighter" Emerson, Powell had opportunities to demonstrate his followership skills and to develop his relatively untested leadership ability. As a follower, Powell was quick to comprehend Emerson's vision of reforming the Eighth Army, which was suffering badly from poor discipline, low morale, and racial tension. Emerson's solution was an active "pro-life program" that emphasized fierce group competition, strenuous physical training, live ammunition exercises, and basic academic education.

Although Powell believed that the Gunfighter could be overzealous in his methods, he was truly inspired by him and executed enthusiastically his boss's reforms. Like Emerson, Powell understood the motivational value of leading by example, and he participated fully in the battalion's grueling physical regimen. He understood that by following his commander, he was leading his own men. In Korea, as in previous assignments, Powell also observed and reflected on the varying leadership styles of his superiors. Powell was especially impressed by Brigadier General Harry Brooks, who balanced the Gunfighter's unbridled energy with "stability, coolness, and common sense." Powell's performance in Korea was not flawless, however. One night, he foolishly participated in a brawl that erupted in the officers' club. Emerson's decision to ignore the fracas reminded Powell of a valuable lesson he had learned in Germany: leading strictly by the book was not always the wisest course of action. Powell's overall performance in Korea made a lasting, positive impression on his colorful boss, who concluded, "Goddamn, this son of bitch can command soldiers. He was charismatic. He really raised the morale . . . of [his] unit. . . . He sure as shit showed me what he could do as a commander."[18]

By spring 1976, Powell had been promoted to full colonel and was serving as the commander of the Second Brigade of the 101st Airborne Division at Fort Campbell, Kentucky. There, he continued to demonstrate an extraordinary ability to succeed both as a follower and as a leader by consistently drawing on lessons he had learned. Powell admired the intelligence and confidence of his division commander, Major General John A. Wickham Jr., who would become an important mentor. Powell was forced, however, to contend most directly with his immediate superior, a brusque assistant division commander, Brigadier General Weldon C. "Tiger" Honeycutt, who "may have been the most profane man in the army." Upon his arrival at Fort Campbell, Honeycutt made perfectly clear to Powell that his new brigade was the worst-performing unit at the post. "We've got three infantry brigades," the general snapped. "Yours is dead-ass last. . . . So fix 'em. Now get your ass outta here." The situation only worsened for Powell when he discovered that his was the only brigade not invited to participate in the annual Reforger war games in Germany.[19]

Powell's response to the challenging circumstances was that of an exemplary follower: he saw it as an opportunity to excel. Through effective leadership, Powell fulfilled his boss's vision of a better-performing Second Brigade. One of the keys to his success was setting high standards for his people, especially his junior officers. For example, he decided that, while the two other brigades of the 101st Airborne were exercising in Germany, all of his officers and many of the enlisted personnel would earn prestigious air assault badges, which required passing a grueling physical test. Again leading by example, Powell, then thirty-nine years old, passed the test himself before informing his officers, including the chaplains, that they must become air assault qualified by winter. All of the officers met the challenge, save one chaplain who broke his leg and transferred out. When Powell's superiors returned from Europe, they were greatly impressed by his initiative and the unit's accomplishments. By successfully following his commander's orders, Powell had effectively led his soldiers.[20]

After only one year at Fort Campbell, Powell's growing reputation as a superb soldier led to a Pentagon appointment as the executive military assistant to John Kester, the de facto chief of staff for Harold Brown, President Jimmy Carter's defense secretary. During the next four years, Powell went on to serve as a military assistant to three deputy defense secretaries: Democrats Charles Duncan and W. Graham Claytor Jr. and Reagan Republican Frank Carlucci. These four years at the Pentagon resembled advanced graduate work in the realpolitik of institutional followership and leadership. He paid particular attention to the tense relations between the Defense Department's civilian leadership and its top military brass. Powell watched with some amazement Kester's power plays on behalf of Secretary Brown, which often came at the expense of the JCS. Powell found himself in the middle of turf wars, but as an exemplary follower, he remained loyal to his superiors, even though many of their decisions decreased the authority of the army's top generals. In 1979, when he became the military assistant to Charles Duncan, Powell, then forty-two years old, received promotion to brigadier general, making him the army's youngest general officer.[21]

During the Carter years, Powell also learned valuable lessons about tactical preparation and crisis management. In April 1980, the president approved Desert One, a joint military mission to rescue fifty-three American hostages held in Iran. The mission proved to be a complete debacle and led to the death of eight soldiers. Powell had no role in the rescue attempt, but he knew that he could learn from it. He analyzed the operation and noted severe flaws in planning, communications, weather forecasting, and chain of command. Beyond the mission's failure, Powell also studied the administration's approach to conveying the bad news to the American people. He judged its management of the affair a "public communications fiasco," for among other things, the administration refused to fully and quickly disclose the central facts of the tragedy and failed to admit that it had committed gross errors. Powell was learning from the mistakes of his leaders.[22]

After Ronald Reagan defeated Carter in the 1980 presidential election, Powell stayed on briefly at the Pentagon under Defense Secretary Carlucci. Fearing that he "was becoming more politician than soldier," however, he sought a field assignment and was gladly transferred to Fort Carson, Colorado, where he served as the assistant division commander for operations and training with the Fourth Infantry Division (Mechanized). As had been the case at Fort Campbell, Powell's new duty station presented him with a challenging leader-follower situation. His new boss, Major General John W. Hudachek, had a negative reputation as a no-nonsense, coercive, and dictatorial leader. Moreover, although Powell was a fast-rising brigadier general, his personal credibility with Hudachek suffered because of his relatively limited command record and his lack of direct experience leading tank soldiers. Wisely, Powell set out to enhance his credibility with both his boss and his subordinates by qualifying as an expert M-60 A1 tank gunner. Initially, this effort seemed to have positive effects. After several months, however, it was obvious to Powell that Hudachek's excessively controlling leadership style severely undermined the division's morale and performance. Because Hudachek's high-profile wife operated in a similar fashion, she had the same negative effect on soldiers' spouses. Powell, as the assistant division commander, served as "the buffer, lightning rod, and father confessor" between the post's disgruntled soldiers and spouses and the commanding general and his wife. The post's climate became so objectionable that Powell felt an obligation to broach the subject with his boss. In this instance, Powell's great challenge as a leader came from his position as a follower. Not surprisingly, neither Hudachek nor his wife appreciated his attempt to play the honest broker.[23]

Powell's standing with the commanding general suffered further when he approached Hudachek with another unsolicited recommendation, this time regarding troop readiness. Powell suggested that the division's performance could be enhanced by switching from the traditional annual general inspection to a perpetual surprise inspection process whereby individual companies were inspected at different times of the year. In the end, when it came to writing Powell's annual efficiency review, Hudachek rated the brigadier as being merely satisfactory, praising his ability as a "staff officer" and a "trainer" of soldiers but failing to praise his potential as a division commander. Powell believed that Hudachek's less than glowing review would derail his army career. "I had blown it," he thought. "Still, I had no regrets. I had done what I thought was right. . . . I was not going to whine or appeal, get mad at Hudachek, or go into a funk. I would live with the consequences." Exemplary followers are concerned about the well-being and performance of their units and subordinates, and when they demonstrate initiative and propose innovative solutions, they always run the risk of offending narrow-minded, egotistical leaders. Nevertheless, effective followers, guided by integrity, remain committed to their personal convictions and professionalism and are willing to be held accountable for their behavior.[24]

Fortunately for Powell, outside Fort Carson he possessed a reputation as a stellar subordinate, and this contributed to his reassignment to Fort Leavenworth in 1982. As Powell later confessed, his professional career had suffered "a gut wound," but he "survived." Powell's ability to survive, even advance, in the coming years was greatly enhanced by the direct intervention of several mentors. In the case of Fort Carson, Lieutenant General Julius W. Becton Jr. had learned of Powell's problems with the uncompromising Hudachek and had contacted General Edward C. Meyer, the army chief of staff. Shortly afterward, Powell was moved. He served successfully in Kansas for a year as the deputy commanding general of the Combined

Arms Combat Development Activity. Becton wrote to Powell, "No odds too great to overcome—even Hudachek notwithstanding." In 1983, much to Powell's chagrin but to the betterment of his career, he was reassigned to the Pentagon. This transfer was orchestrated by General Wickham, Powell's old Fort Campbell mentor, who had succeeded Meyer as the army's chief of staff. For the next three years, Powell served as the senior military assistant to Caspar W. "Cap" Weinberger, Reagan's defense secretary. It was another political—not command—assignment, but it secured for Powell a second star.[25]

Powell had attained the vaunted rank of major general, but his work under Secretary Weinberger largely demonstrated his exemplary followership skills. He described his staff position as "the Secretary's chief horse holder, dog robber, and gofer," but a significant part of Powell's job was to act as Weinberger's gatekeeper, controlling people's access to the defense secretary and helping him to manage his time. "I was a juggler," Powell later wrote, "trying to keep the egos of three service secretaries, four service chiefs, the Chairman of the Joint Chiefs, and other Pentagon pashas all in the air at once." Powell was ever the student of power and leadership, actively expanding his intelligence by observing and reflecting on the events, issues, and people around him. During those three years, he was particularly attuned to problems associated with crisis management; he studied America's withdrawal from Lebanon, its invasion of Granada, and the Soviet Union's downing of a Korean civilian jetliner.[26]

Weinberger's personal philosophy regarding the proper use of American military force had a pronounced and lasting influence on Powell's foreign policy outlook. Within the Reagan administration, Weinberger jousted frequently with Secretary of State George Shultz over the proper application of U.S. military power, with the former arguing for increased restraint. On 28 November 1984, a month after 241 marines were killed in Lebanon, Powell accompanied his boss to the National Press Club, where the defense secretary articulated the so-called Weinberger doctrine. Weinberger argued that American military force should be applied only as a last resort to protect vital national interests. Moreover, there should always be clear political and military goals to guide armed conflicts, and the objectives should have the support of Congress and the public.

Throughout his tenure under Weinberger, Powell performed his followership duties exceptionally well. He emerged from the position with a superior reputation not only for his commitment and competence but also for his intellect, trustworthiness, and honesty. In a 1986 assessment of Powell's performance, Weinberger wrote that "he was directly involved in every issue I faced as Secretary of Defense," and "in every way, Major General Powell's performance was unfailingly superlative. . . . Soldier, scholar, statesman—he does it all."[27]

In June 1986, after serving Weinberger for three years, Powell finally secured a premier leadership position as the commander of the V Corps in West Germany. Recently promoted to lieutenant general, Powell would lead seventy-five thousand soldiers, a superb opportunity to demonstrate to any doubters that he was an "able commanding general," not just a Pentagon politico. After less than six months, however, he was recalled yet again to Washington, DC, to serve in another critical followership role. In the aftermath of the Iran-contra affair, Frank Carlucci, now Reagan's national security advisor, recruited Powell to serve as his deputy. Carlucci knew Powell to be an ideal follower: intelligent, confident, experienced, loyal, positive, honest, and collaborative. It was Carlucci's opinion that over the years Powell had developed into "the world's best staff officer"; with his "upbeat and inclusive style and sense of humor, combined with his military bearing and crisp efficiency, [he] radiated competence and confidence." Above all, Carlucci needed Powell's superior organizational skills to help "impose order and procedure" on the National Security Council, which was left "rudderless, drifting, [and] demoralized" after the departure of renegades John Poindexter, Robert C. McFarlane, and Oliver North.[28]

Powell performed superbly at the National Security Council for two years, during which time he succeeded Carlucci as Reagan's national security advisor. Among the keys to his success as a follower were his willingness to assume responsibility, take the initiative, and work tactfully alongside other high-ranking White House officials.

These ideal followership attributes were especially valuable at the time because of Reagan's passive managerial style of delegating governing authority and responsibility to members of his cabinet. Reagan's passivity, according to Powell, "placed a tremendous burden on us. Until we got used to it, we felt uneasy implementing recommendations without a clear decision." At one point, Carlucci complained to Powell, "My God, we didn't sign on to run this country!" To compensate for the shortcomings of Reagan's leadership style, Powell and Carlucci created and led a policy review group that improved the communication and coordination of policy between departments and agencies, including the Defense and State departments, the JCS, the Central Intelligence Agency, and the office of the vice president.[29]

During the Reagan presidency, Powell developed good relations with Vice President George Bush, and only days after he won the 1988 presidential election, Bush invited the general to join his cabinet as the director of the CIA. Powell declined the offer, opting instead to become the commanding general of Forces Command, a leadership position responsible for the readiness of all U.S.-based army reservists, guardsmen, and active duty soldiers—nearly 1 million troops. The command position brought Powell a fourth general's star, but his tenure at Forces Command proved short lived. In August 1989, President Bush announced his intention to nominate Powell for the position of chairman of the JCS. Powell's biggest booster was Carlucci, the former defense secretary, who championed the general as "one of Washington's best problem solvers . . . a right-hand man who delivered results. . . . [who] had strong views and would push for them but . . . knew when to follow orders and fall in line with the boss."[30] The Senate confirmed Powell's nomination on 20 September 1989. The exemplary follower had become a preeminent leader.

Volatile political events in Panama immediately tested Powell's leadership and followership skills as the senior military advisor to President Bush and Defense Secretary Cheney. Powell, with the full support of the JCS, advised Bush and Cheney to intervene to protect U.S. citizens and the nation's access to the Panama Canal. When administration officials secured the cooperation of Guillermo Endara, the rival of corrupt dictator Manuel Noriega, Bush approved Operation Just Cause. The American military quickly overwhelmed the Panamanian Defense Forces. Endara was sworn in as the country's new president, and Noriega was captured and sentenced to prison in Florida. Twenty-four Americans died in the fighting along with approximately three hundred Panamanian soldiers and civilians.

For Powell, as both a follower and a leader, Operation Just Cause proved a valuable learning experience. He had studied President Bush's approach to decision making and had observed "the cool and solid" Cheney throughout the crisis. At one point, however, Cheney had sharply reminded Powell of his subordinate status. He complimented Powell's initiative and decisiveness: "You're off to a good start as chairman. You're forceful and you're taking charge. That's the way I want it." But Cheney balked at Powell's attempt to control all information sent to the secretary's office. The defense secretary made clear that he wanted information from multiple sources. "I was being shown my place," Powell wrote. He knew that "when the dust settled on this invasion, I would still be an advisor; but [Cheney] and the President would have to bear the responsibility." Beyond his followership role, Powell had performed well as the senior military officer during the Panama campaign. In that capacity, he labored to protect the tactical decision-making authority of the field generals. When twice the White House issued battle orders "from the sidelines," he approached Secretary Cheney to inform him that he "did not want to pass along any more such orders," that "we've got a perfectly good competent commander on the ground." After the successful operation, Powell willingly admitted that leadership mistakes had been made. To capture the Punta Paitilla airport, for example, only a small squad of U.S. Navy SEALs had been deployed, though a larger infantry unit would have been more appropriate. Four sailors died in that operation. There also had been insufficient planning to bolster the new Panamanian government and its security forces. Finally, the Pentagon had failed to accommodate the needs of the U.S. press corps. Powell's continual reflection on his experiences and the events and people around him furthered his ability to follow and lead successfully as the chairman of the JCS.[31]

Over the course of his military career, Powell came to believe that ideal subordinates were those who learned from past experiences, anticipated future events, and initiated plans of action to help their superiors define and achieve organizational objectives. Powell himself had routinely demonstrated such qualities of effective followership, and they remained fully evident during his years as chairman. "More than intelligence and discipline," journalist David Halberstam writes, Powell possessed "an exceptionally refined sense of anticipation, so important in a bureaucracy . . . the ability to sense what was going to happen next, and thereby to help his superior stay ahead of the play."[32] Providing sound guidance and advice to one's superiors is a key attribute of an influential and effective follower.

Powell demonstrated his skill in this arena when he decided, independent of the president and defense secretary, that his "main mission" was to convince them, his JCS colleagues, and Congress of the need to downsize and restructure the U.S. military. "My thoughts were guided simply," he wrote, "by what I had observed at world summits, by my experience at the NSC, by what I like to think of as informed intuition. I was going to project what I expected to happen over the next five years and try to design an Army, Navy, Air Force, and Marine Corps to match these expectations." While serving in the Reagan administration, Powell was among the few who had grown increasingly certain that the cold war was coming to a close. It had become clear to him that Soviet leader Mikhail Gorbachev "was a new man in a new age offering new opportunities for peace." In May 1989, as the commanding general of Forces Command, Powell had shared publicly his crystallizing view of a radically new future. In his speech "The Future Just Ain't What It Used to Be" (later reprinted in *Army* magazine), Powell declared the Soviet Union a "bankrupt" and "benign" enemy and intimated that Communist Poland, Hungary, and Czechoslovakia would one day press for admission to the North Atlantic Treaty Organization. Amid such fast-changing geopolitical realities, Powell argued, America's armed forces must make significant changes. His views were controversial. Powell also believed that as the decline of the Soviet threat became more apparent, Congress would move to cut the defense budget and thus force a military restructuring on the Pentagon. Anticipating the latter, Powell recognized the need for his superiors to seize the initiative: "We had to get in front . . . if we were to control our own destiny. . . . rather than having military reorganization schemes shoved down our throat."[33]

For the next several years, Powell oversaw the development of a "base force" plan. It was designed to greatly reduce the size of the U.S. military while maintaining its capability to fulfill several vital missions: to serve as a nuclear deterrent, to fight two simultaneous wars (across both the Pacific and the Atlantic), and to manage smaller, localized "hot spots" such as Panama. Powell encountered skepticism among administration officials and the JCS about the probability of a declining Soviet threat and thus the appropriateness of a drastically reduced defense budget. Nevertheless, Powell pursued his "missionary work" inside the White House, the Pentagon, and Congress. By August 1990, nine months after the fall of the Berlin Wall, Powell's visionary base force reorganization strategy had won the support of the president and defense secretary. It had not been an easy road to acceptance. "At times," Powell recalled, "I had been discouraged by setbacks and had almost given up hope. . . . The changes envisioned were enormous, from a total active duty strength of 2.1 million down to 1.6 million. . . . The plan . . . effectively marked the end of a forty-year-old strategy of communist containment."[34] In originating and championing the highly controversial base force plan, Powell had personified the independence, foresight, determination, and moral courage of a leader achieving his goals by being an exemplary follower.

Powell continued to demonstrate those important characteristics in the prelude to the Persian Gulf War. On 1 August 1990, the Iraqi Republican Guard invaded Kuwait. The Bush administration determined quickly that it was in the United States' vital interests to mount a defense of neighboring Saudi Arabia, and within a few days, American forces mobilized to defend the Saudi kingdom. Less clear and more complex was the issue of whether the United States should wage a war to liberate Kuwait. During a National Security Council meeting in which support for Saudi Arabia was reconfirmed, Powell directly posed the challenge to the president. To liberate Kuwait "would be the NFL, not a scrimmage. This would mean a major confrontation." His was a bald geopolitical judgment, and he immediately "detected a chill in the air." Powell realized that as the president's military advisor, he might have exceeded his role within the administration. Regardless, the general believed it was crucial that all potential policy objectives be put on the table. The cabinet meeting concluded without an answer to the Kuwait question. Shortly afterward, Defense Secretary Cheney chastised Powell for raising the issue at all, stating, "You're not Secretary of State. You're not the National Security Advisor anymore. And you're not Secretary of Defense. So stick to military matters." While Powell agreed that he had "overstepped," he did not regret pushing his superiors to clarify their policy objectives: "There had been cases in our past, particularly in the Vietnam period, when senior leaders, military leaders, did not force civilians to make those kind of clear choices, and if it caused me to be the skunk at the picnic . . . [they could all] take a deep smell." From the Vietnam experience, Powell had learned that the most responsible followers and leaders asked their superiors penetrating questions about important and difficult issues.[35]

Consistent with the qualities of an exemplary follower, Powell also sought to provide his bosses with different options for achieving their goals. The administration's ultimate objective became the ejection of Iraqi forces from Kuwait. General Powell advised caution regarding an offensive engagement with the 1-million-man Iraqi army, and he articulated the benefits of an alternative defensive containment policy supplemented by economic sanctions. Powell feared that Bush might opt prematurely or unnecessarily for war. Brent Scowcroft, Bush's national security advisor, was especially impressed by Powell's intellect and tactful ability to render independent judgments that were at times contrary to the thinking of his superiors. "Colin was very good that way," he wrote. "I never heard him contradict

Dick Cheney directly, but by the end of the meeting, you always knew where Colin stood. He was very deft at things like that. Colin kept thinking—longer than I did or Dick Cheney did, and probably longer than the president." On 24 September 1990, Powell met with Bush and Cheney at the White House. The general laid before them the various options, including containment and sanctions. "Thanks, Colin," the president responded. "That's useful. That's very interesting. It's good to consider all the angles. But I really don't think we have time for sanctions to work."[36]

With Bush leaning toward an offensive campaign, Powell shifted his thoughts to advising the president on the best strategy for defeating the Iraqi military and liberating Kuwait. With this change of focus, Powell continued to fulfill his responsibilities to the president even as he provided guidance to his subordinates to reorient their planning. Powell was alarmed when he learned that Bush hoped to prosecute the war by applying air power alone. Instead, Powell advocated a comprehensive war campaign that would combine massive air, land, and sea forces to capture the initiative and crush the Iraqi army. Given Bush's predisposition, the challenges for Powell were to construct a persuasive war plan and to amass sufficient forces in the region in a time frame that was acceptable to his anxious leader. To solve these problems, Powell relied extensively on General E. Norman Schwarzkopf, the American commander of Central Command who was made responsible for the defense of Saudi Arabia.

In working under Bush and Cheney and over Schwarzkopf during the Persian Gulf crisis, Powell again found himself in the complex dual roles of follower and leader. Moreover, Schwarzkopf's volatile personality and coercive demeanor complicated Powell's position between the senior civilian leadership and senior ranking field commander. On several occasions, a skeptical Cheney asked Powell if the hot-tempered Schwarzkopf was the best person to execute the president's military policy. Although Powell recognized Schwarzkopf's shortcomings, he believed him an extremely capable commanding general, and he consistently supported him in discussions with Cheney and the president.[37]

By early October 1990, with Schwarzkopf stationed in Saudi Arabia to oversee the buildup of an international defense force, Powell was under pressure from his superiors to produce an offensive war plan aimed at removing Iraqi forces from Kuwait. Powell telephoned Riyadh to seek a preliminary strategy from his field general. "I got no goddam offensive plan," Schwarzkopf hollered, "because I haven't got [sufficient] ground forces." Powell explained that he needed an attack plan, period. Ultimately, Schwarzkopf submitted a draft plan, but officials in the White House and Pentagon deemed the limited, unimaginative ground offensive "a loser." Powell pressured his field general to revise it.[38]

Powell himself collaborated with a select group of JCS war planners, and in late October he flew to Saudi Arabia to assist Schwarzkopf in devising a new, bolder ground attack plan. He also wanted to reassure Schwarzkopf that he had his complete confidence and support. Powell appreciated that his field general did not want to enter into battle without adequate forces; indeed, they both wanted to wage the war with overwhelming power. "Don't worry," Powell informed his general; "you won't be jumping off until you're ready. We're not going off half-cocked." To Schwarzkopf this was very welcome news. He later wrote, "I felt as though [Powell had] lifted a great load from my shoulders." For his part, President Bush had all but decided to eject Iraqi forces from Kuwait, but he would rely on the expertise of his military subordinates. "Colin Powell, ever the professional," Bush later wrote, "wisely wanted to be sure if we had to fight, we would do it right and not take half measures. He sought to ensure that there were sufficient troops for whatever option I wanted, and then freedom of action to do the job once the political decision had been made. I was determined that our military would have both." Having faithfully served the president, Powell was able to "lead up," convincing Bush to hold off the attack until adequate forces had been marshaled in the theater.[39]

In his memoir, Powell elaborated on the constant challenges of his dual leader-follower roles during the Gulf crisis:

> Between [Bush's] impatience and Norm Schwarzkopf's anxieties, I had my own juggling act. Norm displayed the natu-

ral apprehension of a field commander on the edge of war, magnified by his excitable personality. I had to reassure him constantly that he would not be rushed into combat. At the same time, the President was leaning on me: When are we going to be ready? When can we go? Dealing with Norm was like holding a hand grenade with pin pulled. Dealing with the President was like playing [the role of] Scheherazade [in *Arabian Nights*], trying to keep the king calm for a thousand and one nights.[40]

On 30 October 1990, Powell returned to Washington, DC, to update Bush and his war cabinet on both the buildup and positioning of defensive forces in Saudi Arabia and on a new offensive strategy for liberating Kuwait. At the conclusion of the presentation, Brent Scowcroft asked what size force was needed to effectively execute the offensive strategy. Powell stated, bluntly, a half-million troops. The figure astonished many in the room. Cheney, however, made clear that he and the JCS supported the Powell-Schwarzkopf estimate. Bush asked, "Colin, are you sure that [airpower alone] won't do it?" Powell responded that it would not. After further deliberations, the president reached a final decision: he would implement Powell's recommended offensive strategy "in three months if sanctions did not work and the Iraqis were still in Kuwait."[41]

On 6 January 1991, with Iraqi forces still occupying Kuwait, President Bush ordered Powell to initiate a war against Iraq in nine days. The first phase of Desert Storm, which featured relentless aerial bombing against Iraqi installations and armed forces, lasted for more than a month. During this time, Powell emerged as the public face of war through his televised press conferences detailing the campaign's progress. On 22 January he provided a curt but memorable articulation of the administration's war plan: "Our strategy in going after this army is very simple. First we are going to cut it off, and then we are going to kill it." But to kill the Iraqi army, Schwarzkopf needed to launch a major ground offensive. When Cheney and Powell visited him in early February, the field general believed that the ground phase of the war would commence as early as 21 February. This information was conveyed to Bush, who was anxious to achieve victory. On 18 February, the president wrote in his diary, "The meter is ticking. Gosh darn it, I wish Powell and Cheney were ready to go right now."[42]

A few days after Powell returned to Washington, Schwarzkopf adjusted his timetable, proposing to delay the ground offensive, G day, until 24 February. Powell thought the postponement overly cautious, but he chose to support his field general and so advised delay to a disappointed president and defense secretary. On 20 February, Schwarzkopf, citing a bad weather forecast, advocated further delay of the ground war until 26 February. Under immense pressure from his civilian leaders to win the war as quickly as possible, Powell needed to communicate to his subordinate the president's strong desire to launch the ground offensive. Powell also wanted to reaffirm his ongoing respect for Schwarzkopf's position as the commander in the field. When Powell confronted him over the telephone, Schwarzkopf threw a tantrum, screaming, "You're pressuring me to put aside my military judgment out of political expediency. I've felt this way for a long time!" Powell yelled back, "My President wants to get on with this thing. My [defense] secretary wants to get on with it. *We need to get on with this.*" After regaining his composure, he told Schwarzkopf, "We've just got a problem we have to work out. You have the full confidence of us back here. At the end of the day, you know I'm going to carry your message, and we'll do it your way." Only minutes after this heated exchange, Schwarzkopf telephoned Powell to say that the poor weather was clearing and that he would launch ground forces on 24 February, as planned.[43] By fulfilling his responsibilities as a follower, Powell had led Schwarzkopf to initiate the ground attack.

After only three days of ground operations, American-led forces captured some seventy thousand Iraqi soldiers while suffering relatively low casualties. When coalition war planes began decimating the Iraqi army as it fled Kuwait, journalists dubbed the freeway leading from Kuwait City the "highway of death." With this rapid success, Powell's thinking turned to the "nearing endgame," and his actions demonstrated how the morality and sense of personal responsibility of exemplary followers can positively influence the decisions of their leaders. Having achieved the key objective of liberating Kuwait, Powell worried about the ethics of prosecuting a war when an enemy was obviously defeated. He believed that the administration "presently held the high moral ground" but could "lose it by fighting past the [point] of 'rational calculation.'" He shared his concern with Schwarzkopf and decided to advise Bush and Cheney to conclude the war sooner rather than later. At the White House on 27 February, Powell informed the president, "It's going much better than we expected. The Iraqi army is broken. All they're trying to do now is get out. . . . We don't want to be seen as killing for the sake of killing, Mr. President." Bush agreed. He suspended the offensive campaign the very next day. Years later, when critics carped that the war had been ended prematurely, Powell wrote, "I stand by my role in the President's decision to end the war when and how he did. It is an accountability I carry with pride and without apology." In a 1992 interview, Powell charged that "had we [gone to Baghdad], we would have gotten ourselves into the biggest quagmire you can imagine trying to sort out 2,000 years of Mesopotamian history."[44]

Powell continued to serve as the chairman of the JCS for two and a half more years, but his superb followership and leadership during the Persian Gulf War marked the zenith of his military career. "And there is no doubt in my mind," Schwarzkopf testified, "that General Powell was the best man for the job during this crisis. Not since General George Marshall during World War II had a military officer enjoyed such direct access to White House inner circles—not to mention the confidence of the President. Powell could get decisions in hours that would have taken another man days or weeks." President Bush also praised Powell for his successful performance as an exemplary follower and a leader: "If there's anybody that has the integrity and the honor to tell a president what he feels, it's Colin Powell, and if there's anybody that is disciplined enough and enough of a leader to instill confidence in his troops, it's Colin Powell."[45]

During his final year in uniform, Powell served as the senior military advisor to President Bill Clinton and to Defense Secretary Les Aspin, and though he came to like both men personally, he often found the work exasperating. The first major issue he confronted in the Clinton administration concerned the ban on homosexuals in the military, which Powell described as "the hottest social potato tossed to the Pentagon in a generation." During the presidential campaign, Clinton had promised to end the ban, a policy shift that was widely opposed within the armed forces. Powell, ever candid and loyal, informed Clinton that he personally supported the ban but would faithfully execute the president's proposed policy if so ordered. On this controversial issue, Powell again demonstrated the traits of an ideal follower who leads by supplying his leaders with a creative solution to a vexing problem. Powell suggested that the military could simply "stop asking about sexual orientation when people enlist. Gays and lesbians could serve as long they kept their lifestyle to themselves." In September 1993, Clinton and the Congress adopted Powell's recommended policy of "don't ask, don't tell."[46]

Leaders in the untested Clinton administration also relied on Powell's counsel during foreign policy crises that emerged in the Balkans and in Somalia. During the latter part of the Bush administration, Yugoslavia had begun fragmenting into smaller nation-states. In April 1992, the Bosnian parliament declared its independence from Yugoslavia, sparking a civil war between supporters of the new government and the Bosnian Serb population, which was backed by Belgrade. Although a crisis was increasingly evident, Powell supported Bush's decision not to intervene militarily, given the absence of both a defined American political objective and a clear exit strategy for U.S. forces. For many in the administration, Bosnia was a European problem. Clinton, on the other hand, had promised that the United States would take a much more active, though unspecified, role in resolving the conflict. In meeting after meeting on the Bosnian question, Powell, the model follower, drew on his vast experience and expertise to provide the new president and his foreign policy team with options for military intervention. Moreover, he again demonstrated his willingness to stake out an unpopular position. Fearing a Bosnian quagmire, he emphasized that larger policy goals needed to be articulated prior to selecting the appropriate level of military engagement. "My constant, unwelcome message at all the meetings on Bosnia," he later wrote, "was simply that we should not commit military forces until we had a clear political objective." Madeleine K. Albright, then the U.S. ambassador to the United Nations, thought Powell's firm stance was overly cautious. She asked him outright, "What's the point of having this superb military that you're always talking about if we can't use it?" Powell found the question deeply disturbing, but he had the support of others, including Secretary Aspin. Despite his campaign rhetoric, President Clinton never articulated a distinct policy on Bosnia. He refrained from intervening in the Balkans until circumstances deteriorated into a humanitarian disaster, after Powell had retired from the military.[47]

Unlike its hesitation in the Balkans, the Bush administration intervened in Somalia in 1992 when a severe famine developed. For Powell, as the leading general of U.S. armed forces and as a follower of the president and defense secretary, it proved a difficult problem to manage. Believing that hundreds of thousands of lives could be saved, Powell supported a mission of mercy but advocated a limited and well-defined military commitment. In December 1992 Bush approved Operation Restore Hope to quell the civil disorder caused by local warlords and to ensure the safe delivery of UN relief supplies. By April 1993, three months into the Clinton administration, Powell believed that Operation Restore Hope's key objectives had been met. He flew to Mogadishu to inspect the ongoing transfer of U.S. military operations to UN personnel. By June, with American soldiers withdrawing from Somalia, supporters of warlord Mohammed Farah Aidid had killed twenty-four Pakistani soldiers and wounded many more who were serving under UN auspices. The UN, which had recently enlarged its mandate in Somalia from humanitarian relief to political and economic reconstruction, authorized the capture of Aidid. This shift in policy, supported by the Clinton administration, had the effect of recommitting the U.S. military to the theater.

When Major General Tom Montgomery, the commanding U.S.

general in Somalia, requested airplanes and helicopters from the Pentagon, Powell advised Clinton and Aspin to approve the request, which they did. Powell was inclined to apply overwhelming force and to support the tactical recommendations of his field commanders, but he and Secretary Aspin also feared the consequences of escalation without the reestablishment of precise strategic objectives. "It was exactly what Powell hated," reports David Halberstam: "mission expansion, slipping toward an open-ended commitment." As a result, Powell opposed, at least initially, the deployment of army rangers, the Delta Force, and heavy armor to Mogadishu, and he advised the administration to conduct a thorough policy review on Somalia. The latter advice was not heeded. By 22 August, U.S. commanders in the field convinced Powell, and thus Aspin and Clinton, that they absolutely required the capabilities of the rangers and Delta Force soldiers to execute their mission. A month later, Powell reluctantly backed Montgomery's request for the delivery of Abrams tanks and Bradley armored vehicles. The Clinton team, under mounting congressional pressure to withdraw all U.S. forces, blocked this recommendation. On 30 September, the day of Powell's retirement, he met with the president at the White House. The outgoing chairman warned Clinton, as he had a sympathetic Aspin, about the increasingly tumultuous situation in Somalia: "We can't make a country out of that place. We've got to find a way to get out, and soon." Only a few days later, eighteen U.S. soldiers were killed in a bloody and frantic firefight in Mogadishu, where guerrillas had shot down two Blackhawk helicopters. The carnage appalled the American people, and their reaction led Clinton to conduct a full policy review and eventually to withdraw the soldiers.[48]

Somalia marked an anticlimactic, even tragic end to Powell's stellar military career, yet the public did not hold him responsible for the debacle. In fact, a 1994 opinion poll ranked Powell as the nation's most popular leader, scoring him well ahead of all contenders, including President Clinton. The trajectory of Powell's career, from ROTC cadet to chairman of the JCS, was nothing short of astounding. In a career that featured minimal time in senior command billets, his skills and behavior as a highly effective follower, especially as an advisor, accounted for much of his professional success. In 1999, when an interviewer asked him to explain why he had been selected as chairman, Powell unwittingly described many core attributes of his exemplary followership, including dependability, commitment, passion, intrinsic motivation, moral conduct, initiative, and risk taking: "I worked very hard. I was very loyal to people who appointed me, people who were under me, and my associates. I developed a reputation as somebody you could trust. I would give you my very, very best. I would always try to do what I thought was right and I let the chips fall where they might. . . . It didn't really make a difference whether I made general in terms of my self-respect and self-esteem. I just loved being in the army. I wasn't without ambition but ambition wasn't fueling me."[49] Such qualities, not coincidentally, are also at the heart of effective leadership.

Central to Powell's developmental success were his constant reflection on his experiences and his study of and engagement with role models and mentors. Powell was always seeking to learn from others' examples, whether good or bad, to enhance his own capabilities as a follower and leader. Early on, cadet Ronnie Brooks inspired Powell to aim for excellence in the military profession. In Germany, captains Miller and Louisell taught their green lieutenant about human fallibility and the need for "humane leadership." From generals such as DePuy and Emerson, Powell came to value the intellectual traits of independent judgment and creative thinking. At the Pentagon and White House, Powell learned equally from his many civilian mentors, including Fred Malek, John Kester, Cap Weinberger, and Frank Carlucci.[50]

Over the years, as Powell reflected on the nuances of leadership, he concluded that "leadership is all about followership," that success in one role is tightly intertwined with success in the other. In fact, it is evident that many of the core personal factors that contribute to exemplary followership also contribute to ideal leadership. Powell's army career illustrates not only the commonalities of effective followership and leadership but also the reality that all military officers, even those in prominent command positions, must serve in concurrent roles as followers of others.[51]

Notes

1. Colin L. Powell with Joseph E. Persico, *My American Journey* (New York: Random House, 1995), 411, 423.

2. McCain quoted in Karen DeYoung, *Soldier: The Life of Colin Powell* (New York: Knopf, 2006), 209.

3. Ibid.

4. Powell, *My American Journey*, 352, 380.

5. See Robert E. Kelly, "In Praise of Followers," *Harvard Business Review*, November–December 1988, 142–48; Robert E. Kelly, *The Power of Followership: How to Create Leaders People Want to Follow, and Followers Who Lead Themselves* (New York: Doubleday/Currency, 1992); Ira Chaleff, *The Courageous Follower: Standing Up To and For Our Leaders* (San Francisco: Berrett-Koehler, 1995); and Sviatoslav Steve Seteroff, *Beyond Leadership to Followership* (Victoria, BC: Trafford, 2006).

6. Powell, *My American Journey*, 17, 21, 28.

7. Ibid., 36–38.

8. Quoted in DeYoung, *Life of Colin Powell*, 37.

9. Powell, *My American Journey*, 56.

10. Quoted in DeYoung, *Life of Colin Powell*, 43.

11. Powell, *My American Journey*, 85, 88, 89, 95.

12. Ibid., 117, 126.

13. Ibid., 136.

14. Gettys quoted in Howard Means, *Colin Powell: Soldier/Statesman–Statesman/Soldier* (New York: Fine, 1992), 147, 152.

15. Powell, *My American Journey*, 54, 57.

16. Ibid., 102, 87, 144.

17. Ibid., 158, 167, 173, 166; Malek quoted in Means, *Colin Powell*, 174–75.

18. Powell, *My American Journey*, 186; Emerson quoted in Means, *Colin Powell*, 181.

19. Powell, *My American Journey*, 211.

20. Ibid., 214.

21. DeYoung, *Life of Colin Powell*, 115–18.

22. Powell, *My American Journey*, 249.

23. Ibid., 260, 272.

24. Ibid., 269, 270, 271.

25. Becton quoted in ibid., 281; DeYoung, *Life of Colin Powell*, 129.

26. Powell, *My American Journey*, 289, 298.

27. Weinberger quoted in DeYoung, *Life of Colin Powell*, 125.

28. Powell, *My American Journey*, 316, 331; Carlucci quoted in De-Young, *Life of Colin Powell*, 149, 157.

29. Powell, *My American Journey*, 334, 338.

30. Carlucci quoted in Bob Woodward, *The Commanders* (New York: Simon and Schuster, 1991), 108.

31. Powell, *My American Journey*, 419, 425, 426, 429, 432.

32. David Halberstam, *War in a Time of Peace: Bush, Clinton, and the Generals* (Waterville, MN: Thorndike, 2001), 427–28.

33. Powell, *My American Journey*, 436, 341, 437.

34. Ibid., 452, 454, 458.

35. George Bush and Brent Scowcroft, *A World Transformed* (New York: Knopf, 1998), 324; Cheney quoted in Powell, *My American Journey*, 464–66; "Oral History: Colin Powell," *Frontline: The Gulf War*, http://www.pbs.org/wgbh/pages/frontline/gulf/oral/powell/1.html.

36. Scowcroft quoted in Wil S. Hylton, "Casualty of War," *GQ*, June 2004, 5; Bush quoted in Powell, *My American Journey*, 480.

37. Powell, *My American Journey*, 492–93.

38. Ibid., 483–85; Schwarzkopf quoted in ibid.

39. Ibid., 487, 498; H. Norman Schwarzkopf with Peter Petre, *It Doesn't Take a Hero* (New York: Bantam Books, 1992), 367; Bush and Scowcroft, *World Transformed*, 354.

40. Powell, *My American Journey*, 498.

41. Ibid., 489.

42. Ibid., 509–10, 514; Bush and Scowcroft, *World Transformed*, 472.

43. Schwarzkopf, *It Doesn't Take a Hero*, 436, 443; Powell, *My American Journey*, 516.

44. Powell, *My American Journey*, 519, 521, 527; Powell quoted in DeYoung, *Life of Colin Powell*, 212.

45. Schwarzkopf, *It Doesn't Take a Hero*, 325; Bush quoted in De-Young, *Life of Colin Powell*, 216.

46. Powell, *My American Journey*, 547, 572.

47. Ibid., 576.

48. Halberstam, *War in a Time*, 472; Powell, *My American Journey*, 588.

49. DeYoung, *Life of Colin Powell*, 250; Powell quoted in Edgar F. Puryear Jr., *American Generalship: Character Is Everything; The Art of Command* (Novata, CA: Presidio, 2000), 229.

50. Powell, *My American Journey*, 46.

51. Jay F. Marks, "Leadership Is All about Followership," *Oklahoman*, 22 March 2006, http://www.newsok.com.

Recommended Reading

Ambrose, Stephen E. *Eisenhower*. 2 vols. New York: Simon and Schuster, 1983–1984.

Arnold, Henry H. *Global Mission*. New York: Harper, 1949.

Catton, Bruce. *Grant Moves South, 1861–1863*. Edison, NJ: Castle Books, 2000.

———. *Grant Takes Command, 1864–1865*. Boston: Little, Brown, 1960.

Coffey, Thomas M. *Hap: The Story of the U.S. Air Force and the Man Who Built It, General Henry H. "Hap" Arnold*. New York: Viking, 1982.

Connelly, Owen. *On War and Leadership: The Words of Combat Commanders from Frederick the Great to Norman Schwarzkopf*. Princeton, NJ: Princeton University Press, 2002.

Cox, Caroline. *A Proper Sense of Honor: Service and Sacrifice in George Washington's Army*. Chapel Hill: University of North Carolina Press, 2004.

Daso, Dik A. *Architects of American Air Supremacy*. Honolulu: University Press of the Pacific, 2002.

———. *Hap Arnold and the Evolution of American Airpower*. Washington, DC: Smithsonian Institution Press, 2000.

Davis, Burke. *Marine! The Life of Chesty Puller*. New York: Bantam Books, 1991.

DeYoung, Karen. *Soldier: The Life of Colin Powell*. New York: Knopf, 2006.

Duncan, Francis. *Rickover: The Struggle for Excellence*. Annapolis, MD: Naval Institute Press, 2001.

———. *Rickover and the Nuclear Navy: The Discipline of Technology*. Annapolis, MD: Naval Institute Press, 1990.

Eisenhower, David. *Eisenhower at War, 1943–1945*. New York: Random House, 1986.

Eisenhower, Dwight D. *Crusade in Europe*. Garden City, NY: Doubleday, 1948.

Ellis, Joseph. *His Excellency George Washington*. New York: Knopf, 2004.

Ferling, John. *The First of Men: A Life of George Washington*. Knoxville: University of Tennessee Press, 1988.

Flexner, James T. *Washington: The Indispensable Man*. Boston: Little, Brown, 1969.

Gordon, Michael R., and Bernard E. Trainor. *The General's War: The Inside Story of the Conflict in the Gulf*. New York: Little, Brown, 1995.

Hoffman, Jon T. *Chesty: The Story of Lieutenant General Lewis B. Puller, USMC.* New York: Random House, 2001.

Holland, Matthew F. *Eisenhower between the Wars: The Making of a General and Statesman.* Westport, CT: Praeger, 2001.

Jasper, William F. "The Real Hal Moore." *New American,* 25 March 2002.

Lengel, Edward G. *General George Washington: A Military Life.* New York: Random House, 2005.

Marshall, George C. *George C. Marshall: Interviews and Reminiscences for Forrest C. Pogue.* 3rd ed. Edited by Larry I. Bland. Lexington, VA: George C. Marshall Foundation, 1996.

———. *The Papers of George Catlett Marshall.* Edited by Larry I. Bland and Sharon Ritenour Stevens. 5 vols. Baltimore: Johns Hopkins University Press, 1981–2003.

Moore, Harold G. "Battlefield Leadership." 16 December 2003. http://www.au.af.mil/au/awc/awcgate/documents/moore.htm.

———. "Hal Moore on Leadership in War and Peace." *Armchair General,* September 2004.

Moore, Harold G., and Joseph L. Galloway. *We Were Soldiers Once . . . and Young.* New York: Random House, 1992.

Perret, Geoffrey. *Eisenhower.* New York: Random House, 1999.

Pogue, Forrest C. *George C. Marshall.* 4 vols. New York: Viking, 1963–1987.

Polmar, Norman, and Thomas B. Allen. *Rickover: Controversy and Genius.* New York: Simon and Schuster, 1982.

———. *Rickover: Father of the Nuclear Navy.* Dulles, VA: Potomac Books, 2007.

Powell, Colin L., with Joseph E. Persico. *My American Journey.* New York: Random House, 1995.

Rockwell, Theodore. *The Rickover Effect: How One Man Made a Difference.* Annapolis, MD: Naval Institute Press, 1992.

Roth, David. *Sacred Honor: Colin Powell; The Inside Account of His Life and Triumphs.* Grand Rapids, MI: Zondervan, 1993.

Sherry, Michael S. *The Rise of American Air Power: The Creation of Armageddon.* New Haven, CT: Yale University Press, 1989.

Simon, John Y., ed. *The Papers of Ulysses S. Grant.* 28 vols. Carbondale: Southern Illinois University Press, 1967–2005.

Simpson, Brooks D. *Ulysses S. Grant: Triumph over Adversity, 1822–1865.* Boston: Houghton Mifflin, 2000.

Smith, Jean Edward. *Grant.* New York: Simon and Schuster, 2001.

Sobel, Brian M. "Hal G. Moore: The Legacy and Lessons of an American Warrior." *Armchair General,* September 2004.

Stoler, Mark A. *George C. Marshall: Soldier-Statesman of the American Century.* Boston: Twayne, 1989.

Truitt, Christy. "An American Soldier." *East Alabama Living,* Spring 2005.

Woodward, Bob. *The Commanders.* New York: Simon and Schuster, 1991.

Contributors

LARRY I. BLAND, PhD, former editor and project director, *The Papers of George Catlett Marshall* (George C. Marshall Foundation, 1977–). Bland was the author of numerous articles on General Marshall and was the managing editor of the *Journal of Military History*, which is jointly supported by the Marshall Foundation and the Virginia Military Institute.

CAROLINE COX, PhD, associate professor of history, University of the Pacific. Cox is the author of *A Proper Sense of Honor: Service and Sacrifice in George Washington's Army* (University of North Carolina Press, 2004). She was a West Point Summer Seminar Fellow in 2004 and a recipient of the Army Historical Foundation's LTG Richard G. Trefry Distinguished Writing Award in 2005.

THOMAS L. "TIM" FOSTER, MBA, president of the consulting firm TAF Inc. From 1963 to 1994, Foster worked closely with Admiral Hyman Rickover (and subsequently for Rickover's two successors, admirals McKee and DeMars) as business executive (budget, procurement, logistics, congressional liaison) for the U.S. Naval Nuclear Propulsion Program. Foster has earned two Presidential Meritorious Rank awards and the Department of Energy Meritorious Service Award.

COLONEL JON T. HOFFMAN, MA, JD, U.S. Marine Corps Reserves. Hoffman is the author of *Chesty: The Story of Lieutenant General Lewis B. Puller, USMC* (Random House, 2001) and *Once a Legend: "Red Mike" Edson of the Marine Raiders* (Presidio, 1994). He is the former deputy director of the Marine Corps History and Museums Division and is currently serving as chief of the Contemporary Studies Branch at the U.S. Army Center of Military History. Hoffman is writing a biography of General Lewis W. Walt.

KERRY E. IRISH, PhD, professor of history, George Fox University. Irish is the author of "Apt Pupil: Dwight Eisenhower and the 1930 Industrial Mobilization Plan" (*Journal of Military History*, 2006) and *Clarence C. Dill: The Life of a Western Politician* (Washington State University Press, 2000). He is writing a biography of General Dwight D. Eisenhower.

HARRY S. LAVER, PhD, associate professor of military history, Southeastern Louisiana University. Laver is a former instructor of military history at West Point and the author of *Citizens More Than Soldiers: The Kentucky Militia and Society in the Early Republic* (University of Nebraska Press, 2007) and "Preemption and the Evolution of America's Strategic Defense" (*Parameters: U.S. Army War College Quarterly*, 2005). Laver is writing a book on the military leadership of generals George Washington, Ulysses S. Grant, and Dwight D. Eisenhower.

FRANÇOIS LE ROY, PhD, assistant professor of military history and modern Europe, Northern Kentucky University. Le Roy is the author of "Mirages over the Andes: Peru, France, the United States, and Military Jet Procurement in the 1960s" (*Pacific Historical Review*, 2002), and he has recently presented papers on D-day and memory, French arms sales to Libya, and women in aviation. Le Roy serves as the historian for the Tri-State Warbird Museum and directs the Military History Program at Northern Kentucky University.

JEFFREY J. MATTHEWS, MA, PhD, MBA, associate professor and director of the Business Leadership Program, University of Puget Sound. He is the author of numerous history and leadership articles as well as the book *Alanson B. Houghton: Ambassador of the New Era* (SR Books, 2004). Matthews is writing a leadership biography of General Colin L. Powell.

COLONEL H. R. MCMASTER, PhD, U.S. Army. McMaster is currently serving as a senior research associate at the International Institute for Strategic Studies and special assistant to the commander of the Multinational Force Iraq. He is the author of the award-winning book *Dereliction of Duty: Lyndon Johnson, Robert McNamara, the Joint Chiefs of Staff, and the Lies That Led to Vietnam* (HarperCollins, 1997). He was commissioned upon graduation from the U.S. Military Academy at West Point in 1984 and returned to West Point to serve as an assistant professor in the Department of History from 1994 to 1996.

DREW PERKINS, graduate student of history, Northern Kentucky University. Perkins served in the Eighty-second Airborne, U.S. Army. As a student, he has helped to collect and compile many videotaped interviews for the Library of Congress's Veterans History Project, a constitutive part of the American Folklife Center.

Index